Margaret.
Happy Birthday
to my dear friend.
May reading this book
give you much inspiration
Lovingly
Jue
30'

# HOPE
## Against
# HOPE

### THE ANCHOR OF OUR SOUL

# Nancy Missler

**KHW**
KING'S HIGH WAY

"The Lord bless you
and keep you;
the Lord make his face
shine on you and
be gracious to you;
the Lord turn his face
toward you and
give you peace."
Numbers 6:24-26

*Hope Against Hope*

All Scripture quotations are from the King James Version of the Holy Bible.

Published by The King's High Way Ministries, Inc.
P.O. Box 3111
Coeur d'Alene, ID 83816-0347
www.kingshighway.org
(888)775-5464

Cover and interior design by Koechel Peterson and Associates, Mpls. MN

ISBN: 978-0-9906571-0-1

Printed in the United States of America

I want to dedicate this book to my beloved husband, Chuck, who after 57 years of marriage has been the vessel God has used to enable me to "see" the Savior's Hand in the darkest time of my life. Thank you, my darling, for your never-ending love, your care and your concern. I love you!

This book is also written to all my dear Christian brothers and sisters who, like me, are experiencing the Dark Night of the Spirit and the Valley of the Shadow of Death.

Be encouraged. There is hope. God is a real and personal God. He is faithful and He loves us, even though at the moment we might not see it nor our circumstances show it. Be assured, God knows our every need and is working "all things together for our good." He is a God who can be known and seen even in the darkest of times....That's our hope! That's the "anchor of our soul."

Without hope, we will drift away from the Lord, lose our bearings and eventually drown. The only way we can ever make it through our hard times is by doing what Moses did. He had hope and was *able to endure* because he "saw Him who is invisible." (Hebrews 11:27)

It is my heartfelt prayer that this book, written in the most difficult time of my life, would help you to do just that—"see Him who is invisible"—as you walk through your own darkness and confusion.

En Agape,
Nan

# TABLE OF CONTENTS

# Detailed Table of Contents

"TO ALL THE BELOVED OF GOD,

CALLED TO BE SAINTS.

GRACE TO YOU AND PEACE FROM

GOD OUR FATHER,

AND THE LORD JESUS CHRIST."

ROMANS 1:7

# INTRODUCTION

Throughout the New Testament the word "beloved" is used adoringly as an adjective describing how God's children are dear, highly esteemed and favored in His eyes. The Greek word for "beloved" is *agapetos.*

When Nan completed the final manuscript of this book, I had the privilege of reviewing it with her. We took several days praying over each page and asking the Lord to change, correct or add anything that might help His *agapetos*—His beloved—to understand more clearly not only how to approach His presence here and now, but also how to be prepared and equipped for what He has in store for them in the future.

This is an in-depth study of what "hope" really means and how critical it is, especially for the times in which we live. So I encourage you to take the time to really grasp and understand what you are reading. Practical application as to how to "hope in the Lord" when everything else in your life is going haywire is so essential, particularly in these "end times" when we are battling the world, the flesh and the devil daily. God wants His *agapetos* to really know not only how much He loves them, but that He will be faithful to fulfill His promises to them in His timing and in His way. Hoping in His Love and knowing we are His *agapetos* truly becomes the "anchor of our soul."

I pray this book leads you not only to a much deeper understanding of God's personal Love for you, but also how "hope" in that Love will lead you directly into His presence, allowing you to "see Him who is invisible" and preparing you for what He has planned in the future.

In that Love,

Debbie Holland
Executive Director of King's High Way Ministries

"Hope deferred maketh the heart sick;

but when the desire cometh,

it is a tree of Life."

PROVERBS 13:12

PREFACE

# H

ave you ever felt hopeless?

Have you ever felt as though you are literally walking through the Valley of the Shadow of Death? Have you ever felt as though you wanted to run but there was nowhere else to go? You pray and you pray and you pray, but the Lord just doesn't seem to answer. Instead, everything gets worse and worse.

This book is about the incredible blessings of HOPE—what hope really is; why it's so vitally important, and how hope is our only "anchor" when everything around us is crashing and burning. God is not only the Author of all Love, but the Bible is also His message of "hope" to a dying world.

My motive for writing is simple: *I see hopelessness everywhere;* not just in non-believers, but widespread in the Christian Body. And since I am living in a similar hopeless situation right now, I want to use my own experience to help others walk through their difficult times without falling away, but instead, letting those same circumstances push them even closer to the Lord. Without hope, it's a proven fact we will become barren, infertile and totally lifeless, and the enemy will come in, kill our dreams and destroy our faith. I know, because I've recently been there! Proverbs 13:12 says that without hope, our heart will become sick and no "fruit" will be produced in our lives. My prayer is that the Lord will use my words not only to help others "step out of the flame and into His Arms," but also help them turn their challenging situations into a "well of blessing."[1]

Someone said to me recently: "You don't die if you lose your faith, but you do die if you lose your hope." And, oh, how true this is!

Consider a few other comments written to me in the past year about "hopelessness":

- "My vision has been destroyed, so I have no reason to go on."
- "I've lost my meaning, my purpose and my hopes and dreams, all at one time."
- "I've lost my partner, my business, my family, my home and friends in a period of a few months."
- "I feel broken, torn, weak and lost. I know that God is the answer, but I don't seem to be able to reach Him anymore."
- "I'm undone, lost, abandoned, thrown out and have never felt more alone in my life."
- "It's like I'm being spun around and around...and I've ended up in a barren desert."
- "I'm adrift, having lost my anchor, and yet not knowing how to recover."
- "What I have heard from the Lord is not what's happening in my life."
- "I'm numb. It's like I've been thrown out but don't understand why."
- "I feel gutted...."
- "It's like I've been hit with a Mack truck...."
- "I am living on a tightrope with tigers on every side."

- "I feel like Jesus did in Matthew 27:46 when He said: 'My God, my God, why have You forsaken me?'"
- "He tells us other places in the Bible that He will never leave us nor forsake us. Where is He now?"
- "I feel just like Paul did in 2 Corinthians when he said: 'I am pressed out of measure, above strength, despairing of life itself. I am troubled, perplexed, persecuted, cast down, delivered over unto death.'"[2]

The most common comments I have heard are:

- "Where is the Lord in all of this?"
- "Why would He allow me to crash and burn like this? It's cruel."
- "As with Job, the thing I greatly feared has come to pass in my life."
- "I don't know where to go, who to turn to or what to do. I feel totally lost."
- "My hope is dashed. Only my bed is comfort, in that, I am able to forget my misery. I don't want to go on living like this. The life has gone out of me and my soul is crushed. I don't have the strength to endure."
- "I'm shattered."
- "I feel like Job must have…"

These are just a few of the comments that believers have written me; there are hundreds more.

Hope is like a golden cord connecting us to heaven. The more we cling to this cord, the more we can allow the Lord to bear the weight of our burdens and to draw us closer to Him.

Charles Spurgeon once said: "Hope…is like a star, not to be seen in the sunshine of prosperity, but only to be discovered in the night of adversity." From my own perspective, especially now, this is so true.

Charles Spurgeon once said: "Hope... is like a star, not to be seen in the sunshine of prosperity, but only to be discovered in the night of adversity."

I've wanted to write a book on "hope" for four years now. Three years ago, I completed my first draft, but after everyone read it, they all very politely said, "Something is still missing." So I put it aside for a year. One year ago, however, the Lord showed me exactly what was missing from that first manuscript—"personal experience." That was the day I was told I had a malignant melanoma in the mucous area of my nose (a stage three subcutaneous cancer, not a skin cancer), and only the removal of my entire nose area would save my life. The doctor went on to say that if I did nothing, it would be fatal within a few months. Wow! Is there any more "personal experience" involving the loss of hope that one could have? My whole family was there, and all of them burst into tears.

After praying and contemplating what the doctors had said, I decided that I had to make a choice. Either let God use the whole experience for good and share it with others or feel sorry for myself, go downhill and literally die. So I thought there be no better time (nor greater personal experience) than to finish this precious book that I began over four years ago...when life was going so smoothly. So as I write these chapters, bear in mind that the Lord is teaching me these very same things. There's a huge difference between writing a book "from the head" (knowledge based) and writing a book "from the heart" (experienced based). This book is fully written from my heart, not only to encourage others going through similar difficulties, but also for me as I face many other tough and challenging situations ahead.

Hopelessness occurs when you pray and pray and pray and nothing happens—nothing changes. In fact, just the opposite occurs. Everything continues to turn out against you. In my own situation, I got to the point where I didn't even know how to pray anymore. I had expected so many miracles to come out of my ordeal this year, but instead everything backfired and turned downhill.

I received another letter last week that said almost the very same thing: "What about the change we all waited for God's Love to bring? What happened to the zeal we once knew as we reached out to grasp the pearl of great price? We felt incredible feelings, sang inspiring songs, listened to awesome testimonies, experienced spiritual revelation and absolutely believed in miraculous intervention. Why then have so many of us lost our focus? Why do so many of us want to turn back?"

The question on all of our minds is: How do we reconcile God's Word with the traumatic things that so many of us are going through right now?

Most of my life I've had hope in Christ, but it always seemed more like a cerebral or intellectual thing, not a tangible asset. In fact, over thirty years ago when I first began teaching, I could not have told you the difference between "hope" and "faith" even if I wanted to. But after all the earthshaking things that the Lord has allowed in my life since then, and specifically in the last few months, He has not only shown me what "hope" is but also the importance of intimately knowing His faithfulness and His trustworthiness. Hope means trust! These are some of the things I pray I will be able to convey in this book. Through my difficult experiences of the last year, the Lord has shown me how to "see" His Hand in the darkness, which gives me the hope and the endurance

I need to carry on. I not only have faith that Christ is who He says He is, but I also have the trust and the hope that He will perform His promises to me in His perfect timing and way. I know He loves me, and I know He will keep His Word no matter what I see, no matter what I feel and no matter what I think. No matter how long it takes, no matter how bad it gets and no matter what I have to go through, *I know He will work all these things together for my good.*[3]

What Paul says in Philippians 1:12–14 really gives me courage: "But I would ye should understand, brethren, that the things which happened unto me [Paul] have fallen out rather unto the furtherance of the Gospel; so that my bonds in Christ are manifest in all the palace, and all other places. And many of the brethren in the Lord, waxing confident by my bonds, are much more bold to speak the Word without fear."

This is what I'm praying this book might help to bring about—the confidence to walk toward the unknown future no matter what is occurring in your own life, with the ability to "see Him who is invisible," just as Moses did in Hebrews 11:27.[4]

Second Corinthians 4:17–18 validates this and tells us that our short time of distress here on earth will result in God's greatest blessings in the future: "Our light affliction, which is but for a moment, worketh for us a far more exceeding and eternal weight of glory. *While we look not at the things which are seen [tangible things], but at the things which are not seen [not tangible]; for the things which are seen [tangible] are temporal; but the things which are not seen [not tangible, the spiritual things] are eternal.*"

## THE REAL REASON FOR OUR SALVATION

The Christian life is like a "race."

Listen to how Hebrews 12:1 explains it: "Wherefore seeing we also are compassed about with so great a cloud of witnesses, let us lay aside ever weight, and the sin which doth so easily beset us, *and let us run with patience the race that is set before us..."*

And whether we like it or not, if we are believers, we are already enrolled and entered into that race. The goal—or the finish line—I believe, is what Philippians 3:14 calls "the prize of the high calling of God in Christ Jesus." The prize of the high calling of God is the ability to rule and reign with Him in the coming kingdom. Our life here on earth is simply the training ground for that privilege. "Hope" is a vital part of God's plan. Without hope, we'll never reach that goal or that finish line.

What's so sad is that **many of us have not been taught the real reason for our salvation.** Thus, we haven't really understood *why* we have been called by God, *what* God expects of us here and now or *where* He is taking us in the future. Consequently, the question remains: If we don't understand what our future "goal" is, how can we be expected to have hope to weather our present circumstances? Naturally, we won't have the confidence, the trust or the perseverance we need to endure the dark times.

As we will see, hope finds its fullest expression in *endurance under trial.*[5] That's why hope must be a "living hope."[6] Like faith, hope cannot depend upon something we experienced three years ago. It must be a living day-to-day hope based upon God's Love and His faithfulness today. Then we'll be able to cross over that "bridge" toward the future and see that Tree of Life on the other side.

As Proverbs 13:12 reminds us, "Hope deferred maketh the heart sick; but **when the desire cometh, it is a tree of Life.**" This simply means that when the understanding of the promise does become real and tangible, it will produce much "fruit" in our lives. This is my prayer for this book....

"We are troubled on every side,

*yet not distressed;*

we are perplexed, *but not in despair;*

persecuted, *but not forsaken;*

cast down, *but not destroyed;*

ALWAYS BEARING ABOUT IN THE BODY

THE DYING OF THE LORD JESUS,

*so that the Life also of Jesus might be made*

*manifest in our body."*

2 CORINTHIANS 4:8-10

CHAPTER ONE

# My Story:
## *The Valley of Baca*
## *and*
## *the Shadow of Death*

We began the preface with the questions: Have you ever felt hopeless? Have you ever felt as though you are literally walking through the Valley of the Shadow of Death? Have you ever felt as though you just wanted to run, because you pray and you pray and you pray but the situation just gets worse and worse?

That's exactly how I've felt over the last few months. The following is my own story so you know where I am coming from as I write.

Four years ago I set out to write a book on "hope," not only because I saw it as an essential part of the Christian life, but also because I saw many believers struggling in this critical area. So it seemed like a very timely subject. It took me a year to write the first 300 pages, but I knew in my spirit that something was missing. It was not complete. Even when I took it into the King's High Way ministry for a review, they were all very sweet, but told me the very same thing—"Something is missing. It's not complete." (Little did I know how relevant and personal *this subject of hope would become* in the next few months.)

I prayed and asked God to show me what exactly was missing from that first manuscript. Well, He certainly did.... He literally allowed me to go through my own Valley of Baca, my own Valley of the Shadow of Death and my own Valley of Weeping so I could "personally experience" what was missing. The following is how it all happened.

I was visiting my daughter when she noticed a bump (or a lump) on the side of my nose. She kept insisting that I go and see a doctor. To me, it really wasn't a big deal, as I normally don't go to the doctor. I have always been so healthy. Finally I gave in and went to see my primary care doctor. He was concerned enough to refer me to an eye, ear and nose specialist who biopsied the lump and one week later told me it was a malignant melanoma. He then referred us to a cancer surgeon, who candidly and straightforwardly said that either part of my face and nose should be removed or I would have less than a year to live. That scared all of us to death. The following day he called, and I asked him point-blank if I was "his mother," would he put her through that kind of an operation. He candidly said "no way." But he also said that if I didn't do anything at all, the melanoma would work fast, spreading to my brain and other organs, and I would have perhaps only a couple of months left.

I was in a total daze when I heard all of this, but I believed with all my heart that God was involved in some way and that He would do a "miracle." I would somehow be healed, perhaps lead many others to Christ in the hospital, and lots of "fruit" would be produced from the whole experience, etc.

Because of the horrific news, however, we thought it probably a good idea to get a second doctor's opinion. We then went to another cancer specialist who was absolutely adorable and encouraged us to fight the cancer in any way we could. He referred us to a radiation on-cologist who happened to work closely with many of the surgeons at the famous Mayo Clinic. Because my case was so rare (1 in 100,000), the Mayo surgeons agreed to see me. Unfortunately, my insurance was not what they wanted, but because they had never operated on someone with my condition, they miraculously made an exception and took me as a training example. The Mayo doctor said she might be able to get the cancer from the inside of my nose (without having to remove it and do such radical surgery). That, obviously, is what I was praying would happen. At the same time, she introduced me to a plastic surgeon who would do the reconstruction if needed. He said that in the thirty years that he had been practicing, he had never seen a cancer like mine nor had he ever operated on one.

To be honest, I was terrified.

## THE MIRACLE

The first miracle is that Mayo Clinic did take me and that those two surgeons operated on me. They were able to keep the top of my nose but had to remove my entire septum (the bone and cartilage that support the nose). They then put in stents to hold up the skin on the top of my nose until such a time that they could reconstruct a new nose for me. They believed they got all the cancer, as the margins around the area where the cancer was were clear on the scans.

My sister-in-law kept telling me: "It's a gift. They got all the cancer. It's a gift." However, I must be honest and say that when I first saw my face after this surgery, I wept for hours. I do praise God for getting all the cancer at the time, and it was a gift, but I've had to choose daily *by faith* to stand on this, because over the next several weeks everything began to go wrong.

One week after the major operation to remove the cancer, we had to call 911 because we couldn't stop the bleeding from my nose. I have an AFib heart condition that requires me to take a blood thinner daily.

The doctor knew this but mistakenly told me to continue taking it. Well, it definitely was the wrong decision because the next morning I woke up bleeding so profusely that they rushed me to the ER. This also proved to be a mistake, because in the ER they left me on a makeshift (hard) table for eight hours, bleeding continuously. They checked me maybe five times the entire day (never changing my dressings or my clothes, thus I bled all over myself, the table and the floor).

Finally, at close to 5 PM (we had arrived there at 8 AM), my surgeon's assistants came in and proceeded to pull out the metal wires (the stents) holding my nose skin in place. This absolutely traumatized me. (Picture the entire top of your nose held up by stents—small poles. When you pull these out, your nose comes crashing down as there is no septum to now hold it up.) They did all of this without any anesthesia or painkiller. It was probably the worst moment of my entire life (I'd give birth to five babies in place of this). It was horrific. I kept calling out "Jesus! Jesus! Jesus!" Over and over again, I cried out in pain and asked them to please stop. They wouldn't and seemed completely unsympathetic. The young intern doing the procedure kept saying to me, "I know what you are going through," when he obviously did not! (I almost punched him in the face!) Like Job, I cried out in agony to the Lord, "Why have you forsaken me, Lord?" It was absolutely devastating. Finally, they gave me two transfusions and sent me, thankfully, to the main hospital.

I know if it hadn't been for the Body of Christ praying for me that day, I would never have made it through....

Things kept going wrong, nurses kept getting offended and the doctors were often sarcastic and belittling. Rather than draw these people toward the Lord in us, which is what we had hoped God would do, they fled from us. It was so strange. It was as though the enemy had this huge inroad and monstrous stronghold and he wasn't going to give it up for anything. In the midst of this spiritual battle and the intense pain, it became very difficult for me "to see" the Lord's Hand, which affected my hope and my trust. I had expected so many miracles to happen, but after time passed and things kept going from bad to worse, my question to God became: "Where are You, Lord?"

That's why all the loving e-mails from hundreds of brothers and sisters all over the world were so precious to me at that time. I have no doubt that I would not have made it through the above ordeal without their prayers and their intercession. Those prayers kept me alive. And now I know why they kept me alive—to be able to write this book.

Ten days after the above incident, I was scheduled for reconstruction surgery. But I was so weak and had lost so much blood that I was worried about even making it through the operation. The doctors convinced me that the surgery had to be done quickly, because without the stents holding my nose up, it would begin to collapse and shrink on its own (like a pig's nose). So something had to be done and done quickly. The operation turned out to be seven hours long. Ten days earlier, as I said, they had cut the top part of my nose off and laid it back on my forehead in order to remove the old septum. This time they took a strip of skin from the left side of my forehead (from my hairline down to my left eyebrow), twisted it downward to become the liner and the blood source for the new nose cartilage that they had built from a cadaver rib bone. They laid the strip of skin

*I had expected so many miracles to happen, but after time passed and things kept going from bad to worse, my question to God became: "Where are You, Lord?"*

down first, propped the new septum on it and then pulled the old nose skin down and sewed it back in place.

The hard part of this operation was that they had to temporarily (for at least two weeks) leave a huge "bridge" for a blood source distribution between my forehead and my nose. This stuck out from between my eyes about one-half inch. It seemed to get infected quite easily, because they never changed the bandage. They must have had their reasons, but it looked pussy and dirty with dried blood most of the time.

The final operation was when they took away this "blood source" bridge and refined some of the bumps on the newly reconstructed nose.

I wish I could say I sailed through all of these operations like a "saint." But I didn't. I was sick to my stomach most of the time, not only from the surgery but also from the medications they gave me afterward. I experienced nausea, dizziness, sinus headaches and congestion, double vision, infection, diarrhea, constipation, heart pain, mouth rash (from air tubes), boils and gums inflamed. You name it, I had it! I truly thought a lot about Job during this time.

## THE BODY OF BELIEVERS

Again, I would never have made it through this Valley of the Shadow of Death if it had not been for all the prayers of the saints. That's where I did see God's Hand! Thousands wrote and encouraged me. Even when I couldn't put my glasses on my new and very sore nose, I would hold the glass frame up with one hand and read the e-mails, continually being blessed by the constant prayers, stories and Scriptures, etc.

I felt so loved by all my sisters and brothers from all over the world who were such an encouragement, especially during these extremely difficult times. I didn't have the faith to fight the fight, but they did for me. Someone even wrote me: "Your ministry has meant so much to us as the Body, *now we are here for you.*" They surrounded me with their love and carried me through with their prayers. Another wrote: "Jesus' face is also scarred, but it only adds to His beauty."

## The Pain

Over the next several months, much of the "mind-set" that I was in came from the insanity of the pain. I didn't really know what pain was until then. As I said, I'd rather give birth to five babies than go through that again.

"Cancer" (medically and personally) can be defined as something that has taken over, controlled, permeated, usurped and defiled a whole system or another person. It brings with it a spirit of disunity, anxiety, insensitiveness—certainly not the "fruit of the Spirit" but the fruit of "the flesh." This is exactly what the cancer did to me. It was the first time that I had ever really experienced the *physical part* of "the flesh" (i.e., the pain). I've talked in all my books about "the flesh," but I had never really experienced the physical side of it. I had been through the ups and downs of huge emotional and mental calamities but never unending physical pain.

Medications and drugs seem to bring out the worst in me, i.e. "the flesh" in all its brilliant colors. Second Corinthians 1:8 describes how I felt: "pressed out of measure, above strength and despairing of life itself..."

It was an excruciating time with indescribable anguish. Everything was hitting the ground. I was sick to my stomach all the time, yet I'd have to take my antibiotic medicine (to prevent rejection), which made me even sicker. Consequently, I kept losing weight (25 pounds), because I couldn't keep anything down.

Some of my inner thoughts were:

*Father, I feel so alone. No one really understands. And no one can make the pain go away for me.*

*This is the biggest battle of my life.*

*I'm unable to do this.*

*I hurt and am so dependent upon others for everything. I'm not used to doing this. I hate it!*

*Lord, is this what the "fellowship of Your sufferings" means?*

And, of course, I couldn't stand to look in the mirror. The horror that I saw was overwhelming. Philippians 3:8 tells us to "count all things but loss for the excellency of the knowledge of Christ." I thought I had done that before! I've said that verse a hundred times, but now it had taken on a whole different meaning and was so difficult to do.[7]

**Hopelessness occurs when you pray and pray and pray and yet everything continues to turn out against you.**

## BECAME HOPELESS

We began this book by speaking about "hopelessness." So, yes, I can now say that I have personally experienced hopelessness in a variety of ways. I have *physically, emotionally, psychologically, mentally* and *spiritually* been hopeless one time or another in the past year. **Emotionally**, I have been separated from all that I know and love—my beloved husband, my family, my home, my friends, etc.; **physically**, I have gone through the hardest year of my entire life, from being told I had only two months to live to encountering pain that was unbearable to where I now must bear scars on my face for the rest of my life; **mentally,** I have lost the vision that Chuck and I had for our future venture together in New Zealand; **spiritually**, I have lost the daily and wonderful love of my precious ministry team at King's High Way; and **financially,** it's been one of the hardest years of my life, as you can imagine.

Hopelessness occurs when you pray and pray and pray and yet everything continues to turn out against you. I got to the point where I didn't even know how to pray anymore. As I said, I expected so many miracles and so many good things to happen that I was a taken back when they didn't occur as I had hoped, but even got worse.

My lack of faith (not seeing any answers to my prayers) caused me to become a murmurer. I continually complained and grumbled. My expectations of what God was going to do and my presumption He would do it "my" way prevented me from seeing the Lord in the middle of the crisis and from hearing His Word. These things are not necessarily sin, but because I held on to them and didn't recognize the damage they were doing, it led to doubt and unbelief, which was sin. As Scripture says, "...whatsoever is not of faith is sin." (Romans 14:23) Thus I needed to confess them as such. I didn't see that then, so I just continued to ask God to remove the pain. But still, He didn't. All He kept saying to me is: "My grace is sufficient for you, and My strength comes into its own when you are weak."[8]

Here's where the confusion comes in for many of us. We read a Scripture or get a promise from God that ministers to us. We interpret that promise or that Scripture in our own mind, but when it doesn't materialize in the way we thought it would, we get confused and discouraged.[9] That's what happened to me. It's not that God was unfaithful to me, it's that I jumped to my own conclusions about His timing and His way of fulfilling His promises. As the previous Scripture states, God's strength only comes about when we are "weak" (when we are clean, open, willing and trusting in His faithfulness alone).

It's only when I began to honestly confess my doubt and "let go" of my own interpretation and my own expectation of what God was going to do, and instead "grab ahold" of the fact that **God will be faithful** to me no matter what happens, that I began to have some victory in my life.

Hebrews 11:27 tells us that the only way Moses endured his trials and the darkness in his life was by daily "seeing the Lord who is invisible" in the midst of the fire. **He saw God's faithfulness in the middle of his trials, which gave him the hope to carry on.**[10]

## The "Valley of Baca"

Let me back up a little and tell you one of the things that God did do, which I didn't see at the time but in retrospect was such a huge blessing.

About six months before my cancer scare, a puzzling incident occurred. Chuck and I had just given an Agape Weekend conference in New Zealand and all the participants were standing around saying their good-byes. One of the precious men who had attended the conference with his wife came up to me and said, "In the future, this may help you. This may be what you will be looking for." Then he said, "It's Psalm 84." Now, bear in mind, this man had absolutely no knowledge of the book that I was attempting to write on hope, nor could he know about the medical situation that would shortly arise and consume my life. Now, in looking back, this Scripture absolutely blows me away:

Psalm 84:5–7 states: "Blessed is the man *whose strength is in Thee*; in whose *heart* are the ways of them. Who passing through *the valley of Baca* ["valley of tears"] make it a *well*; the rain also filleth the pools. They go from *strength to strength*, every one of them..."

The "Valley of Baca" was an actual place in Israel. It was an arid stretch of land that the believing pilgrims had to pass through on their way to worshiping the Lord at the temple in Jerusalem. This is an important fact to remember—*before the pilgrims could worship in the temple, they had to traverse the Valley of Baca.* The Valley of Baca is equal to the desert of Sinai on the way to the "promised land" and was known for its difficult terrain.[11] (Note especially verse 5 that tells us that these were definitely "believers." One commentary even said that verses 4 and 5 refer to "those who set their hearts on the *high road.*" I, of course, loved that because *the King's High Way* is the name of our ministry.[12])

These believers obviously experienced much weeping as they passed through this barren land. The Valley of Baca was known for its darkness and its black shadows. It reminds me of Job's comments in Job 3:5 where he refers to the "blackness of the day," "thick darkness" and the night as "barren, where no shout of joy can be heard.[13]

The point of Psalm 84:5–6 is that even though these "believers" experienced the darkness and confusion of the Valley of Weeping, they were able to turn it around and "make a well." In other words, they knew how to trust the Lord in the midst of the darkness and let the whole experience make them stronger. These pilgrims made this valley, this gorge, this canyon, into a valley of praise and a well of water. It says *they went from strength (in the Lord) to more strength (in the Lord).*[14]

As a side note, going "from strength to strength" means to become an **overcomer**. It's the Old Testament word *gibbor*, which means putting off the old clothes and putting on the new. I wanted to alert you to the connection between being an overcomer and going from strength to strength because we will mention this often in this book.

Isaiah 40:31 says: "those who wait upon the Lord [those who see the Lord in the midst of their difficult circumstances] will renew their strength." This is exactly what is happening here. These believers are given supernatural "strength" in order to overcome and make it through their ordeal.

Scripture tells us that the only way our strength can be made perfect, or complete, is when we are emptied of self and filled with the Lord. In other words, only in our weaknesses (our emptiness) can we become strong in Him.[15]

*The place that God answers our prayers and the place where He finally turns our darkness into light, our trials into blessings and our confusion into understanding is our own Valley of Baca.*

But here's the best part. "Strength to strength" in the Psalm 84 passage actually means *to put on* a new set of clothes. Yes, it means "a change of clothes." But remember, in order to *put on* new clothes, we must first *put off* our old ones, and that's the difficult part.[16] (Remember this when we talk in Chapter Nine about the ritual of the priests in Solomon's Temple. After the priests had given everything to God in the Inner Court, they were required to "change their clothes" before they could progress on to worshiping the Lord at the Incense Altar in the Holy Place.)

For now, just remember that going "from strength to strength" actually means changing our clothes by putting off our old ones and putting on Christ's new ones.[17] It means to overcome. Unfortunately, this doesn't happen automatically. I so wish it did! No, in order to do this, our own continual "choice" is always involved.

***The whole point of Psalm 84 is that the pilgrim takes the hard, difficult and dark times and turns them into "a well full of blessings." And so he goes from strength in the Lord to more strength in the Lord.***

The bottom line is: The place that God answers our prayers and the place where He finally turns our darkness into light, our trials into blessings and our confusion into understanding is our own Valley of Baca. This is the time that we finally relinquish total control of our lives over to Him, in spite of the darkness, in spite of the confusion and in spite of our circumstances. That's when He will turn "our" strength into "His" strength. That's when He will use every bit of our trial for His glory. And that's when He will give us the supernatural ability to overcome and to carry on. Hebrews tells us over and over again that it's only after we flee to the Lord for refuge and consolation that we can enter into His rest.

We will expand on the Valley of Baca, the Valley of Weeping and the Valley of Tears—its difficulties, its barrenness, its darkness and its blackness—in Chapter Six.

Another side note: I want you to be aware of the number of times that David refers in Psalm 84 to the temple of God. I just want you to be aware of a very important connection between the temple of God and the Valley of Baca, which hopefully you will see later. First, the "man who dwells in the house of God" (v. 4); next, the "man who longs for the Courts of the LORD" (v. 1); and finally, the "man who would rather be a doorkeeper in the house of God" (v. 10, "where a day in His court is better than a thousand" that dwell in the world, with all its riches). All these references to God's House in Psalm 84 are significant, not only because they refer to the Lord in His temple, *but also because they refer to weeping, darkness and clouds on the way to worshiping in His temple.*

Could this be the pattern God has designed for our own lives? We'll look more at all of this in Chapter Nine.

## THE "SHADOW OF DEATH"

The Valley of Baca refers to a time of weeping and tears, so it could also be called "the Valley of the Shadow of Death." Psalm 23:4 says: "Yea, though I walk through the valley of the shadow of death, *I will fear no evil; for Thou art with me; Thy rod and Thy staff they comfort me."*

In Scripture, "rod" means God's Word.[18] It's *an instrument that corrects.* And "staff" means His Spirit of support and comfort.[19] It's *an instrument of guidance.* We will talk more in later chapters about the significance of God's rod and staff. But notice here that even though this believer walks through the hardest times of his life (the Shadow of Death), he still knows that God is with Him and that His rod and staff comfort him.

Why does God allow some of these really difficult situations into our lives? This is a very difficult concept for many. Most of us want to think that *if* we do the right things and love God, we will get blessed, but *if* we do the wrong things and don't love Him, we will get punished. The concept that good people experience bad things is so difficult for us to swallow. His ways are definitely not our ways, completely past our own understanding, and totally unsearchable.[20]

## THE "SECRET PLACE OF THUNDER"

This difficult period of time can also be known as "the secret place of thunder," the place where Scripture says that "God tests us." Psalm 81:7 speaks of how Moses was tested at the waters of Meribah, called the "secret place of thunder." This is referring to the incident in Exodus 17:1–8 where the Israelites doubted and murmured against God, and thus the enemy got a foothold. When Moses held up his "rod," the invasion stopped; but when he let the rod down, the enemy advanced. Note how the enemy gained entrance when Moses laid his rod down (symbolic for God's Word), but how the enemy was held back when Moses held the rod high.

God is continually testing us to see if we really trust Him. Interestingly enough, trust and hope are essentially the same thing. Do we still hope in God when He allows the unthinkable into our lives? Do we, like Moses, hold up the Word of God when the enemy advances, or do we, like I did, drop the Word and let the enemy in. When I did this, the enemy came in like a "flood." I didn't pass God's personal test at my "waters of Meribah." Psalm 81 tells us that if we call on the Lord when we are in trouble, He will answer us in the secret place of thunder. This is the place He tests our faith.[21] So, in essence, *He answers us by testing us!* Wow!

Put this alongside Hebrews 4:12 and it blows your mind: "For the Word of God is living and powerful and sharper than any two-edged sword, piercing even to the dividing asunder of the soul and spirit, and of the joints and marrow and is a discerner of the thoughts and intents of the heart."

The Word of God then is the vehicle or the medium that exposes what is of the soul and what is of the spirit. And that cutting and piercing of the two hurts. It occurs in the "secret place of thunder."

## DARKNESS FROM ABOVE

The Valley of Baca and the Place of Thunder are among the many places in the Bible that speak about darkness. Darkness is simply an absence of light. But even more importantly, it's a darkness that God allows. Listen to Isaiah 50:10: "Who is among you that feareth the LORD, that obeyeth the voice of His servant *that walketh in darkness and hath no light? Let him trust in the Name if the LORD and stay upon his God.*" Notice that the person who is being spoken of not only "fears the Lord" but also "obeys His voice." Consequently, this Scripture is talking about a believer who is faithful and obedient. And yet it says he walks in darkness and has no light. God exhorts this person to continue to trust in the Lord and remain strong.

Many of the trials that God allows into our lives come with an absence of light and are definitely "tests" directly from Him. Scripture calls them "the fire of testing." Psalm 66 speaks about this and says that God proves us and tests us as silver. If we understand what He is doing and how to endure the darkness and the fire, we will come out as "gold" in the end. So, yes, God allows these afflictions, these difficulties and the darkness, but only with the purpose of renewing our strength and turning these times into a "well of blessing."[22]

Hear me clearly, however: *God does NOT cause these night seasons or our valleys of Baca; He just uses them for His purposes.* We'll expand more on this in Chapter Six.

Also remember what Charles Spurgeon said: "Hope...is like a star, not to be seen in the sunshine of prosperity, but only to be discovered in *the night of adversity.*"

This is the time the Lord continually asks us the question: "Do you trust Me?"

## TRUSTING HIM IN THE DARK TIMES

If you read the book of Job, you'll see that he talks a lot about this darkness, blackness and the shadow of death. One of the places is Job 19:8–10 where he says: "You [speaking about the Lord] have fenced up my way and set darkness in my path. You have stripped me of my glory. I am gone. *You have removed my hope like a tree.*" It's interesting that Job associates darkness here with the loss of hope. Even Jesus, as He was crucified on the Cross, spoke about "being forsaken and abandoned" by His Father and then darkness covered the land.

In Chapter Six, we'll discuss exactly what God's plan is for calling us and how He goes about implementing it. But for now we just need to know that He calls us for fellowship—He loves us and wants an intimate relationship with us. In order to do that, however, He must conform us into His image of holiness, and that means we must learn to trust Him in the "dark times."

Many of us have made previous commitments to trust our lives to the Lord (in fact, we've probably done this many times before), but because everything went "haywire," we gave up. In His Love, God returns and once again asks: "Will you trust Me in the darkness this time? Will you hope in Me now? Will you once again rely upon Me?" This happens over and over and over again, until we finally get the message and learn to trust and hope in a Father whom we don't always see, whom we don't always understand and whom we don't always know what He is doing. (Isaiah 55:8–9)

One thing I have learned over the last few months is that it's much easier for me to "trust God" going through difficult *circumstances*

EVEN JESUS,
*as He was crucified on the Cross,*
*spoke about*
"being forsaken and abandoned"
by His Father

AND THEN DARKNESS
COVERED THE LAND.

than it is to trust Him going through *constant physical pain*. Pain wears you down and can become unbearable at times. You choose to trust God and you choose and you choose, but if you don't know His Word by heart and haven't memorized His promises, it's very difficult to hold on. This is where pain and the darkness certainly got the best of me. And this is where many turn to "other things" to ease the constant pain, and then, unfortunately, they get hooked. Certainly, I now understand how easy that would be.

My point is that it's important not only to be *in* the Word every day, but also **to memorize** some of God's promises so that if you are "taken out," as I was, you can still hold on. You can still trust Him in the dark and you can still see His Handprint. It's physically dark, yes, but spiritually it's light.

Unfortunately, it also works the other way around. When you don't trust Him and you don't recognize His Hand of Love in all the little things around you (both the spiritual realm and the physical realm are dark), you will falter and sink. So the lesson I am learning through all my hard and dark times is that if I can continue to confess my lack of faith, make faith choices to trust Him anyway and continue to speak forth His Word, I'll have a better chance to endure the tough circumstances, better eyesight to see His Hand in the darkness and thus more perseverance to make it through the physical pain. (2 Corinthians 1:9)

## THE PRESENCE OF GOD IN THE DARKNESS

Remember that many, many Scriptures throughout the Bible associate God's presence with darkness and "a thick cloud." Consider Exodus 19:9, where God says to Moses: "Lo, I come to thee in a thick cloud." And Exodus 34:5: "And the LORD descended in the cloud and stood with him." And Exodus 40:38: "...for the cloud of the LORD was upon the tabernacle by day and the fire was on it by night." Even in the New Testament, John 12:29 says: "they heard the thunder in the cloud," speaking of God's voice, and they were fearful.[23]

These Scriptures seem to suggest that God's presence is simply obscured in darkness, so we must not think of "darkness" in itself as being something bad or fearful or scary. Exodus 20:21 states: "And the people stood afar off, and Moses drew near unto the thick darkness *where God was.*" Second Chronicles 6:1 says: "The LORD hath said that He would dwell in the thick darkness." And Psalm 97:2 adds: "Clouds and darkness are round about Him..."[24]

Even in Solomon's Temple, the Scriptures say that the Holy Place was so filled with the cloud of God's presence that the priests were unable to minister.[25]

*Consequently, it's important to understand that many of the times we are walking "closest to the Lord," we will experience His presence in the form of a cloud or darkness. But the Holy Spirit will be there with His "chain of Hope," leading us directly to the Lord's Feet and His Love.* (We will expand on this in Chapter Nine.)

Just as the saints in the Valley of Baca and the Valley of the Shadow of Death experienced darkness, shadows and the cloud of His presence on their way to worshiping, we will experience the same. In our darkness, He is always there. He never will leave us nor forsake us, nevertheless He may be shrouded in a cloud around us. Remember Isaiah 50:10: "Who is among you that feareth the LORD, that obeyeth the voice of His servant *that walketh in darkness, and hath no light? Let him trust in the Name if the LORD, and stay upon his God.*"

## THE MOST IMPORTANT SCRIPTURE

Last night as I was preparing for bed, the Lord brought to my mind the Scriptural answer as to "how we see the Lord in the midst of our dark seasons." Proverbs 3:5–6 tells us: "Trust in the LORD with all your heart; and lean not to your own understanding. In all your ways acknowledge Him, and He *will* direct your paths." Notice that *if we* trust in the Lord and *if we* acknowledge Him, *then He* will direct our paths.

Now this doesn't mean we emotionally feel like trusting Him or mentally just say "I trust You," but that we simply choose *by faith* to trust Him. That trust then leads to "acknowledging" Him in all our ways. *The word "acknowledge" in this Scripture means to "see Him right in the middle of our situation."* As Moses did in Hebrews 11:27, it means we are to "see Him who is invisible" and to "acknowledge His presence" in the midst of the darkness.

This is the way it works: If we are a cleansed vessel, *and if we choose by faith to trust in God's faithfulness, it frees Him to perform His will in our situation, which allows us to see His Hand of Love (acknowledge Him) and gives us the strength we need to endure the trial.*

So, remember, "acknowledging Him" means seeing Him in the little things. And this is what will give us the endurance to persevere on.

If, however, we are not a cleansed vessel (see Sanctification Steps in Chapter Eight) and we don't choose by faith to trust in God's faithfulness, then God's Hands are really tied and He won't be able to accomplish His will in the situa-

We can never stop hoping in the Lord no matter what our circumstances are, no matter how we feel and no matter if we understand what He is doing or not.

tion, which then makes it impossible for us to "see" His Handprint of Love (or acknowledge Him) or have the strength to endure the trial.

We will refer to Proverbs 3:5–6 over and over again as we proceed through this book. But for now, this Scripture is the answer to our question of how do we take our hard times and make them into "a well of blessing." Again, *if we* trust in the Lord and acknowledge Him in all our ways (see Him in the midst of our circumstances), **then He** will direct our paths. But it also works the other way around: If we cease to trust Him, and we don't acknowledge Him in *all our ways*, then He will be unable to direct our paths.

What this is saying is that we can never stop hoping in the Lord no matter what our circumstances are, no matter how we feel and no matter if we understand what He is doing or not. Even if we don't see His hand, we must continually choose by faith to trust in His promises and acknowledge Him in all our ways. He will come through. Remember that when we say "continue to trust in the Lord," this doesn't mean we must "feel" like trusting Him. It's not a feeling choice we are making, but a faith choice. We will discuss the difference between faith choices (non-feeling choices) and emotional choices in Chapter Eight.

Proverbs 3:5–6 then is one of the first Scriptures you should memorize, because it's critical to your understanding of how we "hope" in the Lord and see Him in the midst of the darkness and the fire. Hoping and acknowledging Him are the only things that will allow us to keep on seeing Him and enduring.

"Trust in the LORD with all your heart; and lean not to your own understanding. In all your ways, acknowledge Him, and He *will* direct your paths." (Proverbs 3:5–6)

# CHAPTER ONE—VALLEY OF BACA

1. Memorize 2 Corinthians 4:8–10.

2. Why does hopelessness occur in our lives?

3. What is the connection between having faith to believe, confessing our own sin and seeing God's Hand in our trials?

4. In Psalm 84, what does the "Valley of Baca" stand for?

5. Psalm 84:5–7 tells us that even though believers experience much darkness in this "valley," they were able to turn it around and "make it a well" of blessing. How did they do that? What does going from "strength to strength" mean?

6. Second Corinthians 12:9 gives us the answer as to how our strength is renewed. Write this Scripture out and explain it as best you can.

7. In order to go from "strength to strength" in Psalm 84, what did these believers have to do? In other words, before we can go on to having more strength, what must we do first?

8. The place that God answers our prayers and turns them into "a well of blessing" is our own Valley of Baca experience. (Psalm 84) Are you in a similar place right now? Has God encircled you with darkness, confusion and trials? Explain.

9. Psalm 81 tells us that sometimes when we call upon the Lord and are in trouble, He will answer us at the "waters of Meribah." What does this mean?

10. How many times does David refer to the temple of God in Psalm 84? Why is this important?

11. Why does God continually "test" us?

12. How does Hebrews 4:12 fit into this testing place?

13. Why the darkness and the loss of light?

14. The Bible says that God's presence is often obscured in darkness. What are some of the Scriptures that validate this?

15. What is one of the most important and helpful Scriptures as to how we can SEE God in the midst of our trials?

16. What happens if we don't do this? Explain.

"That by two immutable things,

in which it was impossible for God to lie,

we might have a strong consolation,

    who have fled for refuge

    to lay hold upon the hope set before us;

which hope we have as an anchor of the soul,

        both sure and steadfast,


        and which entereth

        into that within the veil..."

HEBREWS 6:18–19

# What Is Hope?
# Why Is It so
# Important?

What is "hope," and why is it so critical?

*Hope is as important to us as the air we breathe or the water we drink.* It's what drives us forward and what sustains our dreams! It's what helps us persevere through our tribulations, and what enables us "to endure as seeing Him who is invisible."[26] Hope is the fuel of our soul. If we have hope, we can withstand anything! If we lose our hope, we'll often lose our faith.

The word "hope" is a noun, not a verb. It's not only something we can possess, it's also something we can lose.[27]

Hope is the Greek word *ELPIS* (*Strong's* #1680), which means "to anticipate, usually with pleasure; to expect; to trust and to have confidence."

Romans 8:24–25 describes hope this way: "For we are saved by hope: but hope that is seen is not hope: for what a man seeth, why doth he yet hope for? But if we hope for that we see not then so we with patience wait for it."

So "hope" means confidently stepping out on God's promises and being assured of His trustworthiness, even though we can't see *how His promises will be fulfilled* or *when they will be answered.* Hope is knowing that God will be faithful to keep His Word, no matter what we see or what we feel. Hope is knowing that God will do exactly what He has promised *in His way.* It's the patient, disciplined and confident waiting for and expecting the fulfillment of all of God's promises *in His timing.*[28]

Hope is the security to withstand and endure the struggle (and the wait) between receiving the promises and their fulfillment in our lives.

> *Hope is the security to withstand and endure the struggle (and the wait) between receiving the promises and their fulfillment in our lives.*

There are many things in life that we naturally "hope" for—personal possessions, better jobs, closer relationships, good health, etc. All of these are important, but I believe the most important "hope" we can ever have (and the hope that will affect our lives more than anything else) is *hope in the Lord, not only "hope" in Him for the future but also "hope" in Him for our everyday lives.*[29]

Hope is being so *secure* in the Lord, so *trusting* of Him and so *leaning* upon Him, that *no matter what* happens in our lives, including every scenario we can imagine, we will never doubt His Hand.

This is the kind of hope that this book is about...the kind of hope that allows us to walk through our tough times trusting that the Lord will work everything together for good, no matter what we see, what we feel or what we think. It is one thing "to believe" something, but it's a totally other step to walk that belief out in the midst of the fire. Hope means stepping out on God's promises and being assured of His trustworthiness, even though we can't see how they can ever possibly be fulfilled. It's the kind of hope that allows us to "see the Lord who is invisible" in the midst of our trials.

Hebrews 6:19 tells us that "hope" is the "anchor of our soul." Consequently, when we lose our hope, we not only become confused and disoriented, but we also end up tossing, turning and eventually sinking and drowning.

## Two Types of Hope in the Lord

Now, what makes this subject of hope rather difficult and confusing is that there are really two types of hope in the Lord. First, there's an "**eternal**" hope that involves His phenomenal promises for the future; but there is also an earthly, "**temporal**" hope that involves our day-to-day *personal* trust in Him here and now. This second type of hope (our temporal hope) is where so many of us are struggling and sinking at the present time. Most believers have some knowledge of the first kind of hope (our eternal hope) and are confident that Christ will soon return, bringing with Him His kingdom and fulfilling all His glorious promises. But the temporal, day-to-day, living here-and-now hope is not often taught in churches or in Bible studies. Consequently, this is where many of us are getting tripped up and confused, especially when our circumstances do not play out as we expect they would.

Our "eternal hope" is based on God's promises for the future, whereas our present earthly "temporal hope" is based upon God's promises for today (and these may or may not be fulfilled in the way we think they should be or in the way we interpret them). In difficult situations, we grasp ahold of God's promises and translate them the way we understand them. But when those promises don't come to pass in the way we thought they would, we lose hope and thus our endurance to make it through. When this occurs, we end up confused and disheartened, and, of course, the enemy rejoices.

Remember Proverbs 13:12 tells us that "hope deferred maketh the heart sick, but when the desire cometh, it is a tree of life." Hope is exactly that. When we embrace it by faith, it's a tree of Life. But without it, we will wither and die. When we have hope, regardless of our circumstances, the Life of God can flow out of our hearts into our souls, making each of us a "tree of Life"—embracing His Life not only for our ourselves but also for others. When we lose hope, however, we cut off God's Life and are unable to receive His Love or pass it on to others.[30] We are not "a tree of Life" as He desires, but a tree "devoid of Life," a shriveled up tree.

Here's an interesting comment a lady sent me recently about this very thing. She is quoting from one of Don Frito's newsletters:

"Dr. McNair Wilson, a well-known cardiologist says, 'Hope is the medicine I use more than any other. Hope can cure nearly anything.'"

Don, himself, continues: "Very interesting! My dictionary says that hope is 'to look forward to with desire and reasonable confidence.' Believers [can be] filled with hope—not only for the distant future, but for the here and now—even when in the fiercest trial. It was from a prison cell that Paul urged fellow believers to be filled with hope and to 'rejoice always.'[31] Isaiah, centuries earlier, understood that hope renews and energizes us. 'Those who hope in the LORD will renew their strength. They will soar on wings like eagles; they will run and not grow weary, they will walk and not be faint.'[32] Hope enlarges our dreams and redefines our landscape so that we 'overflow with hope by the power of the Holy Spirit'[33] [giving us] more hope than we need, so that we can pour out on those around us. Discouraged? Weary? Fearful? Allow 'the eyes of your heart [to] be enlightened so that you will know the hope to which He has called you,'[34] then move forward with desire, joy and confidence. Hope is better than medicine. It can cure everything, if rooted in Jesus."

## HOPE IS THE "ANCHOR OF OUR SOUL"

"Hope" is, then, confidently stepping out on God's promises and being assured of His trustworthiness, even though we can't see *how His promises will be fulfilled* or *when they are going to be answered*. Hope is knowing that God will be faithful to keep His Word, no matter what we see or what we feel. It's knowing that God will do exactly what He has promised in His timing and in His way.

Hope is really the "anchor of our soul." In other words, it's our personal tie to, attachment for and our connection with the Spirit of the Lord (our link or yoke to Him). Thus, when we lose that link, that bond or that tie with Him, we'll lose our mooring, our way and end up drowning.

Listen to what Hebrews 6:18–19 has to say about hope:

"That by two immutable things, in which it was impossible for God to lie, we might have a strong consolation [*comfort*], who have fled for refuge **to lay hold upon the hope set before us. Which hope we have as an <u>anchor of the soul</u>, both sure and steadfast, and which <u>entereth into</u> that within the veil**..." (In Chapter Nine, we will explore this term "within the veil" and see its significance and its real meaning.)

The *Living Translation* of Hebrews 6:18–19 says it even a little clearer: "So God has given us both His promise and His oath. These two things are unchangeable because it is impossible for God to lie. Therefore, we who have fled to Him for refuge can take new courage, *for we can hold on to His promise with confidence. This confidence [or hope] is like a strong and trustworthy anchor for our souls. It <u>leads us through the curtain of heaven</u> into God's inner sanctuary*..."

This Scripture is telling us that "hope" is not only *the anchor* that is going to keep us from going off course in our walk of faith, but it's also *the lifeline* that is going to allow us to penetrate behind the veil and lay hold of God in the midst of our trials. It's what will keep us steady and enable us to "see the Lord" in our circumstances. Hope is what connects the world we are living in with the one to come. In other words, hope is the link to our future. I like to call it my "chain of hope." (This will become clearer as we proceed in the book.)

In essence, Hebrews is telling us that hope is like an anchor that needs to be secured "behind the veil" (meaning in the Holy of Holies of the temple where God dwells). This is what will hold our soul in place during the difficult times and yet at the same time allow us to see His Hand in the midst of the trial.

Hope is knowing that God will be faithful to keep His Word, no matter what we see or what we feel.

### WHAT IS AN ANCHOR?

An anchor is really made up of two parts: 1) the anchor itself and 2) the chain or the connection from the anchor to the object that is holding it in place. The anchor is nothing without the chain that holds the two objects together.

Hope is like that. It's really two parts. It's not only the heavy "anchor" itself that holds us in place and keeps us from straying and floating away in storms; it's also the chain or the connecting "tie" or "bridge" that allows us to cross over the crevasses and the gorges and experience God's presence.

*One part of the anchor holds us in place and keeps us steady, while the other part of the anchor keeps us tied to the Lord and His Love behind the veil.*

Hebrews 11:27 tells us that Moses not only "forsook Egypt and didn't fear the wrath of the king," but he also "endured as seeing Him who is invisible." Hope is what allows us to do the very same two things; persevere in our circumstances, but also see the Lord's Hand in them. Somehow, in all of Moses' trials, his hope in God's faithfulness allowed him to continue to see Him in the fire.

In Biblical terms, an "anchor" (*Strong's #45 Annkura*) is a mooring or a fixed point of reference that keeps one on course while enduring a storm.[35] That's exactly what hope does. *It holds us in place, keeps us in line, immovable, firm, set solid, stable, unyielding, steady, strong, secure, inflexible, persistent, rigid, steadfast, unshakable, unswerving, fixed, constant, faithful and reliable* while we are waiting to see what God is going to do. From now on we'll call it our "chain of hope."

It's interesting because Amos 7:7–8 talks about an anchor being like a "hook" or a "plumb line." It's used to denote strength and power. There are many kinds of anchors, but one of the most famous is called the ELPIS anchor (see the front cover of this book), which is the Greek word for "hope." You also can see the CROSS on this anchor. The anchor is also associated with the "fish," which is one of the symbols of the Savior. The union of these two terms expresses, "***Hope in Jesus.***"

## Hope is also a Bridge

So hope is not only the anchor that holds us in place, it's also the "plumb line" that keeps us on course while we are waiting.[36] Hope seems to find its fullest expression in *endurance under trial*. First Thessalonians 1:3 calls it "the patience of hope."

*"Hope" is like <u>a bridge</u> between God's promises and their fulfillment in our lives. It's like the link or the connection between our faith and His Love.* This is why it is so incredibly important. Hope is what allows us to see Christ in the middle of our tragedies. It's what allows us to cross over the valley, the river or the chasms in times of peril. It's the "zip line" or the cord from the present to the future. It describes the anticipation we might feel as we proceed toward the goal of "the prize of the high calling in Christ Jesus"[37] and emphasizes the race that we are in.[38] This is why I sometimes define hope as "the bridge to the unseen."

Hope is what bears the tension between *the now* and *the future.* It's the confident expectation of good *by Christ*, of deliverance *by Christ* and of salvation *by Christ*, no matter what our circumstances are or how long it takes.[39] It's expecting a miracle from the Lord, no matter what shape or form that miracle takes.

The Scripture that really ministers to me is Romans 5:5, which says that "hope never disappoints"—it never makes ashamed. In other words, hope in its fullness makes it impossible to be satisfied with the here and now, even though we can't see where we are going or how it will turn out. I think I am finally here now—knowing that all of this will somehow turn out for God's glory because I know that **He** is faithful.

Of course, the ultimate hope (our eternal hope) is that Jesus will soon return and bring with Him His kingdom.[40] Our hope will only be fully and completely realized then.[41] In Titus 2:13, this is called the "blessed hope" or the glorious appearing of the great God.[42]

## HOPE MEANS TRUST

I find it absolutely fascinating that the word "hope" and the word "trust" actually come from the same Greek root. Hope is the Greek word *elpis* (*Strong's* #1680) (O.T. #8615), which means the confidence, trust and assurance that the things we have believed in (and had faith in) are true and will come to pass. It's the conviction that "what we have had faith in" *will* happen. It's the expectation that God's promises are true and will come to pass in His timing and way. The hard part is that, in the meantime, we must keep on patiently walking and waiting for His Word to materialize.

The word for "trust" is the Greek word *elipizo* (*Strong's* #1679), which means to expect or to have confidence in.[43] "Trust" is not only depending upon God's promises for the future, it's also expecting God's Spirit to get us through the trials and the difficulties of today.

Hope and trust are so closely related that several of the Bible translations use them interchangeably. The King James Version of the Bible translates *elipso* as "trust," whereas the Revised Version of the Bible translates the word as "hope."

When we say "trust" God, we simply mean we trust in HIS faithfulness. Hope is saying the exact same thing—we are trusting in God's faithfulness to us no matter what we see, feel or understand in the natural. ***"Hope" includes not only trusting in, relying upon and having confidence in the Lord, but also acknowledging His presence in the dark time. Hope is seeing Him who is invisible.***

## TRUSTING GOD IN THE DARKNESS

So the word "hope" comes from the same root word as the word "trust." This, to me, is what Matthew 16:24 is referring to when it talks about picking up our crosses and "doing" what He has asked us, whether we feel like it or not and whether we understand it or not!

Regardless of our feelings, our circumstances or how the other person responds to us, we must trust God to work out our life experiences as He wills. Now, it's so easy to just "say" that, but it's quite another to actually "walk" it out. Hope and trust are both involved in the latter. Second Corinthians 8:11 says that we must not only have a readiness to will (to choose) but also a readiness to perform (take an action).

Trusting God in the darkness is difficult because quite often we feel one way, and yet by faith we must choose to act in another way. This is where many of us fall down. It's easier to trust God if we actually can "see" Him at work. If we can't see Him, and things are going the opposite of what we thought they would, trusting Him becomes very difficult. And yet that's the whole point of being able to trust someone, isn't it? You have confidence in that person even when all the evidence points the other direction.

God is asking us to choose to depend upon Him no matter how long it takes to accomplish His will and no matter how He chooses to work out His will. We must have the confidence that He will not only work out the circumstances according to His will, but that He will also align our feelings with the faith choices we make and fill us with His Spirit.

## An Example: Joseph (Genesis 37:3—41:43)

An incredible example of this is Joseph in the Old Testament. If you recall, Joseph was Jacob's firstborn son by Rachel. Joseph was loved more than any of his older brothers. This, of course, caused the brothers to hate him. Finally, the brothers came up with a plan to get rid of Joseph by selling him to some traveling merchants. These merchants then turned around and sold Joseph to an Egyptian officer in Pharaoh's army named Potiphar.

Even through all these horrific circumstances, the Scriptures tell us over and over again that the Lord continued "to be with" Joseph and watch over him. (Genesis 39:2) It says that Joseph even "found grace" with Potiphar. But, unfortunately, Potiphar's wife was not as "full of grace" as her husband. She was sexually attracted to Joseph, so she tried to compromise him by tempting him to "lie with her." (Genesis 39:7) Joseph refused and fled. She then called her husband's men, lied about the whole affair and accused Joseph of initiating the situation. When Potiphar heard about the incident, he threw Joseph out of his house and into prison. (Genesis 39:20) But again, Scripture tells us that even in prison the Lord was with Joseph and watched out for him. And through a series of events, Joseph (who had the gift of interpreting dreams) was called to render clear the dreams of Pharaoh.

Pharaoh was so pleased with Joseph's interpretation that he freed Joseph, gave him his own ring, and put new silk garments on him with a gold chain about his neck. Eventually, Pharaoh made Joseph ruler over all of Egypt, and through him, all of Israel was blessed. (Genesis 41:43)

*Trusting God in the darkness is difficult because quite often we feel one way, and yet by faith we must choose to act in another way.*

You can see God's Handprint over the entire story of Joseph and how He wove the horrific things that happened to Joseph and turned them into blessings.

But in the middle of these trials, I'm sure Joseph had the same reaction that we might have. Hopelessness. And yet now, because we can stand back and in hindsight see the whole story, we realize that God never forgot Joseph. He never stopped loving him. He was with him the whole time, faithfully working out His perfect will. And look what happened in the end. Joseph became the chief ruler of a whole nation, a country that would ultimately control the whole world. Here's a perfect example of how if we are hopeful and patient, ***God will "work all things together for good."***[44]

He is faithful, and that's what we must put our hope in.

Other examples of men who had "hope" even in their darkest "night seasons" are Job, Abraham, Moses, and many others. All of these men clung to hope even though their situations were dire. In like manner, we must be open to learning the same lessons.

Hebrews 11:33–40 also describes some of the other ways God tested the Old Testament saints: "they were faced with stopping the mouths of lions; they quenched the violence of fire; they were tortured, encountered trials of mocking, chains and imprisonment; they were sawn in two, stoned, tempted, slain with a sword; they wandered; were destitute, afflicted and tormented."

These were some of the "dark" periods of time that these heroes of faith had to withstand in order to learn to trust the Lord completely. We, then, are not the only ones to encounter darkness. Since most of us are unable to learn what God is trying to teach us through our own reason, our own intellect or our own emotions, God teaches us by darkening these areas of our soul and forcing us to rely only upon the *eyes of our spirit* as He did with the Old Testament saints. As with Moses, God is teaching us to *"see Him who is invisible"* during the hard times. If you read Hebrews 12:10–14, you'll note how it says that only "if" we endure chastening, we will be "partakers of His holiness," but without holiness we'll not be able to "see Him."[45] In other words, if we are not "clean," we'll be unable to behold Him. (See Chapter Eight, Sanctification Steps.)

Many of us will struggle in this new realm of faith just as a swimmer fights the powerful current that draws him into deeper water. Unless the swimmer quiets his fears and calmly rests in the water, he will drown. The believer, likewise, will drown in this dark time unless he learns to be still and to quiet his soul. God is simply using the darkness to accomplish His will in us and to form such unshakable trust that we'll be able to advance to impregnable fellowship with Him. He is teaching us to rely upon *His* faithfulness to perform *His* promises in *His* timing and *His* way, whether we understand what He is doing or not. Consequently, *the way we respond to the darkness is extremely important and will determine our whole spiritual walk.* Whether we advance, withdraw or simply stay where we are will decide our degree of intimacy with Him.

This is why it's so critical that we understand the importance of hoping in Him—trusting in His faithfulness—even in the darkness. If we don't, we will fight Him the whole way and *never* advance beyond this stage. Some of us will even grow impatient and seek a means by which we can escape. Others of us will become paralyzed and immobile in the place of thunder. But if we understand what He is trying to do, we'll be able through endurance to cooperate fully with Him and learn the lessons. These are the believers who can say, "Though You slay me, yet will I trust You."[46] "Though everything in my life is upside down, and I don't understand a thing that You are doing, I will still hope in Your Love and faithfulness."

This is where I am now. I trust Him completely even though everything in my life is upside down and I don't have a clue as to why all this has happened and is happening. In spite of it all, I still hope and trust in His Love and faithfulness.

## WHY HOPE IS SO IMPORTANT?

Hope, then, is critical, not only as "the anchor of our soul," but also as "the tie" or "the connection" or the "bridge" to the presence of God.

As we said, hope is what allows us to withstand our present struggles. It's what allows us to go across the chasms, the gorges and the valleys in our life, *knowing* that God will be faithful to do as He has promised, no matter how long it takes. Hope is what allows us to "see" the Lord in the midst of our trials and trust that He will get us through. I can't imagine what people who don't know the Lord do when they are told horrific things such as I was told one year ago. "If you don't do this, you'll have two months to live." If someone doesn't know where they are going when they die or what their life here has been about, what do they do with this information? Hope is what gives us the endurance to walk over that bridge toward the unseen, continually communicating with the Father "behind the veil," knowing, at least, where we are headed and unconditionally relinquishing the time frame to Him. The veil that Hebrews 6:18–19 is referring to is the veil to the Holy of Holies in Solomon's Temple (in the Old Testament) where God Himself dwelt. It validates that our "hope" in God's faithfulness is what will penetrate that veil of His presence and join us with His Spirit.

# HOPE

is the *only thing* that helps us "to see Him"

who is **INVISIBLE** in the midst of our trials,

WHICH THEN GIVES US THE STRENGTH

TO ENDURE *and* TO OVERCOME.

So the answer to why "hope" is so important is *that hope is the only thing that helps us "to see Him" who is invisible in the midst of our trials, which then gives us the strength to endure and to overcome. In other words, it's the link, the tie and the bridge to our future—our "chain of Hope."*

*If we don't have hope*, it's like falling down a slippery slope (constantly gaining momentum) and not having anything to hold on to. *If we don't have hope*, it's like drifting on a fragile and ill-equipped life raft in the middle of an ocean with the sharks encircling us, just waiting for them to attack. And finally, *if we don't have hope*, it's like being trapped in an avalanche plummeting downhill until we are totally stripped, even of our desire to live. As Job says in Job 17:11, 15: "My days are past and my purposes are broken off.... Where now is my hope?"

If I didn't have hope right now in God's faithfulness to "work all things together for my good," I might as well give up, let go and die. Letting go of His Hand right now would cause me to lose my mooring, frantically thrash about and then drown.

Maybe you can now understand why Romans 8:24 emphasizes the fact that we are literally "saved by hope." Hope is not only an essential part of our salvation, it's also critical for our sanctification, without which our future will be impaired.

Hope, however, as we have seen can become faint, trembling and feeble as we wait for God's touch, especially if we have it all mapped out in our own minds as to how He is going to act. As I mentioned earlier, I was shattered when my situation didn't turn out as I thought it would. Remember Proverbs 13:12: "Hope deferred maketh the heart sick..." It certainly did mine.

Many believers, under heavy and fiery trials, have lost their anchor. They have lost their trust in the Lord, strayed from their mooring and severed their tie to the Lord "behind the veil."

## An Example: Wharf Rats

Let me give you a small but very graphic example of what hope is and what it does. It's rather a gross example, but it really gets the point across. The late Chuck Smith of Calvary Chapel Costa Mesa tells the story that...

Some psychologists decided to do an experiment on some Norwegian wharf rats. They wanted to see how long it would take for these rats to drown. Why they did the experiment in the first place, I don't understand. Nevertheless, they put the rats in a huge tank of water, let them flounder and begin to go under. It took only 17 minutes for this to happen. But just before the rats went down for the last time, the psychologists rescued them, pulled them out, dried them off and took care of them for the next few days.

Two or three days later, the psychologists again put the same rats in another huge tank of water to see how long it would take them to drown this time. The rats survived a whopping 37 hours!

What made the difference? How were the rats able to survive over 36 hours longer the second time around? The reason is that the rats had "hope" that someone would rescue them, as they had been in the past!

And it's the same with us. Once we know and experience God's faithfulness, we will hold on unconditionally because we know He will be faithful to do the same for us in the future. Experiencing God's Love and faithfulness in the past is what will allow us to "hope for the same" in the future. This kind of hope is what sustains us in suffering and gives us the strength to endure the waiting process.[47] Remember Moses. He *knew by experience* that God would be faithful to His promises so he was able to endure.

Hope demonstrates its character by the steadfastness with which it waits. Hope is a place of shelter, refuge, security and safety. It's a rock and a shield where we flee for protection.[48] It's also the glue that gives us endurance. Once we know God's personal Love and we see His faithfulness over and over again, we'll be able to stand and endure the winds and the storms of the future. This is what will keep us firmly fixed on course. Hope, therefore, is what helps us to patiently bear the tension between the now and the future.[49]

## Hope is the Connection to Intimacy

*Hope, therefore, is the connection or the tie to the Holy of Holies where God dwells.* It's not only the anchor that holds us steady, it's the "chain of hope" that leads us right to the Lord's presence. First, there's faith; then, there's hope, and finally, there's Love.

"Faith" seems to show itself in the Inner Court of the temple, but "hope" shows itself in the Holy Place.[50] And "Love" shows itself in the Holy of Holies where God dwells.

As we will see later, the priests in Solomon's Temple had a very important ritual to carry out every day. The Inner Court was for the cleaning of "sins," whereas the Holy Place was for a deeper inner cleansing and for worshiping the Lord. The priests had to literally carry "hot coals of fire" from the Brazen Altar in the Inner Court right on into the Incense Altar in the Holy Place. This ritual will become very important to us as we begin to see the parallel between what the priests were required to do in order to be in God's presence and what the Lord wants us, as believers, to do to be in His presence. The Brazen Altar in the Inner Court was for the cleansing of sin, whereas the Incense Altar in the Holy Place was for intimacy and fellowship with the Lord of Love. We will cover all of this in more detail in Chapter 9. Hope plays a "big part" in this Scriptural analogy.

Second Corinthians 3:18 tells us that we must learn to spiritually "see through the glass darkly." In other words, God teaches us His life principles through different "patterns," parables and analogies in the Bible. I believe the temple and what the priests were required to do there is a model or a design of what God requires each of us to do in our own lives. It's an overview of God's plan.

In closing, ask yourself: What is it that gives *you* hope? What is it that gets *you* through the hard times, the trials and the storms? Who do *you* trust when your world is crumbling around you?

Read the words of Michael Card's song called "Soul Anchor":

*Though the wind is ragin' all around*
*And even though the waves may rise*
*There's a place of stillness in the storm*
*And you can find it if you will believe*
*It's a soul anchor, hold on to the hope*
*It's a soul anchor, just hold on to your courage*
*Before we call, He answers us with hope*
*We are so sure of what we're waiting for*
*And certain of the things we do not see*
*For we are told by the One who cannot lie*
*And in this hope is our security*
*So, hold fast, draw near!*

## SCRIPTURES ON HOPE

Lamentations 3:24
Colossians 1:27
Hebrews 11:1; 6:18–19
1 Peter 3:15
Romans 15:13
Psalm 31:24; 42:5; 71:14
1 Peter 1:8, 13
Hebrews 11:13

# CHAPTER TWO—WHAT IS HOPE?

1. Memorize Hebrews 6:18–19.

2. What exactly is "hope"?

3. What are the two types of hope, and how do they differ?

4. Why is it that when our hope is "deferred," our hearts become sad and we wither and die? Have you ever been here?

5. Hebrews 6:18–19 tells us that "hope is the anchor of our soul." What exactly is an anchor, and why is hope associated with it?

6. Hebrews 6 tells us that "hope" is like the chain that keeps us tied to the Lord "behind the veil" (in the Holy of Holies). Explain exactly what this means. Can you give a personal example? (Hebrews 11:27)

7. Scripture tells us that hope is not only like an "anchor" holding us in place, it's also like a chain, bridge, link or a cord between what two things? (2 Corinthians 1:10; 1 Timothy 4:10)

8. Romans 5:5 tells us that "hope never disappoints." Can you explain what this means?

9. How are the words "hope" and "trust" related? Define each of them.

10. Why is trusting God in the darkness so very difficult? Give a personal example.

11. Why is this type of unconditional hope and trust so very important?

"Now faith is the substance

of things hoped for,

*the evidence of things not seen.*"

HEBREWS 11:1

# CHAPTER THREE

# How Does Hope Differ from Faith? Why Do We Lose Hope?

L ast chapter we spoke about "hope" and its critical importance in our lives.

Hope is like the link between our faith and God's Love. First Corinthians 13:13 even validates this: "Now abideth *faith, hope* and *Love*, these three; but the greatest of these is Love." Faith, hope and Love are three of the most important and basic themes of the Bible. To me, they are the three main "pillars" of the Christian walk.

Faith, hope and Love are also alluded to in Colossians 1:4–5, which says: "we have heard of your *faith* in Christ, of the *Love* you have for all the saints and the *hope* which is laid up for you in heaven." They are also referenced in 1 Thessalonians 1:3: "Remembering without ceasing your work of *faith*, and labor of *Love* and patience of *hope* in our Lord Jesus Christ, in the sight of God and our Father..." And finally they appear together in 1 Thessalonians 5:8, which talks about faith and Love being like our breastplate and hope our helmet of salvation.

***Faith*** *can be defined as believing in God's Word.* ***Hope*** *is trusting that God's Spirit will perform His Word* *in His timing and way. And <u>Love</u> is the fulfillment of God's Word—that Tree of Life—at the end of the bridge.*

Another way of saying this is: ***Faith is the promise believed; hope is the promise walked out, and Love is the promise fulfilled.***[51]

All three of these pillars are extremely important, but what I never saw before is that "hope" is the actual link or the connection or the tie between ***our*** faith and ***His*** Love. Notice that "faith" and "hope" are things that *we* must do, whereas Love—whether it's God's Love to us or God's Love through us—is something ***God*** does.

Let's explore each of these three pillars in a little greater detail.

## FAITH

"Faith" is what saves us. Ephesians 2:8–9 validates this: "For by grace you are saved through faith and that not of yourselves; it is a gift of God: not of works, lest any man should boast."

*Faith is not a "feeling," it's simply the choice to believe and then the choice to act upon that belief.*

Hebrews 11:1 defines faith for us: "Faith is the <u>substance</u> of things hoped for and <u>evidence</u> of things not yet seen." <u>Substance</u> (*Strong's* #5287) in this Scripture means support, essence, assurance and foundational. And <u>evidence</u> (*Strong's* #1650) means the proof of something or the conviction about it.

Faith is made up of a series of choices we make to do His will by "faith," not our feelings. It's the constant choice not only to believe what the Lord says in His Word, but also to step out in that belief. As 1 John 5:4 tells us, faith is the victory that overcomes the world, the flesh and the devil. Ephesians 6:16 tells us that faith is like a "shield," and it's the way we quench the darts of the enemy. Faith is not a "feeling," it's simply the choice to believe and then the choice to act upon that belief. It's the unequivocal strong conviction that no matter what happens God will never leave us nor forsake us. Only through faith can a human being leave his familiar comfort zone and move out into the realm of the unknown.

Faith is synonymous with abandonment to God's will, and that means being "obedient unto death."[52] It's looking away from ourselves and looking only to Him.[53] He is Who we depend upon, Who we lean upon and Who directs our lives.

## Hope

Hope, on the other hand, is trusting in God's Spirit to actually bring His Word to pass. It's faith, yes, but it's taken one step farther. It's not only the conviction that God's promises are true, *it's the confidence and the security to withstand and endure the struggle (and the wait) between receiving the promises and their fulfillment in our lives.* Hope is not only the "anchor" that keeps us steady while we are waiting for their fulfillment, it's also the "bridge" that will ultimately get us to our goal—seeing His Love and faithfulness in our lives. As Hebrews 10:36 says, "We have need of endurance so that after we have done the will of God, we will receive the promise."

Maybe you can now begin to understand how critical "hope" is. Hope is how we stay connected to the Lord during the difficult times. Remember the Israelites. They had faith, but when it came to persevering in the hard times, they lost their hope and never made it to the promised land.

*So hope is what gives us the power to remain sure and steadfast to the end of the race. It's what allows us to "see Him who is invisible" in the middle of our trials—the chain of hope tied directly to the Lord of Love.*

Hebrews 10:23 confirms this for us: "We must hold fast to our confession of hope without wavering, **because He who promised is faithful**." There's the secret! <u>He</u> who promised is faithful, but <u>we</u> *are the ones who must hold fast*. We are the ones who must "hope against hope" in order to experience His Love and faithfulness. Only then, according to Proverbs 3:5, can He direct our paths. In other words, it not only takes **His** faithfulness, it also takes **our** trust. Hope is not only based on His promises for the future, it also rests on His character. Once we have experienced His Love and His character of faithfulness in the past, we'll have the hope that He will do the same for us in the future. *Hope is simply trusting in the trustworthiness of God to bring His Word to pass.*

Let me read an excerpt from John Bunyan's *Israel's Hope Encouraged*, because it defines "hope" so perfectly. (http://ninetysixandten. wordpress.com/2007/08/18/the-difference-between-faith-and-hope/)

"The promise is like a mighty cable that is fastened by one end to a ship and by the other to the anchor. The soul is the ship where faith is, and to which the hither end of the cable is fastened; but *hope* is the anchor that is at the other end of the cable, and 'which entereth into that within the veil.' Thus faith and hope are getting hold of both ends of the promise; they carry it safely all away. *Faith looks to Christ as dead, buried and ascended; and hope looks for His second coming. Faith looks to Him for justification; hope for glory. Faith fights for doctrine; hope for reward; faith for what is in the Bible; hope for what is in heaven. Faith purifies the heart from bad principles; hope from bad manners."*

So faith and hope are two sides of the same coin. We can't have faith without hoping and trusting in something or someone; and we can't have hope without faith in something or someone. Each depends upon the other. They are linked, and yet at the same time they are very distinctive in their separate functions.

## WHAT'S THE DIFFERENCE BETWEEN FAITH AND HOPE?

This leads to the next question: What's the differences between faith and hope?

When I first began to write this book, I went round and round in my mind as to what the difference was between these two very important subjects. I think I believed they were almost the same thing. And as I have been asking others the same question, it's amazing how many have answered: "Aren't they really the same thing?" In fact, one woman just called the other day and stated that she really couldn't articulate their differences. Well, if we don't know in our head how faith and hope differ, how on earth can we live them out? We can't!

In my studies *and life experiences* over the last couple of years, I've come to the conclusion that "faith" is simply the choice to believe and act upon God's Word, whereas "hope" is the choice to trust God's faithfulness to perform that Word in my life. (It's also choosing to endure all that God allows while we are waiting for His promises to materialize. Thus, we desperately need both faith and hope!)

*In simple terms, think of "faith" as believing in and depending upon God's Word, whereas "hope" is trusting in and relying upon God's Spirit to perform His Word, no matter how long it takes. Hope is what allows us to "see God" while we are waiting.*

Speaking of getting hope and faith confused and mixed up, listen to how the King James Version translates verse 23 of Hebrews 10: "Let us hold fast the *profession of our faith* without wavering…" Now look at how the New King James Version translates the same verse: "Let us hold fast the *confession of our hope* without wavering." Which version is correct? Which one accurately tells us what this verse is speaking about. Is it faith or is it hope? No wonder we often think of them as interchangeable terms. The Greek word here in Hebrews 10:23 is *elipis* (*Strong's* #1680), which means "hope," and not faith (the Greek word for faith is *pistis, Strong's* #4102).

What's tragic about this confusion is that it causes us to be fuzzy in our own understanding of these critical terms. Yes, they work together. But without understanding their significant differences, it will be difficult for us to move forward in our walk with the Lord. I believe this confusion is one of the reasons and one of the causes for so much hopelessness in the Body of Christ right now.

So faith and hope do have different functions, and it is critical that we learn exactly what those differences are.

Think of FAITH as believing in

*and depending upon God's Word,*

whereas HOPE is trusting in

*and relying upon God's Spirit*

*to perform His Word,*

NO MATTER HOW LONG IT TAKES.

## HEROES OF FAITH AND HOPE

Hebrews 11 is a powerful chronicle of men and women who faithfully stepped out into the unknown, believing what God had promised them. These incredible heroes of faith *endured horrific hardships, but continued to embrace God's promises, even though many of them never lived to see them fulfilled.* Verse 7 of Hebrews 11 begins by saying, *By faith* Noah prepared an ark...*by faith* Abraham went out...*by faith* Sarah received the ability to conceive...*by faith* Moses kept the Passover...*by faith* the people of God passed through the Red Sea...*by faith* the walls of Jericho fell down...*by faith* Rahab the harlot did not perish.

The incredible part about these "heroes of faith" is that even though many of them died having never received the actual completion of God promise, *they still had "hope" (trust) that God would in His timing and way perform what He had promised.* Because they knew God's character and they knew He would be faithful to keep His Word, ***they "saw" the fulfillment of His promises afar off.*** Consider what Hebrews 11:13 says: "These all died in faith, not having received the promises, but *having seen them afar off,* and were persuaded of them, and embraced them." That's our commission, too. We must see God's promises fulfilled afar off. We must be persuaded of them and embrace them, even though we may never see them fulfilled in our lifetime. That's the definition of hope!

As Moses did, these heroes of faith "endured as seeing Him who is invisible."[54] They not only had faith, they had hope. They were supernaturally given the power to endure chastening, suffer affliction, subdue kingdoms, wrought righteousness, obtain promises, stop the mouth of lions, quench the violence of fire, escape the edge of the sword, be made strong when they were weak, turn to flight the armies of the aliens, be tortured, mocked and scourged, be imprisoned,

81

stoned, and sawn asunder, be tested and slain with the sword, wander about in sheepskins, be destitute, afflicted and tormented.[55]

Yet these believers still had "hope." That's what allowed them to bear their incredible hardships, trials and persecutions. They withstood these things, not only by having "faith" in God's promises but also by having "hope" and trust in God's character, His faithfulness and His Love. Faith gave them the belief, but hope gave them the strength to weather it all.

One of my favorite definitions of faith has always been Paul's words in Romans 4:20–21 about Abraham: "He staggered not at the promise of God through unbelief; but was strong in faith, giving glory to God; and being fully persuaded that, what [God] had promised, He [would be] able also to perform." This is a wonderful Scripture, but as I study it closer, I believe it refers to both Abraham's faith and hope. The *faith part* is "that he staggered not at the promise of God through unbelief, but was strong in faith, giving glory to God." But the *hope part* is that "he was fully persuaded that, what God had promised He would be able to perform."

*To me, this is the simple difference between faith and hope. "Faith" is the free choice to follow and do what God has counseled us in His Word. "Hope" is the free choice to trust in God's faithfulness and His Spirit to perform that Word in our lives in His timing and way. Saying it another way: Faith is choosing to believe and apply what God says in His Word, whereas hope is relying upon God Spirit to bring it to pass. The first involves "belief"; the second involves "trust." Faith and trust...."staggering not at His promise" but also "being fully persuaded He will perform it."*

In other words, hope must follow faith and then, of course, comes Love.[56]

Faith comes from hearing God's Word, but hope comes from knowing God's character and experiencing His faithfulness. Romans 5:1–5 validates this: "Therefore being *justified by faith*, we have peace with God through our Lord Jesus Christ: by whom also we have *access by faith* into this grace in which we stand, and *rejoice in hope* of the glory of God. And not only so, but we glory in tribulations also: *knowing* that *tribulation worketh patience;* and *patience, experience*; and *experience, hope*: and hope maketh not ashamed; because *the Love of God is shed abroad* in our hearts by the Holy Spirit which is given unto us."

As the above Scripture implies, hope seems to come *after* a certain amount of maturity in our walk with the Lord. It comes *after* we have experienced tribulations, *after* we have been given the power to endure, and *after* we have seen God's faithfulness during the difficult times. Here, again, is the secret! Just as the heroes of faith in Hebrew 11 knew that God would be faithful to perform His promises in His perfect timing and His perfect way, they also knew His character and His trustworthiness. They had seen it over and over again. They also knew that "God is a *rewarder* of them that diligently seek Him."[57] So they trusted Him implicitly.

How about us? Do we have this kind of faith and this kind of hope?

## Why We Lose our Hope

As was said earlier, "We don't die if we lose our faith, but we **do** die if we lose our hope."

How many born-again believers do you know today who have lost their hope and their way? I could name at least ten right now without even having to think about it. In fact, I just received another letter from a precious sister in the Lord that expresses this hopelessness perfectly:

"I am hurting so badly, I just wish God would take me home. I have been of no value here on this earth, and I'm tired. I've done no good here. There is no end to this wretched life. I am not favored, not blessed and never have been. I really don't believe God has anything good in store for me. No matter how much I love God, craziness and abuse have ruled my life, and I cannot escape it. So I am sick of trying. It doesn't matter how much I repent or how much I try to love. I am damaged beyond repair. I am perishing because I have yet to see the goodness of the Lord in the land of the living."

Another brother wrote this two weeks ago: "I am flattened. My vision is destroyed; my dreams shattered. The people I love and had hoped would come to my aid have, instead, left me. As I look around, it's totally dark and it's frightening. I have lost my home, my loved ones, my purpose.... What is left?"

And finally, this one: "Although I have been reading the Word and praying more than ever before, I have been hit with major problem after major problem. I know God's many promises in the Bible and realize that the heavy load is supposed to build my muscles of faith. But, frankly, it has been too hard. Suffice to say, it has been over-whelming even with faith...so I question my faith and question my ability to make it through.... Though I love my family and friends and want to do the Lord's work on earth, I would not mind if I was taken home soon to be with Him."

This last letter reminds me of Isaiah 49:14: "The LORD has forsaken me, and my Lord hath forgotten me." And what Job said in Job 7:20: "Why hast thou set me as a mark against thee, so that I am a burden to myself?"[58]

These letters define hopelessness. They each express "eternal hope" (salvation), but all three seem to waver on their day-to-day temporal hope. Why is this so catastrophic? What's so important about having not only eternal hope but also temporal hope?

Having temporal hope is important because if we think that having eternal hope of "salvation" is the only goal of our Christian life, then why not give up in tough times, just as these letters convey? We know we're already saved. We know we're going to heaven! Why not just "close the door," as we really have no further need for hope. But here's the problem: Yes, we're saved; yes, we'll be raptured, and yes, we're going to heaven. But what will God have us do there? What kind of future responsibility will we have if we have given up so easily down here? We, obviously, won't be fully prepared for heaven; we won't have been made "ready," and we won't have been totally sanctified. What will God have us do in the Millennium when He comes to rule on the earth, and what will that mean for us in eternity?

Whether we like it or not, we are in a "race," and in order to finish that race, we must have "hope." Hope is the connection, the bridge and the zip line to the finish line and the "goal" of our salvation, the mark of the high calling of God that is being conformed into His image.[59]

Now, some of us know what we must do in order to get out of a hopeless state of mind (how to pick up that "chain of hope" again), but others of us do not. This book is intended to help the latter. It's very true that at this present moment God is allowing some very difficult times in many of our lives (mine included)—financially, maritally, emotionally, occupationally, medically, etc. But He is also using these difficult times to push us into trusting Him more, to seeing Him in the midst of the fire and to learning more about His personal Love and faithfulness. (Remember Charles Spurgeon's quote: "Hope is like a star, not to be seen in the sunshine of prosperity, but only to be discovered in the night of adversity.") God doesn't want us to be "lukewarm" believers or "fence-sitter" Christians any longer. He wants us to know Him so intimately that we will never wane in our hope toward Him. Consequently, He is pushing many of us to our limits.

Again, remember Romans 5:3–5, which explains all of this perfectly: "tribulation works patience; and patience [works] experience; and experience [works] hope; and hope maketh not ashamed because the Love of God is shed abroad in our hearts..." In other words, our hard times can (if we allow them to) result in experiencing God's faithfulness to a new depth, which will then bring about renewed hope and trust for our next difficult circumstance. Romans 5 is God's plan in a nutshell: tribulation teaches us patience that then produces experience that provides hope that then results in our knowing His Love to an even greater degree.

Some of us will be able to survive our trials and tribulations because we have seen and experienced His faithfulness in the past, just as Romans 5 says, and we know He will do the same again. Thus we'll have the confidence to endure and to overcome. But others of us, as represented in the previous letters, because we have not experienced His mercy and His trustworthiness in the past, will automatically lose hope and let go of His Hand.

*Hope is the connection, the bridge and the zip line to the finish line and the "goal" of our salvation, the mark of the high calling of God that is being conformed into His Image.*

## What are "Night Seasons"?

A distinctive characteristic of our valleys of Baca and our dark nights is that often heaven "seems" silent. I think this is one of the hardest parts of this period of time. No matter how much we pray, seek God and read His Word, He just doesn't seem to communicate with us as He once did. We don't "hear" Him, "see" Him or "feel" Him as we have in the past. These episodes are sometimes called "night seasons." (I wrote an entire book on this subject, thinking I understood it. Boy, it wasn't until this recent episode in my life that I had a real grasp of what a night season really is.) A "night season" is a series of trials where we think that God has totally left us or abandoned us. And this is what often leads us to hopelessness.

In reality, night seasons are simply Father-filtered periods of time where God teaches us to trust Him more by *depriving us of the "natural" light we have always relied upon* (our own natural seeing, our own natural feeling and our own natural understanding). Even as mature Christians, most of us still walk by the "flesh" (by our *own* emotions and through the eyes of our *own* understanding). This is the reason why many of us have just a lukewarm relationship with God and why we don't know Him intimately. God, on the other hand, loves us too much to allow us to remain in this dispassionate state. He knows that the only way we will ever attain immovable intimacy with Him is by learning to walk by *naked faith* and *enduring hope*—faith and hope that are *not* dependent upon our sight, our feelings or our own understanding. Our trust must be based on His faithfulness and His Love no matter what occurs. The classroom that He often uses to teach us this lesson is called "the dark night of the spirit" or "night seasons."

Take a moment to read Job 30:17–31 as it is a perfect Scriptural example of a night season. In verse 17, Job says: "My bones are pierced in me in the night season: and my sinews take no rest." In verse 20, he says: "I cry unto thee, and thou dost not hear me: I stand up, and thou regardest, me not." And in verse 26, he says: "When I looked for good, then evil came unto me: and when I waited for light, there came only darkness."

Listen also to Isaiah 50:10: "Who is among you that *feareth the* LORD, that *obeyeth the voice of His servant*, [but that] walketh in darkness, and hath no light?" Notice something very important here: **This person not**

*only "fears the Lord," he also "obeys His voice." This person is not only*
*a believer, but an obedient one. Yet he still walks in darkness.*

The dark night, then, is a God-directed period of time when the Lord purposely puts us in a "corner" (in that "secret place of thunder," the valley of weeping or the shadow of death) so we will learn to trust (*elipizo*) Him as never before. It's a place where God tries our faith, tests our endurance and stretches our patience.

A Biblical "night season" is a God-sent, Father-filtered period of time when God allows storms into our lives specifically to strengthen our endurance, our trust in Him and our hope, so we might come to know His faithfulness and His Love in a way we never have before.[60] It doesn't really matter where our trials come from (medical circumstances, death of a beloved one, financial or marital trials, etc.), because God allows them all. Consequently, our response should be exactly the same—to trust Him implicitly, knowing He loves us and knowing He promises to faithfully "work everything together for our good." Even if we don't see how He is going to do it or understand why He is allowing it, we must *choose by faith* to trust Him.

Trials and problems come to *all* Christians, either because of personal sin, the sins of others, the schemes of the devil, or the fallen state of the human race. According to the Bible, a true "night season" is none of these! It's the time when God tries and tests our faith. Again, it often occurs at the "place of thunder" or the "valley of Baca" or "the shadow of death." Listen to James 1:3–4: "Knowing this, that the trying of your faith worketh patience. But let patience have her perfect work, that ye may be *perfect [complete]* and entire, wanting nothing."

That's God's goal—that we might "be complete in Him, nothing wanting" (conformed perfectly to His image). This simply means that others will be able to see Christ in us—experience His Love through us, hear His wisdom and witness His power, in spite of the trials and ordeals we are experiencing in our lives.

The thing that makes a Biblical "night season" so very different from other trials is that there often seems to be no disobedience or any known sin on our part. That's what makes this period of time so difficult. We've already dealt with our sin and our self as much as we can, but the situation continues to loom in front of us. Remember, the Valley of Baca was "on the way to where the believers worshiped." These Christians weren't running from God. On the contrary, they were going toward God when they encountered the night season.

If we could really get behind the Lord and actually see what He sees, we would understand that our "night season" is His way of exposing our hidden, secret habits, our hidden motives, our "self-centered" ways, etc. It's His design to crucify any self-love, self-confidence, self-reliance, self-trust, self-will, self-pity, self-grasping and any other self-interest, self-seeking, self-preservation and self-esteem that God sees in us. These interior attitudes will never change on their own, unless God exposes them and uproots them. So it's *not* necessarily sin that God is focusing on in this night season, but our "self," our *own* plans, our *own* ambitions, our *own* values and our *own* ideals—anything that is not "of God." If these habits and motives and self-centered ways are not uncovered and dealt with, they can, and often do, lead us to more sin. Only God knows the quenching effect they have on His Spirit and His Life in us. And only He knows how to perfectly deal with them.

## "WHY ME, LORD?"

The one question that remains in many of our minds is: "Why, Lord? Why me?" (Especially if we have lost a loved one, or our marriage has failed, or we have lost our job, etc.)

I have asked this question a million times this past year as I was struggling with fear and terrified of the continuing pain. I kept saying, "Lord, I'm willing for this to happen any other place in my body, but why my face, Lord? Why!"

I recently received an e-mail that expressed the same feelings about my situation: "There has been much discussion about 'why God would let this happen to you.' For many young believers it is a hard concept to understand. They really want to apply 'the act right and God will bless you, mess up and punishment will follow.' Why do bad things happen to good people?"

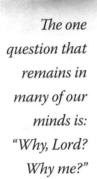

*The one question that remains in many of our minds is: "Why, Lord? Why me?"*

Another letter expresses it this way: "No one knows how deep a struggle cuts except the person in the midst of it. Sometimes the intensity of the struggle does overwhelm the soul. The temptation is always to ask 'why me?' And it's strongest when you have given it all to the foot of the Cross and yet nothing has changed or, in some cases, it's gotten worse."

Notice that Job thought the same thing— that God was actually punishing him.[61]

Unanswered prayer naturally causes us to doubt. We must recognize that having doubt is natural (it's not necessarily a lack of faith). Doubt is the natural result of prayer that's not answered in our timing or in our way. What we must do then is recognize our doubt (not berate ourselves because of it), confess it to the Lord ("Yes, Lord, I am doubtful"), and then choose *by faith* to trust Him no matter what the situation. (Again, we don't have to "feel" our faith choices to follow God and to trust Him. These choices are made simply by faith.) So don't let doubt take hold or it will result in a falling away from the Lord. We'll talk about the "cycle of trust" versus the "cycle of defeat" in the upcoming chapters. We'll also explore *how to make* practical "faith choices."

One of God's answers as to "why" He allows these difficult circumstances is: "Whom the Lord loves, He chastens and scourges."[62] And He makes us partakers of His sufferings by "fiery trials."[63]

Fire is a symbol of God's Love, but it's also an agent of God's correcting, cleansing and purging. He wants to purge us of any self-centeredness, any self-love, and "anything that is not of Him." We all continue to experience these attitudes because we are human. The only one who was "perfect" was Jesus. As we let Him fill us more and more with **His** perfectness, we too can be complete. (We went driving Sunday morning and passed a church with a sign out front that said "no perfect people allowed." We loved what that meant, so we turned around and attended the service.) Jesus is the only One who is perfect, but as we die to our self and allow Him to fill us, we too can become complete in Him.

God wants all our pettiness, spite, revenge, cruelty, foolishness, egotism, possessiveness, addictions and selfishness removed. These things not only affect our communication with Him, they obviously affect our communication with others. And until these things are purged from our spirit, we cannot have the union with Christ that we seek. We must become detached from all our own plans, preferences, praise, success and comforts, and dead to *all* desires but those of the Lord.

Now again, some of these things are not necessarily sin, but because they are obviously "not of God," they can and will quench His Spirit in us. Remember 1 Thessalonians 5:23 and 2 Corinthians 7:1. Both tell us that *believers* not only must have their soul sanctified, they must also have their spirit purified (and that means a "daily" or even a moment-by-moment decision). Only as we surrender these internal attitudes does the crucifixion of spirit become complete.

The question then becomes: ***How does God reveal these specific things to us?***

He uses the current situations in our lives—the difficult situations, the self-centered lives of others and the world of hurt we often find ourselves in. These are the "crosses we have to bear."[64] These "crosses" might result from consequences of past choices, current difficult situations, marital hardships, sexual problems, the death of a loved one, permanent physical ailments or any besetting sin. They can also be long-standing situations or current circumstances. Whatever it is, God will lovingly use them to test our endurance and expose our self-centeredness, but in return (if we allow Him to) He revives our intimacy and shows us His faithfulness in a new depth.

Then, and only then, can we claim with the apostle Paul: "I am crucified with Christ: nevertheless I live; yet not I, but Christ liveth in me; and the life which I now live in the flesh I live by the faith [or the faithfulness] of the Son of God, who loved me and gave Himself for me." (Galatians 2:20)

Only God can answer the "why" question as it pertains to each of our lives. Each of His answers may be different. But ***the bottom line is that God doesn't cause the dark nights in our lives; He simply uses them for His purposes—to conform us more into His image and to teach us to trust and hope in Him to a greater degree.***

God doesn't cause the dark nights in our lives; He simply uses them for His purposes—to conform us more into His image and to teach us to trust and hope in Him to a greater degree.

The bottom line is: "Faith" is simply *choosing to believe God's Word*, whereas "hope" is *choosing to trust the Holy Spirit to perform His Word* in our lives **in His timing and way**. Big difference! So again, faith and hope are two sides of the same coin, and they must work together. Faith is **believing in God's Word** and taking that first step, whereas hope is **trusting God's Spirit to perform His Word** and then waiting for it to happen.

**Hope is the ability to endure our trials by trusting God to lead us forward without any fear.** Trusting Him is different than simply believing in Him. It's putting shoe leather to our belief. It's relying upon His promises even though they make no sense.[65] It's knowing (by faith, not feelings) that He is on our right hand and thus we will not be moved.[66] It's saying and believing, by faith, that no matter what He does to us or allows in our lives, we will trust Him.

## "Faith, Hope and Love, but the Greatest of these is Love" (1 Corinthians 13)

We will be talking about faith, hope and Love throughout this book. First Corinthians 13 tells us that of these three, "the greatest is Love." What exactly is this Love that 1 Corinthians is referring to, and how is it any different from normal human love?

First Corinthians is speaking about God's Love, which is the Greek word *Agape*. What's so unique about *Agape*? First John 4:8 tells us that God Himself is Love. Therefore we are not simply talking about a human love here, but a supernatural Love.

*Agape* is a supernatural Love that is poured into our hearts the moment we invite Christ to be our Savior and to take control of our lives. It's God Himself who comes into our hearts at that moment, and *He is that Love!* Yes, of course, He loves the world and everyone in it, but it's not until we have invited the God of the Universe (Jesus

Christ) into our hearts to be our Lord and Savior (which we will explain in Chapter Four) that we can we personally know His unconditional Love for ourselves.

This personal Love relationship between the Father and us is what makes Christianity so totally different from all the other religions in the world. Christianity is the only belief system where God Himself (who is Love), when asked to, comes to dwell within each of our hearts.

As with faith and hope, we come to know God's Love in various stages. First, we experience His *beginning Love,* and that occurs when we are first born again and are getting used to our new relationship with Him; then we'll experience His *faithful Love* as we begin to encounter various trials and hard times in our lives, and finally, we'll experience His *ultimate consuming Love* when at the end we come to see Him face-to-face.

Knowing His faithful Love, however, is the only way we will make it through our present difficult times.[67]

## DEFINITION OF GOD'S LOVE

Let's define God's Love so we'll understand just how completely opposite this type of Love is from our own human love.

Listen to how Paul describes God's Love in 1 Corinthians 13:4–8:

"[God's] Love suffereth long, and is kind; [His] Love envieth not; [His] Love vaunteth not itself, is not puffed up, doth not behave itself unseemly, seeketh not her own, is not easily provoked, thinketh no evil; rejoiceth not in iniquity, but rejoiceth in the truth; beareth all things, believeth all things, hopeth all things, endureth all things. [God's] *Love never faileth."*

The following is the *Living Bible* translation of the above Scripture that might help you to get the full impact of what God's Love really is:

"God's Love is very patient and kind, never jealous or envious, never boastful or proud, never haughty or selfish or rude. God's Love does not demand its own way. It is not irritable or touchy. It does not hold grudges and will hardly even notice when others do it wrong. It is never glad about injustice, but rejoices whenever truth wins out. If you love someone [with God's Love], you will be loyal to him no matter what the cost. You will always believe in him, always expect the best of him, and always stand your ground in defending him. God's Love never fails."

Jeremiah 31:3 adds a little more definition to what God's Love is: It's an everlasting Love, an eternal Love, a never-ending Love, a timeless Love, an infinite Love, an absolute Love, an ever-living Love, an indestructible Love, a changeless Love and an immovable Love.

The question is: Can you love like that? Can you do and be these things in your own strength? Absolutely not! (At least, I can't!)

God's Love can be these things because it is not a human love. It's a supernatural Love! It's a supernatural Love because it's *not* dependent upon human understanding, human desires, or human emotions, nor is it based upon the other person's responses or the circumstances we are in. God's Love is a Love that is dependent only upon God. And as we begin to understand that He is always faithful, always trustworthy, and always reliable, we'll be able to hope in His Love more and more and more. Therefore, no matter how we feel or what we think, no matter how that other person responds, and no matter what the circumstances we are in, God is always willing to love, even when we can't.

As we said, in the Greek language God's Love is called **Agape**. In the Hebrew, it is called **chesed**. *Agape* Love has two distinct sides to it: One side is a longsuffering and merciful Love; the other side is a strict, firm and disciplinary Love. This means that God's Love can manifest itself either mercifully in our lives when appropriate, or it can manifest itself in strictness and firmness as the occasion demands. Both are facets of God's Love. As we seek God's wisdom and

His discernment for each of our particular situations, He will let us know which type of Love to use.

The Greek word *Agape* was coined exclusively for its use in the New Testament. Therefore, there is no precedent upon which to define *Agape*. Consequently, it's true meaning, nature, and purpose has not always been easily understood. This is why there has been so much confusion in this area and why the enemy of our souls rejoices in that confusion. Let's be educated then and learn exactly what God's Love is and how we can pass His Love on to others.

## CHARACTERISTICS OF GOD'S LOVE

*Agape* has four characteristics that again make it totally opposite from human love:

1) First of all, it's an unconditional Love because it loves no matter what. No matter what others do or how they respond, God's Love keeps on coming. Even if that other person tries to stop that Love from coming, it still flows to him unceasingly. As mentioned previously, it has two sides to it: It has a merciful and longsuffering side to it as well as a tough and discipline side to it. It's God's wisdom that will tell us which type of Love to use for our particular situation.

2) Agape is also a one-sided Love because it doesn't have to be returned in order to be kept alive. In other words, it's not "I'll love you, if you'll love me"; it's "I'll love you no matter what you do!" God's Love is an initiating and unilateral Love, which means it's the first to reach out.

3) Agape is also a freeing Love because it not only frees the person loving from his own expectations and presumptions, but it also frees the one being loved by making no demands upon him and

allowing him to respond from his heart, not from his defenses. In other words, it's a Love that not only lets us be who we really are, but frees the one we are trying to love to be himself. All our relationships will be affected when we love like this.

4) Finally, Agape is an other-centered Love because it always puts the other person's interests above and before its own. C. S. Lewis calls Agape the only "giving-gift Love" there is.

## CHARACTERISTICS OF HUMAN LOVE

Human love, on the other hand, is just the opposite of God's Love.

1) It's a conditional love because it always depends upon what we think, what we feel, what we desire, what our circumstances are and how the other person responds to us.

2) It's a two-sided love because it always says, "I'll love you if you love me. But if you stop loving me, I'll stop loving you."

3) It's a bondage love because we become totally wrapped up with our own presumptions and expectations of the other person. Then the other person is not free to respond from his heart but is often pushed into self-defensiveness.

4) Finally, it's a self-centered love because no matter how selfless it looks on the outside, we will always be loving that other person while hoping to get in return the love, the admiration or the notoriety we so desperately desire.

Human love, therefore, is part of our old nature. We are born with human love. God's Love (*Agape*), on the other hand, only comes when we ask Christ to come into our lives to be our Savior. He is that Love, and He is the One who brings that supernatural Love into our hearts. It's part of our "new creation."

## GOD'S LOVE IS A GIFT

C. S. Lewis once said, "God's Love is the only gift-Love there is." And oh how true is that! God's Love is a gift.

In the original King James Version of the Bible, God's Love is translated *charity,* which is an old English term meaning "unconditional Love in action." The significance of the word charity is that it was a *gift of love with no strings attached.* And that's exactly what God's Love is. It's a Love that loves the poor, the needy, the maimed, and the ugly. It's a Love that originates in the heart of God and keeps on coming, even when the object of that Love refuses to return that Love or even tries to stop it from coming.

God's Love is not only *a gift we receive* from the Father when we are born again at the beginning of our walk with Him. It's also *a gift we learn to give out to others* during our walk with Him, and it will also be *the ultimate gift we encounter* when at the end of our life we meet the Lord in person.

*Agape* Love is critically important not only because it's the goal, the object and the aim of the Christian life here and now (it's proof we have been conformed to His image), but also *because it's going to be the measuring stick, the gauge and the standard by which the Lord will grade us for positions of authority and responsibility in His future kingdom.* Agape is the "fruit" of the Spirit that God will be looking for. It's the evidence that we have been conformed into the image of Christ, His image of Love.[68] Being filled with Him means being filled with His Love, and that's the "fullness of the Spirit" that the Bible continually talks about.

Love is the reason we have been called. Love is the purpose for our lives here and now. And Love is the prize that we are working toward at the end of the road.

Ephesians 3:17–19 summarizes it: "that Christ may dwell in your hearts by faith; that ye, being rooted and grounded in Love, may be able to comprehend with all saints what is the breadth, and length, and depth, and height; ***and to know the Love of Christ, which passeth knowledge, that ye might be filled with all the fullness of God.***" In other words, we must not only *receive God's Love* when we are born again; we also must *abide in His Love* during the hard times and look forward to *His ultimate Love* in the future. In between these two last stages, however, there is quite a sanctification and a purification process (which we will begin to discuss next chapter). This is where we must learn to depend upon His *faithful and enduring Love* as never before. This is the kind of Love that be-comes the basis of our hope. And this is the type of Love that sustains us, supports us and carries us through the hard times while we are waiting for God's promises to be fulfilled.

*C. S. Lewis once said, "God's Love is the only gift-Love there is."*

So faith and hope are attitudes "we" must learn to maintain, whereas *Agape* is God's gift from the very beginning to the very end. (Yes, <u>God</u> gives us a measure of "faith" as a gift when we begin our walk with Him, but <u>we</u> are the ones who must maintain that faith in our walk.[69])

## GOD'S LOVE MUST BE THE BASIS OF OUR HOPE

So why is Love so important in regards to having hope? Love must be the foundation of our hope. We cannot go any further in our walk with the Lord without personally knowing His Love. This is what our present hope must continually be based upon.

*Strong's Concordance* explains that: "God's Love stresses the reci-procity of the relationship, *but will not be abandoned even if the human partner is unfaithful and must be disciplined.* The stronger partner remains committed to the promise but retains the freedom in regards to the manner in which he will implement the promise. ***Love is the goal and the end of all salvation history.""***

Isaiah 16:5 and 2 Samuel 7:15 both tell us that God's throne will be established or built upon God's mercy (His Love). If you recall, His throne is called "the Mercy Seat."

Love is the vehicle God uses to fulfill His eternal plans for mankind. Love was present at creation, is present here and now, and will also be present at the end of the age. Listen to Psalm 136:1–9: *"O give thanks unto the LORD; for He is good: for His mercy [or His Agape Love] endureth for ever. O give thanks unto the God of gods: for His mercy endureth for ever. O give thanks to the Lord of lords: for His mercy endureth for ever. To Him who alone doeth great wonders: for His mercy endureth for ever. To Him that by wisdom made the heavens: for His mercy endureth for ever. To Him that stretched out the earth above the waters: for His mercy endureth for ever. To Him that made great lights: for His mercy endureth for ever: the sun to rule by day: for His mercy endureth for ever: the moon and stars to rule by night: for His mercy endureth for ever."*

God's Love will endure forever. It's the reason for creation, the reason He called us in the first place and the motive behind the "kingdom yet to come."[70]

How can we ever really trust the Lord without knowing His personal Agape Love? How can we cross that bridge to the unseen without experiencing His Love? And what hope do we have without abiding in His Love?

## DIFFERENT SEASONS

So faith, hope and Love are the three fundamental elements of the Christian life. All are critically important, but God often teaches us these principles at different "times" or "seasons" in our walk with Him.[71]

Ecclesiastes 3:1–8 confirms this: "*To everything there is a season, and a time to every purpose under the heaven*: a time to be born, and a time to die; a time to plant, and a time to pluck up that which is planted; a time to kill, and a time to heal; a time to break down, and a time to build up; a time to weep, and a time to laugh; a time to mourn, and a time to dance; a time to cast away stones, and a time to gather stones together; a time to embrace, and a time to refrain from embracing; a time to get, and a time to lose; a time to keep, and a time to cast away; a time to rend, and a time to sew; a time to keep silence, and time to speak; a time to love, and a time to hate; a time of war, and a time of peace."[72]

Ecclesiastes is saying that there are "seasons" God uses to teach us these three pillars. First, there is a season where the Lord lovingly draws us to Himself and we commit our lives to Him and begin our faith walk with Him; then there is a season where He teaches us how to have real and lasting faith; then a season where He shows us the importance of hope, trust and endurance in our different trials; and finally, a season where we experience His Love in such a deeper way that we are able to continually give it out to others and glorify (reflect) Him. First Thessalonians 1:3 expresses it this way: "your work of faith, and labor of Love, and patience of hope." These "seasons" also remind me of John's example in 1 John 2:12–13 where he speaks of "little children" (as those who are learning faith), "young men" (as those who are learning to overcome) and "fathers" (as those who have an intimate relationship with God). Then He repeats this statement a second time. He encourages them to continue to produce "fruit," overcome the enemy and stay strong in the Word.

Now I'm not saying that every Christian will go through the exact same season at the exact same time and in the exact same way. Experience tells us that everyone's walk is completely different and every one of us responds uniquely. But, in general, every Christian (as he progresses in his walk with the Lord) will experience a season where God focuses on teaching him more about faith; a season where God tests and tries his hope, and, of course, a season where the lesson is Love. Now, it's also possible to experience all three of these seasons at the same time or to complete one season, then fall back and have to do the same lesson all over again. So there's no set way in learning to walk out our faith, our hope and His Love, except that we all must experience these three seasons in order to get to the level of maturity that God desires for each of us.

Remember the goal that God has set before us is: "Forgetting those things which are behind, and reaching forth unto those things which are before, I press toward the mark for the prize of the high calling of God in Christ Jesus."[73] What is the "mark"? I believe it's being conformed into His image—His image of Love.

First, however, there is usually a "season of faith."

In my own life (and I will share more about this in coming chapters), my season of faith came when we had to weather not only personal bankruptcy but also corporate bankruptcy. Losing Chuck's job, our home, our savings, our cars and our insurance was one thing, but losing many of our close friends (because of the bankruptcy) was absolutely devastating. When you have a lot of money, it's amazing how many "friends" you accrue; but when you lose your money, position and status, it's funny how many of those same "close friends" quickly disappear! What a test of faith that period of time was for both of us!

Next, there is the "season of hope."

A perfect Old Testament example of a "season of hope" is Moses, because of what was said about him in Hebrews 11:27: he was able to endure (continue to have hope) "by seeing Him who was invisible." That, to me, is the simple definition of hope. Moses not only ***endured 40 years in the desert, he also withstood 40 years in the wilderness.***

Can you imagine 40 years, only to be denied entry to the promised land in the end. I don't know how he could have weathered these extreme testings except by experiencing God's reality, even though He could not be seen. God rewarded Moses' faithfulness by allowing him to be present at the transfiguration in Matthew 17 and also by allowing him to be one of the two witnesses in Revelation 11.

One of our own greatest personal trials of hope came a couple of years ago when our second son, Mark, was taken seriously ill with fourth stage colon and rectal cancer. The doctors gave him little hope of being able to save his organs and prepared him for an illiostromy (a permanent outside bag). Our Mark is a scuba diver instructor as well as a fireman and to be restricted by such physical limitations would end his career in both. We began to pray and hope for the impossible, not only for our son's life but also for his calling as he loves the outdoors and his passion is helping other people. We prayed just like Abraham did: "who *against hope believed in hope*."[74] Against all hope, we trusted the God of hope!

The Lord was absolutely faithful. When they operated on Mark, they discovered they had a sixteenth of an inch left in which it was possible to save his colon. Mark now is continuing his love of firefighting and scuba instructing. "Hope against hope…"

Finally, there is a "season of Love."

A possible Biblical example of those who experienced a "season of Love" might be Jacob and Rachel in Genesis 29. Do you remember how Jacob had to work a total of 14 years in order to win Laban's approval to marry Rachel. Now, there's a true love story and definitely a period of enduring love was experienced. Also, there's the story of Boaz and Ruth. In this case, Ruth (in my opinion) is the example of not only *enduring Love* but also *imparting Love* (passing on God's Love) as she chose to give up everything to follow Naomi into an unknown country. Then, of course, there's her relationship with Boaz and how she displayed tremendous strength and courage by doing what Naomi suggested: going to Boaz, lying next to him and, in short, propositioning him to marry her. This, to me, is another example of "God's Love in action."

Our own season of learning how to love with God's Love is explained in my book *The Way of Agape* as we began to encounter huge trials in our marital life after being married 20 years. But God used it all to teach us about His unconditional Love, which in the end is the only thing that ultimately saved our marriage.

As Ecclesiastes 3:11 tells us: "**He** makes everything beautiful in *His* time."

Notice how Scripture emphasizes the importance of becoming an "overcomer." (See end note.[75]) Overcomers are the ones who will make it through the season of faith, past the season of hope and right into the future kingdom of Love and inheritance. Only the "overcomers" gain victory over the world, the flesh and the devil. They have learned how to refuse the world, forbid the flesh and bind the enemy. We'll talk more about these victorious ones in Chapter Eight.

## Summary: Faith, Hope and Love

So there seems to be various seasons that we, as believers in Jesus Christ, must go through in order to advance across the "bridge to the unseen." In the season of faith, we will learn the importance of obedience and how to walk by faith and not our feelings. In the season of hope, we'll learn how to trust the Lord more and how to endure our difficult trials and tribulations by seeing Him who is invisible. And in the season of Love, we'll learn not only how much God loves us but also how to share His Love with others.

Again, it's *our* faith, *our* hope, but *His* Love!

"Faith" is believing in Christ's promises; "hope" is trusting in His faithfulness to perform His promises in His timing and way, and Love is the fulfillment of His promises. *Our* faith is built upon Christ's Word; *our* hope is built upon His Spirit bringing His Word to pass, and *His* Love becomes the basis of our future inheritance and that "tree of Life" that awaits us at the end of the bridge.

First Peter 1:3–4 tells us: "Blessed be the God and Father of our Lord Jesus Christ, who, according to *His abundant [Love]*, hath begotten us again unto *a living hope* by the resurrection of Jesus Christ from the

OVERCOMERS
are the ones who will make it
*through the season of faith,*

PAST THE SEASON OF HOPE
*and right into the future*
*kingdom of Love*
and inheritance.

dead, to an inheritance incorruptible, and undefiled, and that fadeth not away, reserved in heaven for you, who are kept by the power of God *through faith* unto salvation ready to be revealed in the last time."

God's Love is the gift that sustains us, supports us and carries us through this whole process. We receive His Love at the beginning of our journey; we rest upon His faithful Love during the difficult times in our journey, and His Love will consume us at the end of our journey.

So the three pillars of our Christian walk are: First *faith*, then *hope*, and finally, *Love.* But "the greatest of these is Love."[76]

# Chapter Three—
# How Does Hope Differ from Faith?

1. Memorize Hebrews 11:1.
2. As simply as you can, define what **faith** is, what **hope** is and what **Love** is.
3. Define faith according to Hebrews 11:1. What does the word "substance" mean? What does the word "evidence" mean? Define "faith" in your own words.
4. What is "hope"? Have you ever struggled in this area of hope?
5. What's the difference between faith and hope? Have you ever gotten these two confused?
6. What is the secret to holding fast to God's promises? Give an example in your own life where you held on to His promises "against all odds" because you knew He would be faithful and He would come through.
7. Why do we lose our hope? Have you ever lost yours? (Job 49:14) Explain.
8. "Night Seasons"—what are they, and why does God allow them? Have you ever experienced a night season in your life?
9. What is God trying to accomplish in us by allowing night seasons? (James 1:3)
10. The three pillars of the Christian walk are faith, hope and Love. 1 Corinthians 13 tells us the greatest of these pillars is Love. Can you define Love?
11. What are some of the characteristics of this kind of Love?
12. Why must God's Love be the basis of our hope? Do you know God's personal Love?

*hope*

ABRAHAM…

*"who against hope believed in hope,*

*that he might become the father*

*of many nations,*

*according to that which was spoken…"*

ROMANS 4:18

# TWO KINDS
# OF HOPE—
# HOPE AGAINST
# HOPE

As we said in Chapter Two, hope comes in two forms: one is an *eternal* hope (which means the hope that Christ will return for His own at the end of this age and give us His eternal life); and the second type of hope is a *temporal* hope (which means a present-day experiential hope—believing in the personal promises we have received from the Lord and that will affect our everyday life).

## OUR ETERNAL HOPE

For *a believer*, "eternal hope" is what keeps him going—it's the assurance that his life here on earth is not the end, but there's an unimaginable heavenly kingdom that lies ahead.

First Corinthians 15:51–53, 58 gives us a glimpse of God's incredible promises for the future: "Behold I show you a mystery: We shall not all sleep, but we shall all be changed, in a moment, in the twinkling of an eye, at the last trump; for the trumpet shall sound and the dead shall be raised incorruptible, and we shall be changed. For this corruptible must put on incorruption and this mortal must put on immortality.... Therefore, my beloved brethren, be ye steadfast, unmovable, always abounding in the work of the Lord, forasmuch as ye know that your labor is not in vain in the Lord."[77]

## OUR TEMPORAL HOPE

A believer can also have "temporal hope," because he knows that God is always involved in his life. "Temporal hope," however, is often based upon human expectations and our own interpretation of the Word, whereas Godly "eternal hope" is based on God's solid promises in His Word about the future.

So it goes without saying that Christians should have great expectation and confidence in both types of hope if we understand them properly.[78] The second type of hope—*temporal hope*—is the kind of hope that we will be talking about mostly in this book, because this is the hope that many believers lose when they can't see the Lord in their circumstances. In the midst of their greatest suffering—in their own Valley of Baca—if they can't see the Lord, it becomes difficult for them to "trust Him" and let Him turn the whole situation into a "well of blessing."

*It's one thing "to believe" something for the future; however, it's totally different to "walk out" that belief in the midst of trouble.*

Temporal hope is the kind of hope I see so many struggling with at the present time. It's one thing "to believe" something for the future; however, it's totally different to "walk out" that belief in the midst of trouble. Believing can simply be "having faith" both mentally and emotionally, whereas trusting is "putting your actions" where your heart is. Hope consists of not only *believing in His promises*, but also moment-by-moment *trusting in His faithfulness to implement those promises in His timing and in His way*. Remember Proverbs 3:5–6, which says: "Trust in the LORD with all thine heart; and lean not unto thine own understanding. In all thy ways acknowledge Him, and *He will direct your paths*."[79] As we, by faith, trust in Him and acknowledge His presence even in the darkness, He is freed to direct our paths and give us the strength to endure and to carry on.

This is exactly what hope (both temporal and eternal) will allow us to do. It helps us walk out our faith till the very end. It enables us to walk through the tough times trusting that God WILL work our circumstances out, regardless of what we see or what we understand.

*Eternal hope* is steady and always there. *Temporal hope* comes and goes depending upon what is going on in our lives at the moment, what difficulties we are facing and what kind of warfare we are encountering. Thus temporal hope is where we often get discouraged, let our guard down and fall away. It's also where the enemy comes in "like a flood," trying to kill, steal and destroy our faith.

## A SCRIPTURAL EXAMPLE OF TEMPORAL HOPE AND ETERNAL HOPE

An example of both temporal hope and eternal hope is found in the book of Job. Job didn't understand what was happening to him or why he was suffering so. He couldn't see all that was happening around him from God's perspective. He couldn't hear what the Lord was saying to Satan: "...all that Job has is in your power; only upon himself put not forth your hand."[80] Job 2:7 goes on to say: "Satan went forth from the presence of God and smote Job with sore boils from the sole of his feet unto his crown." Job is very much like us—we can't see the overall heavenly plan the Lord has for us or how He is going to implement it.

Even though Job didn't understand what God was doing and he candidly expressed his feelings, he still chose to trust the Lord in everything. In Job 13:15, he says: "Though You slay me, yet will I trust You." His *temporal hope* was built upon his *eternal hope* that God was real, that He would be faithful and that one day he would be with Him. (Note: this so hits home with me right now. I have just finished my four weeks of radiation and my poor nose is absolutely covered with boils and blisters. They sting, they hurt, and the pain drives me crazy, but all I can say is: "Though You slay me, Lord, I will continue to trust You.")[81]

So it's our temporal hopes that can become "deferred." But that's when our eternal hope must kick in. Like Job, our eternal hope is what helps us "wait" for God's answers.

### FAITH IN THE NIGHT SEASONS

Almost 15 years ago I wrote a book titled *Faith in the Night Seasons*, which was my own chronicle of a personal promise God gave me at a very critical time in my life that I clutched to, held on to, but finally let go of after 10 years of waiting. Reading Chapter One of *Faith in the Night Seasons* might help you understand a little more clearly the difference between God's temporal promises and His eternal promises.

Who knows, maybe this book, *Hope Against Hope*, will have something to do with God's personal promise to me over 22 years ago. We'll see!

Again, the "key" is always His timing and His way, not ours!

### HOPE AGAINST HOPE

That's what makes Romans 4:18 (the title of this book) so very powerful. As believers, we can hope against hope. In spite of what we see with our natural eye, feel with our natural heart and think with our natural mind, we can always hope in God's faithfulness to work all of our circumstances together for our good. Like Abraham, we must trust the Lord to do the impossible. And like Job, we must build our temporal hopes upon our eternal hope no matter what occurs in our lives, no matter how bleak it becomes and no matter how long it takes. In other words, *when our temporal hope falls apart, disappoints us or confuses us (as Job's did and mine did), we must replace it with our eternal hope, which is ever steady and never fails.* Like Job, we must be honest with God and share our innermost feelings with Him, but in the end, like Job, say: "No matter what I see or feel, I still choose to trust You." Our temporal hope will come and go because so much of it depends upon what we understand, what we interpret, what we feel and what we can see. God tells us, however, that His ways are not our ways; and some of His ways are past finding out and far above our own understanding.[82] When everything falls apart in our lives, we must trust, believe and have faith that God somehow will work it all out to our good and to His glory, *because He is faithful.*

So when a promise of God fails to come to pass in the time and the way we thought it would, we must fall back on our eternal hope, which we know to be absolutely true. God in His timing will then fill in the pieces for us. So even though it might "feel" like betrayal from God (in our eyes), the fact is that it's usually just the opposite. Our job is simply to "hope against hope."

## A Personal Example

During one of my setbacks this past year, when I had massive headaches and vomiting and they found evidence that the cancer may have gone to my brain, they put me on powerful steroids to reduce the inflammation and stop the pain. The steroids worked quickly. In fact, they were phenomenal. The day after I was out of the hospital, I cleaned house, drove the car and did all my errands with no problem. What a huge difference the steroids made—no pain at all and massive energy. I remember thinking to myself. *This is great. Keep me on these the rest of my life and I'll be fine.*

When our temporal hope falls apart, disappoints us or confuses us (as Job's did and mine did), we must replace it with our eternal hope, which is ever steady and never fails.

Well, unfortunately, just as the steroids build you up quickly, they also take you down quickly. Give them a few weeks and they absolutely undo you. I got to where I had absolutely no strength. It's as though the life in me just drained out. I had absolutely no energy to do anything.

Thus began the long drawn out process of withdrawal. Boy, now when someone says they are going through withdrawal, I totally understand what they are saying. Three weeks of sweat, weakness like I've never experienced and absolutely no strength at all. I couldn't even walk across the room without fainting. Of course, this affected my heart and my blood pressure plummeted. It was so scary.

In the midst of this trial, God gave me Isaiah 40:29, 31: "He gives power to the faint; and to them that have no might He increases strength.... They that wait upon the LORD shall renew their strength; they shall mount up with wings as eagles; they shall run and not be weary and they shall walk and not faint." He also gave me Isaiah 40:10, which tells me "not to be dismayed" nor to fear because He is with me.

Such a perfect Scripture for where I was. That was my temporal promise. He is going to renew my strength (help me to overcome), and I am going to once again be able to run and not be weary. What a perfect Scripture for me to hope in. I cling to it.

Here's the problem, however: Even though that Scripture was definitely for me at that moment, and I received it and claimed it for myself, God is the One who will implement it in His timing and in His way. It's His decision, not mine. I believe Him, I trust Him and I know it will happen. My job now is to wait...to give Him my temporal hope and to fall back on my eternal hope. This is exactly what "hope against hope" means.

## OTHER SCRIPTURAL EXAMPLES OF THE TWO KINDS OF HOPE

<u>Abraham</u> is probably one of my favorite examples of weathering and experiencing the two kinds of Hope. He and Sarah were told they would have a baby when both of them were way past childbearing age. They waited 13 years before God's promise was fulfilled and Isaac was born. (Compare Genesis 17:16–19 with Genesis 21:1–3; see also Hebrews 11:8–11.) Abraham was in his 90s and Sarah was a little younger. You can read their whole story in Chapter One of *Faith in the Night Seasons*.

<u>Simeon</u>—was promised to see the Messiah born. He waited 20 years to see that promise fulfilled.[83]

<u>David</u>—waited 13 years to become the king as God promised him.[84]

<u>Joseph</u>—dreamed of exaltation but was sold into slavery. He waited years before he found freedom and God's answer to his prayers.[85]

<u>Rachel</u>—God remembered Rachel, even as He does us, when we are too discouraged to believe. Like Rachel, He still remembers us and He remembers His promises to us.[86]

<u>Mary and Martha</u>, Lazarus's sisters—Jesus was four days late in coming to them after Lazarus had died. But instead of performing a simple healing, which is what they had wanted, He actually resurrected Lazarus.[87]

(If the promise turns out not to be in our scheme of things or in our timetable, it simply means God has something better planned.)

Zerubbabel—He waited 10 years for the promise that God gave him to build the third temple. The people did not want the new temple, but Haggai came and encouraged him to try again. The message is to "begin again." Get back on track—get your hopes back—it doesn't matter the time that has elapsed.[88]

How often we have to begin again. How often we need to get our hopes back up and dream again. What the Lord begins, He promises to finish. But as Joel Osteen says, "If it doesn't happen in our timing, He not only has a healing in mind but a total resurrection."

## Both Kinds of Hope are Important

So hope, both temporal and eternal, is critically important. Romans 8:24 tells us: "We are saved [delivered, protected, healed, preserved and made whole] by *hope.*"

Hope—confidence that God will do as He says—must be the anchor of our soul, not only in the good times but also in the difficult times while we are waiting for His answers. With God in the picture, there is always "hope." Hope, therefore, is the *opposite of disappointment.* Even when hope contradicts all that is happening in the present moment, we must do as Abraham is recorded as doing in Romans 4:18, "hope against hope."

God *is* either who He said He is and will perform what He has promised, or He is not. There is no in-between. Thus we must choose to stand strong in our hope, because it's impossible to live in-between. "Disappointed hope" means doing exactly that, living in the middle, halting between two opinions![89] Hope in God is simply the *freedom from wanting anything or anyone but Him.* This is again why Paul tells us that we are "saved" by hope.

Paul's confidence is also expressed throughout Corinthians, Philippians and Colossians. Paul could be joyful even when he was imprisoned because the Lord's presence was always felt. To him, disappointment, despair and discouragement were unnecessary. Paul felt that to submit to these things would be to dishonor his Lord. Just like Paul, we are to put all these things behind us and press on toward the "mark."

We are *not* to look at the things which are seen, but at the things which are not seen, i.e., the "eternal things." Like Paul, if we are engrossed with eternal things, we can walk on firm and stable ground, always finding confidence and joy in God's abiding presence. (This is where I am seeking to walk every day.) When we take our eyes off the Lord, however, and focus on the waves beneath us, we will surely be engulfed and consumed.

*With God in the picture, there is always "hope."*

*Our human existence is not determined by the acceptance of the present or by the recollections of the past, but solely by the expectation of the future.* People without a purpose or a goal or a vision do "perish" as Proverbs 29:18 tells us. This is why when our hope is deferred, our heart becomes sad. Hope not only exists in this life, it also determines our future. When our hope is fixed on God, it will secure all our future expectations. However, if we don't know God's faithfulness and don't understand His Love, especially in the dark times, our hope will become faint, trembling and weak. This seems to be what's occurring now in the Body of Christ. Many, under similar trials to mine, have lost their way in the darkness. They have gotten lost in the confusion, their own mistrust and unbelief and lost their anchor.[90]

God allows trials and storms and confusion into our lives so that we will be able to unconditionally trust Him no matter what we see, what we feel or what we think. Like Abraham, Simeon and David, in the end God will "work all things together for His purposes and His plans." He does love us, and He will be faithful to His promises, even though in the middle of the trial we won't be able to see where we are going or what God is doing. Even at that time, we mustn't let our hope get deferred.[91]

This is the kind of confidence in the Lord that will enable us to see the Lord's Hand in the middle of all our dire circumstances. As Paul says in 2 Corinthians 7:4, he was "exceedingly joyful in all his tribulation." I wonder if Abraham felt this way in the middle of his trial? How about you, can you say the same thing?

Hope involves overcoming, and although it may be painful, it must be reckoned positively. It has to be a "living hope."[92] In other words, we can't depend upon a hope that we had three years ago; it must be a "present-day" hope.

First Peter 1:13 warns us to "gird up the loins of our minds and be sober and *hope to the end* for the grace that is to be brought unto you at the revelation of Jesus Christ." This is exhorting us to be ready for the battle to which we have been appointed. Hope requires us to hold fast our confession of faith without wavering[93] and to be ready to give an answer to anyone who asks us a reason for the hope that is in us.[94]

Hope does *not* depend upon what a man possesses or upon what he may be able to do for himself or even upon what any other human being may have promised him. Hope's fulfillment rests only upon God, His promises for the future, His Love and His faithfulness.

***Hope against hope*** then simply means that in the midst of our trials, our pain and our suffering, we must still believe, proclaim and stand on God's faithfulness and His eternal promises. Even though our temporal hopes are "deferred," we must continue to choose by faith to unconditionally depend upon Him to bring them to pass in His way and in His timing.[95]

## JESUS IS OUR HOPE

The Bible tells us that Jesus Christ is our "hope." Period. End of sentence. End of discussion.

It's Christ's faithfulness and *His* Love that make our hope secure. Without Him, there is nothing to hope for, nothing to depend upon and nothing to look forward to. We are, in every way, lost! "He is the [only] Way, the [only] Truth and the [only] Life."[96] This says that our meaning and purpose in life is all in Him. In other words, if we lose our hope in Him, it follows that we will also lose our own identity, meaning and purpose. And if that is the case, we'll end up completely devastated, shattered and undone. Proverbs 29:18 says it perfectly: "Where there is no vision, the people perish."[97]

So the question becomes, What are we trusting in? Are we trusting in our own righteousness to get us through? Are we hoping in our own power and ability to pave our way? Are we trusting in others to help us? What are *you* trusting in?

The Scriptures very clearly tell us that our hope (both eternal and temporal) should be solely in the Lord Jesus Christ, His promises and His character. He is the source of all believers' expectations and the fountain head of our hope. Thus our trust must always be directed to and centered upon the person of Christ. One of my favorite Scriptures in researching this book has become: "Put not your trust in princes, nor in the son of man, in whom there is no help...[but put your] hope in the LORD [your] God."[98] Also, "None who trust [hope] in the LORD will be desolate."[99]

When our hope is fixed upon Him, it embraces sight, expectation, trust and patient waiting all at the same time.[100] Hope is the only way we won't be tossed about, the only way we won't be turned around and the only way we won't be driven by the winds of change as we wait for God's promises to come to pass.[101] Hope is simply "sure confidence" in God, His Love and faithfulness.[102]

*"Hope," therefore, focuses on the character of God who has promised, not on what is to be given. It's His faithfulness that true hope reveals.*

Now, there is a difference between "beginning" hope (which usually depends upon our own *sight*) and "mature" hope (which comes from *experientially knowing* God's faithfulness and Love). Romans 5:3–5 tells us, "patience worketh experience and experience, hope." In other words, *mature hope is gained only through experience.* That's the tough part. There's a purifying process that we all must go through in order to reach that mature state of hope.

## THE IMPORTANCE OF THE WORD OF GOD

The more I read Hebrews 4:12 about the importance of Word of God in our lives, the more I realize the criticalness of really understanding what this Scripture is saying. Take just a moment to let the words of this Scripture really sink in: *"For the Word of God is quick, and powerful, and sharper than any twoedged sword, piercing even to the dividing asunder of soul and spirit, and of the joints and marrow, and is a discerner of the thoughts and intents of the heart."*

As we progress in this book, we'll talk more about the parallel between the ritual that the priests of Solomon's Temple did in the Inner Court and what we must do in our own personal walk with the Lord. And, hopefully, we'll be able to see the connection between our soul and spirit and why God wants them separated and divided. The Word of God is the instrument God uses in that division.[103]

What this is saying is that we must not only have faith in His Word and speak it forth, we must also trust His Spirit to bring it about. We will learn as we get further into the book that the priests of Solomon's Temple (as they were carrying those "hot coals of fire" into the Holy Place) had to pass the Tables of Shewbread (the Biblical symbol for God's Word) and the Candlesticks (the Biblical symbol for God's Spirit) on their way to worshiping the Lord at the Incense Altar.

The Word of God is not only what divides our soul from our spirit, it's also what combats the lies of the enemy. God's Word tells us that Satan is the "father of lies." And it's only His Word (God's rod) that will help us defeat the enemy and His Spirit (His staff) that will help us traverse the Valley of the Shadow of Death in order to reach intimacy with the Lord.

Boldly speaking forth the Word of God is one of the places I truly fell down in the past year. Memorization has always been very difficult

"Hope," therefore,

FOCUSES ON THE CHARACTER OF GOD

who has promised,

*not on what is to be given.*

for me. Consequently, when I went through my horrific trial of pain, and I couldn't see because I couldn't wear glasses on my new nose, meditating on the Word or speaking it forth became very difficult for me. And the farther down the road I got (away from God's Word), the less I wanted to hear it. I didn't even play music or listen to Scriptures on my iPad or iPhone. How quickly we can slip, sink and drown. Hope through reading the Word of God and speaking it forth to bind the enemy is the only thing that will keep us alive, afloat and stable.

Remember Psalm 1:1–3, which says: "A man who meditates on the Word of God will be like *a tree planted by the river.*" Again, the connection to being that "life giving" tree is hoping in God's Word, not only believing it but also walking it out. We must not only read it, we must also learn to speak it forth in hope.

*Hope, then, is the connection or the vehicle by which the Word of God is implemented in our lives. So whenever we choose to hope for God's promises—and speak them forth—we must have the confidence that God's Spirit will perform them in His way and by His timing. Psalm 130:5 says it so simply: "I wait for the LORD, ...and in His word do I hope."*

## THE AUTHORITY OF THE CHURCH

Talking about the importance of speaking forth the Word of God, we must also understand the authority that God has given us as believers in order to do this.

At our new birth, God not only gives us "His strength" to do His will, He also gives us "His authority" to choose His will regardless of how we feel, what we think or what we want. The Greek word for this kind of authority is *exousia* (*Strong's* #1849), which means "the right to exercise power or the right of the person in charge." This authority originates with God as He is obviously the Person in charge. The Word of God is what gives us this authority and the Spirit of God is what gives us the power. These two phenomenal gifts—the authority and power of Christ—are not only the keys to overcoming here and now, but they are also the keys to the future Millennial Kingdom.

Ignorance of this incredible authority from God has caused untold grief for the Body of Christ. Look around. Are we overcomers? Are we victorious? Are we winning? No way! Divorces, severed relationships, substance abuse, mental breakdowns and hopelessness define the Body of Christ right now. Rather than overcoming, we are being overcome. Lack of understanding in this critical area of authority is one of the reasons we have lost our hope and also why Satan is making such headway in so many of our lives.

Many believers ask: "Do we really have the authority to choose to do something we don't feel, something we don't want to do and something we don't really think will work? Is this Scriptural?" The answer is: "Absolutely yes!" We not only have God's authority to make these type of non-feeling "faith choices," but also His strength to walk these kind of choices out in our lives.

*The Dictionary of New Testament Theology* says: "Our authority is founded in the rule of Christ." We exercise that power only by the authority that *God* has given us. The *Word of God* gives us the authority and the *Spirit of God* gives us the power. This authority and power are truly the "keys to the kingdom," not only here and now, but in the future. Jesus tells us in Matthew 16:19: "I will give unto you the ***keys of the kingdom*** of heaven and whatsoever you shall BIND [forbid] on earth shall be bound in heaven and whatsoever you shall LOOSE [permit] on earth shall be loosed in heaven."[104]

The word "to bind" (*Strong's* #1210, *deo*) means to forbid, to refuse, to shut the door or to bring into subjection. In Matthew 12:29, it is explained quite clearly: "How can one enter into a strong man's house, and spoil his goods, except he first bind the strong man? And then he will spoil his house." The word "to loose" (*Strong's #3089, luo*) means to permit, to open, to allow or to release. It means to release the captive and to let him go.

Binding and loosing are simply Hebrew idioms for exercising the Lord's authority and power. They are "the keys to the kingdom."

Now all of this is only applicable because we belong to Christ—it's His authority and His power. We are just the vessels He uses.

## THE ARMOR OF GOD

Ephesians 6 talks about the importance of "putting on the whole armor of God."

> *Stand,* having our loins gird with Truth
>
> *Having on* the Breastplate of righteousness
>
> And our *feet shod* with preparation of Gospel of peace
>
> Above all, *taking* the Shield of Faith which we will be able to quench the darts of the wicked
>
> *Taking* the Helmet of Salvation
>
> And the Sword of the Spirit, which is the Word of God
>
> *Praying* always in the Spirit

In order to help you in your battle for "hope," I have included some of God's promises that have ministered to me. Remember the enemy wants to kill your hope, steal it away and destroy your faith. Speaking forth God's Word is what helps us to resist him and cause him to flee.

## GOD'S PROMISES

**James 4:7:** "Submit yourselves therefore to God. Resist the devil, and he will flee from you."

**1 Peter 5:8–9:** "Be sober, be vigilant, because your adversary the devil is a roaring lion, walking about seeking whom he may devour.

Whom resist steadfast in the faith knowing that the same afflictions are accomplished in your brethren that are in the world."

**Psalm 107:28**: He delivers us out of our distresses.

**Psalm 107:13**: He saves us out of our distresses.

**Psalm 107:20**: He sent His Word and healed us.

**Isaiah 53:5**: "We are healed by [Jesus'] stripes."[105] We need faith, however, in order to be healed.[106]

**James 4:7**: Submit yourselves to God, *resist* the devil and he will flee from you.

**2 Corinthians 6:7**: In all things we commend ourselves as ministers of God *by the Word of Truth, the power of God and the armor of righteousness.*

**Psalm 34:19**: Many are the afflictions of the righteous, but the Lord delivers them out of all of them.

**Joshua 1:9**: The Lord is with us wherever we go.

**Isaiah 54:17**: No weapon formed against us will prosper.

**2 Corinthians 10:4**: The weapons of our warfare are not carnal; casting down imaginations and every high thing that exalts itself against the knowledge of God; bringing every thought into captivity.

**Jeremiah 17:14**: Heal me, O Lord, and I shall be healed.

**Exodus 15:26**: I am the Lord that heals you.

**Psalm 30:12**: To the end that my glory may sing praise to You.

**Isaiah 41:13**: He will help me.

**Matthew 8:8**: Speak the Word and you shall be healed.

**Acts 14:9**: He had faith to be healed.

**Exodus 15:26**: I will put none of these diseases upon you.

**Luke 9:11**: He received them, spake unto them and healed them.

**Exodus 23:25**: I will take sickness away from the midst of you.

**Psalm 103:1–3**: Who heals all your diseases.

**Jeremiah 32:17**: There is nothing too hard for Him.

**Jude 24–25**: He is able to keep you from falling and present you faultless before God.

**Psalm 145:14**: The Lord upholds all who fall and raises up those that are bowed down.

**Philippians 4:6–7**: Be anxious for nothing and the peace of God which passes all understanding will keep your hearts and minds through Christ Jesus.

**Philippians 1:6**: I am convinced that He who began a good work in you will perform it until the day of Jesus Christ.

**Isaiah 41:10**: Fear not, for He is with us, do not be dismayed for He is our God and He will strengthen us and uphold us.

**Psalm 18:2**: You are my Rock, my Fortress, my Stronghold and whom I will trust.

**Mark 11:24**: Whatever things you desire when you pray, believe that you receive them and you shall have them (difficult Scripture; what happens when you don't receive them?).

**Psalm 119**: Note how many times it says: "I hope in Your Word."

# CHAPTER FOUR—TWO KINDS OF HOPE

1. Memorize Romans 4:18.

2. There are two kinds of hope. What are they, and, in your own words, explain their differences. Can a non-believer enjoy these two kinds of hope?

3. "Hope against hope" then really means what? (Romans 4:18) Can you give a personal example?

4. Why is the Word of God so important while we are waiting for our temporal hopes to materialize? (Hebrews 4:12)

5. The Bible talks about the authority believers have in Christ. What is this authority, and how does it work?

6. Matthew 16:19 speaks about the "Keys to the Kingdom." What is this referring to, and how does it work?

7. In your own walk with the Lord, have you ever had an opportunity to "bind the enemy"? Can you give an example? How about loosing strongholds in your life?

8. Ephesians 6:11–19 talks about putting on the whole armor of God. What does this mean, and how do we actually put the armor on? Explain each step.

9. What are some of God's promises from this chapter that really ministered to you. List them here.

I AM
CRUCIFIED
WITH
CHRIST

*"I am crucified with Christ:*

*nevertheless, I live;*

*yet not I, but Christ liveth in me;*

*and the life which I now live in the flesh*

*I live by the faith of the Son of God,*

*who loved me*

*and gave Himself for me."*

GALATIANS 2:20

NOW I LIVE

CHAPTER FIVE

# CAN WE TAKE
# GOD'S PROMISES
# LITERALLY?
# IS GOD FAITHFUL?

The overriding question in all of this is: Can we take God's temporal promises literally and personally? In other words, can we put our "hope" in the specific things that He says in the Bible that speak to our own situations? Can we be confident in doing this?

I think this is where many of us flounder with "hope." We take His Word personally, and we believe He cares about our lives and that He is directing us in all our ways. But when His personal promises don't come true in the way we thought and expected they would, we get weary, drained and our hope dies.

Here are a couple of examples:

Can the husband who was driving the car when his wife and four children were killed by a drunk driver personally apply "The LORD will fulfill the desire of those who fear Him; He will hear their cry and save them" to his life? (Psalm 145:19)

At the age of forty, can the woman who longs to get married (it's been her sole desire and prayer from childhood) still apply "God will give you the desires of your heart" to her life?

And what about the man who is suffering from chronic headaches so severe that he is not able to work, play with his kids or be the husband his wife needs. Can he apply the Scripture, "I will heal all your diseases"[107]?

All of these questions were written to me from real believers, ones who love the Lord but are stumbling because their prayers have not been answered. These Christians live good and righteous lives, and they all have personal faith in God and hope for the future. The question they are each wrestling with is, "Does God speak personally to us in His Word as He did with Moses or Abraham?" Can we really take His Word and apply it to our own current situation?

David, in the Old Testament, seemed to feel we all can. He wrote:

"Though I walk in the midst of trouble, Thou wilt revive me: Thou shalt stretch forth Thine hand against the wrath of mine enemies, and Thy right hand shall save me..."[108]

"When I cry to You, all of my enemies are turned back..."[109]

"You keep my soul among the living, and You do not allow my foot to be turned back..."[110]

"You will make my enemies flee."[111] "You will save my family."[112]

Like David, most of us are comfortable with the "eternal" promises of God, His future kingdom promises. But unlike David, there are times we don't see Him "uphold[ing] all those that fall and rais[ing] up those that are bowed down." We don't feel Him "being close to those that call upon Him in truth" or "healing the broken in heart and binding up their wounds." We trip over Scriptures that say God promises to "fulfill the desires of them that fear Him" and to "work all things together for good to those who love Him." Can we take these Scriptures personally and literally?

For me, right now, Psalm 103:3 ("He healeth all thy diseases...") is a question in my mind, because we've just been told that the malignant melanoma I had six months ago has returned and there are very few options left for me, except possibly a radical removal of my entire new nose.

Psalm 103:3 states that He will heal ALL our diseases. Can I stand on His Word here and apply this to my own life right now? You bet I can! I can claim this verse for myself while at the same time give God the liberty to implement that healing in His way and in His timing. I must put all of my confidence in Him, leaving Him room to fulfill His Word as He desires. We can't trust Him half the time and mistrust Him the rest. His Word is either *all* true or none of it is true! Romans 4:21 confirms that "we must be fully persuaded that what He has promised, He will perform" in our life in His timing and way.[113] Again, remember all the Old Testament saints we mentioned last chapter believed in God's promises and yet some of them never saw their fulfillment in their lifetime.

Without His personal Word to us at these critical times in our lives, we would just give up and die. As Psalm 119:92 says, "Unless Thy law had been my delight, I should then have perished in mine affliction." Consequently, we are left with having to trust and believe and hope upon the Lord's promises in all the details of our lives, even though we might not understand how they apply to our own situation or how He will manifest them. We must put all of our confidence behind Him.

That's what this book is all about...and what I am totally living right now.

## A WONDERFUL EXAMPLE: POPS!

Let me give you a personal example of "holding on to God's promises" even though we might never see them materialize.

I was not raised as a Christian. Both my parents were Christian

Scientists, which is a sect begun and promoted by Mary Baker Eddy. In fact, my grandparents, whom I absolutely adored, were so heavily into Christian Science for over sixty years that they had become "practitioners," which is similar to being pastors.

After I became a Christian, one of the first people I wanted to share the Lord Jesus Christ with was my grandfather "Pops," because the two of us had become inseparable. I loved him more than all my other relatives. We were "buds" and used to sit for hours and talk "spiritual talk." The only problem was, now that I had accepted Christ as my Savior, the words I used, such as "Jesus," "getting saved," and "eternal life," had totally different meanings than the words Pops used. They were the same words he used, but they had totally different implications to him. His definitions of these things were completely at odds with mine.

At first, we had very friendly discussions with lots of love between us; then our talks became a little more animated, even argumentative, and finally, after I had done an extensive comparative religious study, our chats became more frustrating for both of us. Pops wouldn't budge. There was not a softening on his side at all. Time, I felt, was of the essence now, because he was getting older and already had had several serious illnesses.

Finally, one afternoon, right in the middle of one of our "spiritual discussions," the Lord said to

*Psalm 103:3 states that He will heal ALL our diseases. Can I stand on His Word here and apply this to my own life right now? You bet I can!*

me (almost audibly): "Nancy, stop talking. Begin to pray for Pops and choose by faith to *hope* for your grandpa's salvation." I knew it was the Lord's voice because I would never have thought to do that. In my mind, I thought: *Why not talk it out? How could that hurt? Why be still?* But I knew it was God's voice, not my own, so I began to do as He said. I began to pray for Pops...and to hope for his salvation. Every place I read in the Bible at that time seemed to confirm that approach: "Be still and know that I am God." "Hope in the Lord with all your heart." "I will save your family." "Pray about everything."[114]

At first, I prayed every day, but after six months, not one thing had changed. Pops was still as adamant as ever. Then I began to pray every morning and every night, but still no change. Finally, after a year or so, I slowed down to praying for him every couple of days. But still nothing. After fifteen years of praying for my Pops, and I still hadn't seen or heard anything different, I became very weary. By this time, Pops was in his 80's and getting weaker and weaker by the moment.

During that fifteen-year period, Chuck and I had moved away, begun a whole new life, had babies and were busy doing our own thing. Every time I would think about Pops, the words "pray and hope" came back to my mind. But, privately, I was disappointed because I never saw anything change and fifteen years had gone by.

Finally, I heard that my Pops had died. And, of course, I was devastated.

In my mind, he had never come to know the Lord. "God, You promised! I prayed and I hoped as You told me to do, but nothing ever happened! I don't understand! I did as You told me. Lord, what went wrong?"

I cried for a whole day.

That weekend, we traveled many miles to get to Pops' funeral, and I, most of all, was still very sad, very confused and very discouraged.

After the funeral service was over and I was standing in the middle of the crowd talking to one of my relatives whom I had not seen for many years, a beautiful black lady came up to me and said, "Are you Nancy? Can I speak with you for a moment?" Her name was Deana. I followed her over to the side of the room where we could talk easily. Deana graciously said, "I was your grandfather's nurse for the last couple of weeks of his life. *He gave me specific instructions that I was to find 'Nancy' at this service and tell you that he accepted Jesus Christ as his personal Savior two days before he died."*

Deana, who was also a believer, explained that just before the Lord took Pops home, she had the 700 Club TV program playing in his room when the host of the program asked that if anyone wanted to become a real Christian, he or she should pray with him. Pops grabbed ahold of Deana's hand and out loud gave his life to Christ. He then told Deana that he finally had figured out what I had been trying so ardently to tell him all those years ago. And he made her promise that she would find me at the funeral and tell me he had committed his life to Christ. Deana ended her conversation with me by saying (and this is what makes this story so precious to me), *"God truly is a God of Hope, isn't He?"*

Deana disappeared that night, and I have never seen or heard from her again. Was she real? Was she an angel? *All I know is that God, in His unfathomable way, was incredibly faithful to His promise to me.* "Pray and hope for your grandfather's salvation." It had taken many years, but God brought him to Himself "*in His timing, not mine.*" My Pops is with the Lord now, and I will be able to see and hug him soon. That's all that matters.

Now, it didn't turn out the way I thought it would or the way I would have liked, but God was faithful and it turned out His perfect way.

For those of you who have a "Pops" in your family, don't stop praying for them, don't stop hoping for their salvation and don't stop believing God can bring them to salvation. God is faithful.

"Blessed is the man that trusts in the LORD, and whose *hope* the LORD is."[115]

Again, when I say "the man that trusts in the Lord," I simply mean a man who trusts in God's faithfulness. Hope is simply trusting in God's faithfulness no matter what we see, feel or understand in the natural. That's what I plan to do with my own future, and I'm anxious to see how God is going to have it all play out. Yes, God heals us, but how He will do it is up to Him.

He is faithful....

## God's Faithfulness

Faithfulness is the word *emuwnah* (*Strong's* #530) in the Hebrew, and this word only occurs in the Old Testament. It always speaks of **God's faithfulness toward man.** It speaks of His trust-worthiness, His security, His truthfulness and His honesty toward us.

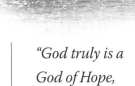

God's faithfulness refers to His "standing in a firm place." This firmness can be described as a peg that is pounded into a piece of wood. That peg becomes so immoveable that even if it's pushed to its limits and breaks off at the point of entry, it still remains firm in the wood. Faithful-

*"God truly is a God of Hope, isn't He?"*

ness means to remain in one place or a fixed position.[116] God wants us to learn "experientially" not only about His dependability but also about His reliability.

Hebrews 11:11 tells us that "hope" is really based upon knowing God's faithfulness.[117]

God's faithfulness is an integral part of the anchor by which we can cross the bridge to the unseen, no matter what is coming at us. It's one of the core issues that will allow us not only to take that initial step of faith but also to keep on walking toward the unseen in hope.

*It's <u>our</u> faith in <u>His</u> faithfulness and Love that is going to give us hope for the future.*

Again, Galatians 2:20 seems to fit in here perfectly: "I am crucified with Christ: nevertheless I live; yet not I, but Christ liveth in me: and the life which I now live in the flesh *I live by the faith [or faithfulness] of the Son of God,* who loved me, and gave Himself for me."

I believe much of the confusion about faith and hope comes from the fact that we haven't been taught about *God's faithfulness*, but the emphasis has always been on *our faith*. Here's an example: "the just shall live by HIS faith." (Habakkuk 2:4) Does this mean, "the just shall live by his (own) faith"? Or does this mean *we live by God's faithfulness to us*? The word "faith" in this Scripture is the same Hebrew word (*emuwnah*) that also means "faithfulness." What this verse might really be saying is that "we live by God's faithfulness toward us." This then becomes the basis of our "hope." God binds Himself to His Word and He is always faithful to perform it. As Jeremiah 1:12 promises, "Thou hast well seen: for I will hasten My Word to perform it."

Consequently, we need to be careful when we talk about faith. Do we mean <u>our</u> "faith" toward God or <u>His</u> "faithfulness" toward us? Some passages we will be talking about will be speaking of God's faithfulness to us, while others will be speaking of our faith toward Him. The only way this all makes sense is if we say: We have *faith* because of "His faithfulness" to us; we have *Love* because of "His Love" toward us, and we have *hope* because of both His Love and His faithfulness. *Hope is the only thing that allows us to apply both His Love and His faithfulness to our lives.* If you keep this in mind, it will help clear up some of the confusion.

Again, hope is the connection between having faith and intimately knowing His Love.

## THE IMPORTANCE OF SEEING GOD'S FAITHFULNESS IN THE LITTLE THINGS

The most important thing we can do in the midst of our worst suffering is see God's Hand and His faithfulness even in the little things.

Seeing Him in the middle of our circumstances means "acknowledging Him." Remember Proverbs 3:5–6: "Trust in the LORD with all thine heart; and lean not to thine own understanding. *In all thy ways acknowledge Him,* and He will direct thy paths."

Notice something interesting. Job did **not** "see" or "acknowledge" God's faithfulness throughout the first part of the book of Job. In fact in Job 9:11, he says: "He [God] goes by me and I see Him **not**; He passeth on also, but I perceive Him not." He does acknowledge his "eternal hope," however, in Job 19:25–26, when he says: "For I know that my redeemer liveth, and that He shall stand at the latter day upon the earth: and though after my skin worms destroy this body, yet in my flesh I shall see God."

What happened that finally turned Job around? In Job 42:5, he says: "I had heard of You by the hearing of the ear, but *now my eye sees You.*" He finally acknowledges God's faithfulness and goodness.

The most important thing we can do in the midst of our worst suffering is see God's Hand and His faithfulness even in the little things.

141

As I look back at my own situation, I can now say that I see God's faithfulness clearly. But, at the time, like Job, I'm not sure I recognized God's faithfulness in the phenomenal connections that became available to me for the best oncology doctors in the country—the radiologist who *just happened* to know the famous Mayo Clinic cancer surgeon; who *just happened* to "make an exception" for me to be her patient; who *just happened* to work with one of the best reconstructive surgeons in the world; who just happened to...etc. That's God handiwork. Then there was the famous oncology surgeon who agreed to see me in five days (it normally takes six to eight weeks to get an appointment with him). That's God's Hand. Lastly, I've had to travel a total of 3,000 miles to see these doctors (five trips, 600 miles each), but not a single car breakdown, flat tire or gas problem. I have an older car, and I traveled alone. That's God's Hand.[118]

The bottom line is: It's so important to look for God's faithful Handprint even when we are going through the darkest times in our lives. We say we "trust God." That means we trust His Love and His faithfulness to protect us, to guide us and to provide for us *no matter what is happening in our lives.*

But there are conditions....

## FIRST CONDITION: YOU MUST BE "BORN AGAIN"

(The rest of this chapter we'll be dealing with some critical—*but deep*—"theological foundational truths." In order to "hope in the dark times," these truths are very important for us to understand. I don't want you to get buried in the next few pages, however, so take your time in reading. Pray and ask God for His supernatural understanding.)

Let's go back to our original question: Can we take God's promises personally? The answer is: yes, of course, because God is always faithful.

But there are conditions on our side and also on His side.

The first condition is that we must truly belong to the Lord. In other words, we need to be "born again." Born again simply means we must have, at one time or another, freely given our lives to the Lord just like my Pops did. This means we have asked Christ to come into our lives to become our Savior. Only then can we begin to personally experience His Love and faithfulness through His Word.

When we are born again, the Bible tells us we receive the gift of God's Holy Spirit who comes to dwell in our hearts. Acts 2:38 validates this: "Repent, and be baptized every one of you in the Name of Jesus Christ for the remission of sins, and ye shall receive *the gift of the Holy Spirit.*" This is the time that God's Spirit unites with our human spirit and gives us a brand-new spirit—a spirit that is now alive and sensitive to the Lord's leading. An analogy might be: The electricity is now turned on by the Master Transformer.

God gives us a <u>body</u> to interact with and be *conscious of the world and others* around us. He gives us a <u>soul</u> so that we might be *conscious of ourselves*—our own thoughts, emotions and desires. And He gives us a <u>spirit</u> so we can be *conscious of, communicate with and have fellowship in the Lord.* In other words, our spirit is our vital "link" to God.

God's Spirit uses our human spirit not only to restore true spiritual communication in our lives but also to carry out the process of our soul's sanctification. *Sanctification simply means the process of restoring our human spirit to its rightful place, as director of our souls. This restoration is crucially important because until our soul is completely submitted to our spirit, our communication with the Lord will be hindered.*

Romans 8:16 tells us very clearly that even after we are born again, we still have a human spirit. This will be very important to remember in the upcoming chapters. "The Spirit itself beareth witness with *our spirit,* that we are the children of God." Consequently, if we truly are "a child of God," His Spirit will always bear witness to us, lead us and guide us through our human spirit.

The true spiritual man is one in whom the spirit rules, *not* the soul. And this can only occur when one is "born again." Only when God's Spirit unites with our spirit can the direction of our lives begin to change. God's will is that our regenerate spirit becomes stronger and stronger, so that it can work alongside God's Spirit to control and govern our soul. Our new spirit will then be able to operate *outwardly* through our soul to communicate with the world and others, while operating *inwardly* toward God and communing with Him.

A "spiritual" Christian is one in whom the Spirit is leading, guiding and directing their soul, whereas a "carnal" Christian is one in whom the flesh (or the soul) is in control. The Lord still lives in a carnal person's heart, but that person has allowed sin and self-centeredness to quench the Spirit's guidance. Thus God's Life is blocked from coming forth.

Pops gave his life to the Lord two days before he died while watching that TV program. As a result, his human spirit was united with God's Spirit and he immediately became one spirit with God. He became a new creation and was born again. Consequently, all the Scriptures that pertain to a true believer, such as "going to be with the Lord" when they die, apply to my Pops. As the thief on the cross did, Pops immediately became one with the Lord that day.

The bottom line is that the Holy Spirit wants to permeate our souls with His Life so that we might "know the Love of Christ, which passeth knowledge, [so we] *might be filled with all the fulness of God.*"[119]

## What Exactly is our Spirit?

Our spirit is like the *power source*, the *energy source* or the *light source* of our lives. It's analogous to a generator or an electric power plant in a

144

huge building. Without its energy and its power, nothing in the building will work. There will be no light, no electricity at all! And it's the same with us. Our spirit is the *life-giving power source* that makes us alive, that quickens us and that gives us life. Its removal means death.

Our spirit exists independently in our body. In other words, it's not material. Proverbs 20:27 likens it to an electric light bulb. "The spirit of man is the candle of the LORD." In order to have light, however, Scripture tells us that our spirit must come in contact with and be united with the Spirit of God. The Spirit of God is the "Master Transformer"; our own spirit is simply the transmitter. So apart from God's Spirit turning our spirit on, it will remain darkened and unlit (not born again).

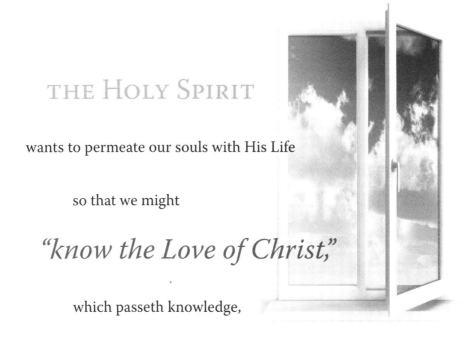

THE HOLY SPIRIT

wants to permeate our souls with His Life

so that we might

*"know the Love of Christ,"*

which passeth knowledge,

so we might be filled with all the fulness of God.

Now the reason we want to focus our attention on our spirit and understand exactly what it is and what it does is because *our hope* is going to be built on the purification of our spirit. If our spirit is purified, our hope will prevail. If our spirit is unclean, our hope will fail....

## WHAT HAPPENS AT OUR NEW BIRTH?

The book of Genesis tells us that at the beginning of time, man's spirit was head over the whole man. But because of Adam's sin and fall (he chose to follow his own will rather than God's), he lost his original union and fellowship with God. In other words, Adam's soul became inflated and his spirit suppressed. Adam's spirit became cut off from its original *source of power*—the Master Transformer (God's Spirit).

At this point, Adam's spirit and soul became comingled, fused or joined, with his soul becoming the ruling and governing force. As a result, the spirit of man could no longer control his body. Thus God could no longer communicate with man or rule him internally, and He had to resort to the laws of nature.

Man's spirit became simply a resident or a prisoner of his soul. So, as was true of Adam, when we are born into the human race, our soul is naturally the dominant force, controlling all that we do.

When we ask Jesus Christ to come into our lives to become our Savior and Lord, however, God gives us the gift of the Holy Spirit. "Repent, and be baptized every one of you in the Name of Jesus Christ for the remission of sins, and ye shall receive *the gift of the Holy Spirit.*"[120]

This is the time that God's Spirit unites with our human spirit and our spirit becomes alive, quickened and regenerated. In other words, the electricity is turned back on by the Master Transformer. Ezekiel 36:27 explains: "I will put My Spirit within you, and cause you to walk in My statutes, and ye shall keep My judgments, and do them." This means that when the Holy Spirit infuses our spirit with new Life, our dead spirit becomes alive again.

What this is saying is that once we become "born again," we become a dual man. We not only have a human spirit, we also have God's Spirit in us. God's Spirit then uses our human spirit like a carrier or a transport to help carry out the process of sanctification and to restore spiritual communication in our lives.

Our biggest difficulty, then, is that our spirit needs to be untangled from our soul and break free from its influence. When our soul becomes defiled, unholy or unclean because of our self-centered, emotional choices, it also defiles our spirit and causes all communication, leading and guiding from the Holy Spirit to be stopped. This blocked communication is what we mean when we say that the Spirit has become "quenched."

All communication and fellowship with God occurs in our spirit, because this is the place where "He meets with us"; this is the place where He dwells, and this is the place where we become one with Him. Thus, when our spirit is cleansed and purified, we are able to communicate and fellowship directly with Him. But as long as our spirit and our soul are intermingled (and not cleansed), our spirit will be suppressed by our soul's influence and our spiritual walk hindered.

As Christians we will always have a human soul and a human spirit. The question is: Which one is in control?

Before we continue to explore how our spirits are purified, let's first understand what our spirit really is and what its function is.

## What are the Functions of Our Spirit?

Our spirit—the place where we communicate with God—has three main functions or operations, and each one is essential to fellowship with the Father.

The three main functions of our spirit are our conscience, our intuition and our communion with God. Briefly, *our conscience* is the place where God teaches us secret things and speaks privately to us. This is where He lets us know what is right and what is wrong and what His will is. *Our intuition* is where God guides and leads us and where we can discern His movements. This is the area where we develop true intimate knowledge of God and experience His revelation and His anointing. The third function of our spirit is where we *fellowship and commune* directly with God. This is where we are to worship the Lord in the spirit.

Let's explore these functions of our spirit in a little more detail.

## CONSCIENCE

All three functions of our spirit are very closely related, so each one depends upon and builds from the other. A pure conscience leads to an undefiled intuition and ultimately to open communion and fellowship with God.

Our conscience is like the inner voice of God. This is where God corrects and protects us. This is also where the Holy Spirit reveals God's will to us. Our conscience is like God's inward monitor. It renders us uneasy when we don't choose to follow His will and gives us peace when we do. Our conscience reprimands us, reproves us, corrects

> All communication and fellowship with God occurs in our spirit, because this is the place where "He meets with us"; this is the place where He dwells, and this is the place where we become one with Him.

148

us and approves us. It is designed to govern our lives and, by doing so, constantly shows us what God's will is.

Our spiritual conscience is our teacher. As Job declares, God's Spirit taught him things that he did not understand. And I can say the very same thing. Throughout the writing of this book, God has taught me things by His Spirit that I neither knew nor understood before. (Even after being a Christian for more than sixty years!)

The first step of salvation is to awaken our comatose conscience. We need a conscience in order to convict us of sin and to make us sensitive to our self-centered ways. Hebrews tells us that Christ's blood has been shed over our conscience so that we *can* have a cleansed and purified spirit. A cleansed conscience is one that carries *no guilt.* Hebrews 10:22 tells us: "Our hearts [are] sprinkled [clean] from an evil conscience, and our bodies [are] washed with pure water." *Thus, a sprinkled and cleansed conscience is the only basis for our spiritual communion with God.* A conscience that is tinged with offenses will not only affect our communication with God but also prevent our sanctification.

Someone once said, *"It's more important to be afraid of one reproach from our conscience than it is from all the condemnation of men in the world."*

So the first step toward sanctification is to abide by our "purified" conscience, which will constantly tell us if we are clean or not. As we grow more and more into a spiritual man, our conscience will grow more and more sensitive and attuned to God's voice. Scripture states that our conscience will not only "bear witness" to us, it will also "condemn us."

As our spiritual life grows, our conscience will begin to show us not only what is right and what is wrong, but also what is of God and what is not. Although many things may *appear* right in our own eyes, they are, nonetheless, condemned by God because they do not originate with

His Spirit. We must learn to be sensitive only to His voice and be willing to eliminate anything that does not bear witness to our spirit.

Now, please don't misunderstand me. We are never going to be perfectly clean or perfectly holy in this lifetime. *There is only One who is, and that's Jesus.* What I am referring to here is dealing daily with the sin and self that God shows us. Since God loves us and wants us completely for Himself, moment-by-moment He will lovingly point out more and more *self* that must be given over.

So, from now on, when I speak of a "sanctified soul" or a "purified spirit," I do *not* mean a totally pure and completely holy person. That will only happen at the resurrection. *I simply mean a person who has dealt with all that God has shown them for that day!*

We also don't have to wait until "all" sin and "all" self is dealt with *before* we can have communion with God and enjoy His presence. That also will take a lifetime! We need only to be faithful to crucify the things that He shows us today! *It's not unknown sin that is going to hinder our communication with God. It's the known sin!*

Our conscience is limited by its own present knowledge. Therefore, it can only guide us by the knowledge it possesses now. God will continue to examine our actions and our motives and will reveal what He finds. Then it will be up to us to deal with the things that "are not of faith." Therefore, our sanctification is going to be totally dependent upon our own willingness to accept the reproach of our conscience and to do whatever is necessary to correct it.

I don't believe that we can make some sort of vague "blanket" or "general" statement of confession by acknowledging *all* of our sins and *all* of our self-centered ways. "Oh, Lord, forgive me for all of my sins." I don't believe this is what cleanses our conscience. We need to let the Holy Spirit, daily, moment-by-moment, reprove and convict us of "specific" things that we have done that are "not of faith." (Yes, our sin was dealt with at the Cross, but it's still our responsibility to ***appropriate*** what Christ did at the Cross every day as we deal with our current sin and self.) As 1 John 1:9 tells us: "If we confess our sins, He is faithful and just to forgive us our sins and to cleanse us from all unrighteousness."[121]

Paul is a perfect example of someone who had a Spirit-filled conscience. In Acts 24:16, he asserts: "I exercise myself, to have always a conscience void of offense toward God, and toward men."[122] I believe God desires the same for us—a clean conscience before God and man. In fact, Scripture tells us we can only serve God when we have a cleansed and pure conscience.

*I believe maturity in Christ can be measured by our responsiveness to our conscience.* A good conscience enables us to receive God's promises, walk by His Spirit and enter His presence. An evil conscience leads us to a lack of faith, being guilt-ridden and walking by the flesh.

## INTUITION

The next function of our spirit is our intuition. Intuition is the attaining of direct knowledge, perception or conviction beyond the means of reason alone. Our intuition and our conscience work closely together. One leads to the next. A pure conscience leads to a keen intuition. In other words, *we can't have discernment if we have a defiled conscience.*

Intuition is simply "spiritual sensing" or spiritual discernment. This is very different from following our own natural instinct or our soulish emotional feelings. Spiritual intuition is adhering to what the voice of the Spirit is saying, as this is how we receive God's instructions. Many Christians do not have this intuitive knowledge because they don't know how to discern God's voice. They don't know how to "walk by or after the spirit." If we don't heed our spiritual intuition, we'll naturally go back to walking after the flesh and adhering to our own soulish thoughts and emotions. *To live and walk in the Spirit means to live and walk according to our intuition.*

A pure spirit will disclose an unmistakable discernment, and this discernment is critical when fighting the enemy. *The enemy can attack us only through our soul and body—through the motions of our flesh.* Therefore, if we are not sensitive to this vulnerability, he will always find a "hole" to keep us his prisoners. Those who adhere to the leading of the Spirit (via their intuition) will be preserved from being deceived in times of confusion.

What is the difference between discerning and judging? To judge someone really means to condemn them, whereas to discern someone means to separate the good from the bad, but this is always done in love. Discernment sees things as they really are, from the Mind of Christ. Jesus always discerned; He never judged.

## COMMUNION AND FELLOWSHIP

In review, our *conscience* is where God teaches us what His will is; our *intuition* is where God leads and guides us and gives us supernatural discernment and revelation. The third function of our spirit, our *communion and fellowship* with God, is unique.

This operation of our spirit requires *our* participation. While teaching and guiding are aspects of God's communication *to us*, communion and fellowship require our communication *with God*. In other words, there is a response needed from us. *Communion is a two-way relationship*, and *only* a sprinkled and cleansed spirit is the basis for this communion.

In order to communicate and fellowship with God, we must possess a similar nature, a spiritual nature. Scripture tells us that God is a Spirit and the only way we can have intimacy and fellowship with

Him is through our purified spirit. Therefore, if our spirit has been quenched because of sin or self, we won't be able to commune with Him as we would like. In fact, we won't even be able to hear Him. Lamentations 3:44 validates this, "Thou hast covered Thyself with a cloud, that our prayer[s] should not pass through."

Most of us attempt to communicate with God in a wide variety of ways. Naturally, we give our soulish thoughts and emotions first place. Consequently, we often overlook the most important way to fellowship with God, which is through our spirit. If we can learn how to constantly surrender and relinquish ourselves to God, He will be able to answer us *in the most miraculous ways.*

# OUR CONSCIENCE

is where God teaches us what His will is;

our intuition is where God leads—

*He guides us.*

*He gives us supernatural discernment.*

*And he gives revelation.*

## WHAT IS THE PURIFICATION OF OUR SPIRIT?

The bottom line is that only as we moment-by-moment crucify the flesh, can we truly walk by the Spirit. As 2 Corinthians 7:1 exhorts us, "Having, therefore, these promises, dearly beloved, let us cleanse ourselves from all filthiness of the *flesh* and *spirit*, perfecting holiness in the fear of God."

*Purification of our spirit simply means a spirit that is freed from all soulish influence.* Our spirit gets polluted through our "flesh." God wants to purify our spirit so that it can be freed of soulish entanglements and begin to direct our lives.

In order for our spirit to become experientially one with God (where He is directing and guiding us), there can be no adulteration from anything that is soulish. He wants us to know His will through our conscience, discern His leading and guiding through our intuition and begin to fellowship and commune with Him in the spirit.[123]

All of our own self-justification, self-defense and self-orientation only betrays an *unbroken and unpurified spirit.* Until our spirit is purified, we will be full of ourselves, full of our own plans, our own ambitions, our own values, our own judgments, our own rationalizations, our own ideals and so on. Many of these things are not sin, but nevertheless, because we build our lives upon them, they can prevent God's perfect will from being accomplished.

This was new to me. I knew our souls needed to be sanctified, but I wasn't aware that the Scripture says our spirits also need to be purified. Without the constant cleansing of our spirit, we will never experience a pure conscience, a keen intuition or sweet fellowship with God. (This is one of those foundational truths that I mentioned earlier that we will build upon in the coming chapters. So be sure to take time to really understand what is being said here.)

God desires that we know His will through *our conscience*, that we discern His leading and guiding through *our intuition* and that we fellowship and *commune with Him* in the spirit. He wants us not only to have a right spirit but also a purified spirit (a spirit with no guile, no searing and no deceitfulness). As the psalmist declares in Psalm 32:2, "Blessed is the man unto whom the LORD imputeth not iniquity, and in whose spirit there is no guile."

*If our spirit does not grow stronger, and the soulish things in our lives become less and less, we have not really grown at all. Real advancement is only measured by the growth of our spirit.*

Eloquent preaching, Bible knowledge and spiritual gifts do not increase our spiritual life. Only the cleansing and purifying of our spirit does. In other words, mental knowledge does *nothing* toward increasing a person's intimacy with Christ or his being conformed into Christ's image. Only the Spirit of God can do these things in our lives. Thus God wants us to be sanctified not only in our soul but also purified in our spirit.

## WHAT IS OUR SOUL?

As long as we are defining what our spirit is, let's also define what our soul is. Then we won't get these intangible parts of our makeup confused. It's really important to understand these basic elements of our personal architecture so we can allow them to function properly. As we said, our spirit is like the power source or energy source of our lives. It's where God's Spirit unites with our own spirit and gives us a brand-new spirit. Our spirit is the *inward power source* of our lives, whereas our soul is the *outward expression* of our lives—it's comprised of our natural thoughts, emotions and desires. In other words, our soul is the "life" we show forth from our bodies (often visible), whereas our spirit is the "source" of that life (always invisible).

The Greek word for our soul is *psyche*, which has a very interesting twofold meaning. Psyche means "it shall have life" or "it shall wax cold." This is a perfect definition because our soul will either be "spirit filled" and have life because of the free flow of God's Life from our hearts into our lives, or our soul will be empty and waxing cold because God's Life has been quenched and blocked from coming forth.

Therefore, you could say that our soul is like a *"neutral area"* (or an open container) that either can be filled with "God's Life" if we have made faith choices to do His will, or filled with "self-life" if we have made emotional choices to follow our own desires.

So there's nothing supernatural about our soul, <u>unless</u>, by our own moment-by-moment choice, it can become filled with God's Life. This is what being "spirit filled" is all about.

Why is this so critical to understand? Because our spirit is the place where God, the Holy Spirit, dwells and the place "He meets with us." When our spirit is cleansed and purified, we are able to communicate and fellowship directly with the Lord. But if our spirit is suppressed by our soul's influence, our spiritual communication is also hindered (i.e., we won't experience God's Love for ourselves, let alone for others).

"Having therefore these promises, dearly beloved, let us cleanse ourselves from all filthiness of the *flesh and spirit*, perfecting holiness in the fear of God."[124] Cleansing ourselves from all filthiness of flesh and spirit simply means we need to be sanctified.[125]

## SANCTIFICATION: DIVIDING OUR SOUL FROM OUR SPIRIT

Sanctification is simply *the process of becoming holy, purified or consecrated.* It's the process of seeing Christ's Life reproduced in us.

Sanctification is the removal of anything in our lives that is unrighteous or unholy. God is not only working to conform us into His image and to instill intimacy, He is also preparing us for His return as the Bridegroom.

We begin our course of sanctification when we first become believers, but we don't finish this cleansing process until we are sanctified *wholly*—body, soul and spirit. *Sanctification is simply the process of separating, dividing and cutting away the soulish things in our lives from the spiritual.* God is the only One who can do this in our lives because He is the only One who knows *what is spiritual* and *what is soulish.* We could never accomplish this separation in our own strength or by our own wisdom.

Our greatest problem is *impurity.* Remember, we have become a "dual" man. Our outward man (our soul) continually affects our inward man (our spirit), and this cannot be. Our inward man needs to be released in order to direct our outward man. In other words, our spirit needs to be set free. The only way this freedom is possible is to divide and separate the two.

In order for this division and this separation to come about, we must be able to "see" what God sees in us. *Seeing is the first step toward dealing with the problem,* and only the Word of God can give us the revelation we need to see what God sees.

"...all things are naked and opened unto the eyes of Him with whom we have to do."[126]

In other words, *to the degree that we allow God's Word and His Spirit to show us our "selves," is the degree to which our spirit can be purified.* Through His Word, God can reveal the motives of our heart and enable us to *see ourselves as we truly are. We are unable to do this for ourselves.* Deliverance comes only when the light of God's Word helps us to see as God sees.

Hebrews 4:12 points out that this process is like "...piercing even to the *dividing asunder of the soul and spirit, and of the joints and marrow,* and is a discerner of the thoughts and intents of the heart."

According to this Scripture, our soul and spirit together are analogous to our *bones,* which consist of joints and marrow. In order to divide our bones, they must be broken, *disunited* or separated. God's Word is like His sword, and He uses the power of His sword to cut, pierce and divide our soul and spirit, just as you would divide the joints and marrow of our bones.

A *joint* is a place between two parts, just as our *soul* is the place between our body and our spirit. *Marrow* means the best part, the innermost part or the essential part from which all of our strength, vitality and life is derived—the richest portion of our bones.

And it's the same with our spirit. Our spirit is the best, the richest and the supremest part of our makeup, because it's where God dwells. Only as our spirit (the *marrow*) is separated away from our soul (the *joint*) can it be sanctified and strengthened and the Life of God truly come forth.

To separate the joints means to "cut across the bones." To divide the marrow from the joint means to "crack the bones" or to "break the bones." There are only two things harder to divide than the joints and marrow, and *that's our soul and spirit.* This is exactly what God does during our "night seasons."

> Sanctification is simply the process of becoming holy, purified or consecrated. It's the process of seeing Christ's Life reproduced in us.

As Job cries, "My bones are pierced in the *night seasons.*"[127]

And Jeremiah says, "He hath broken my bones."[128]

God's whole purpose is to refine us so that our spirit will not be influenced and affected by anything in our outward man or in our circumstances. He doesn't want *anything* to be able to move us from the peace and joy of His presence—from oneness of spirit. He sanctifies our spirit and soul so that He might reproduce Himself in us and we might begin to experience His presence and His fullness, *no matter where we are and no matter what is going on in our lives.*

The lesson here is that if the spirit is truly the *master* of the body, God's presence is always with us, no matter what is occurring in our lives. The enemy wants to steal, kill and destroy us with all the things that happen in our lives, but God wants to use our circumstances, no matter how bad, for His glory.

We can compare ourselves to the priests of Solomon's Temple. After they had sacrificed their offerings on the Brazen Altar in the Inner Court (and had become cleansed), they were allowed to *enter the Holy Place and God's presence.* Once God begins to cleanse us and make us holy, we, too, can boldly approach God's presence in the Holy Place of our hearts.

## What is our Heart?

As long as we are defining what our spirit and our soul are, let's also be clear on what our "heart" is.

For many years I was taught that our heart and our soul were really the same thing. When pastors would tell me that, however, I'd always ask them, "If that's true, why does God tell us in Matthew 22 to 'love Him with all *our heart* and with all *our soul'*?" They must be two different things, because they are two different Greek words! After years of study, I finally came to the conclusion that they definitely are two different things.

Our heart is the place where God's Life—His Love, His wisdom and His power—is created, started and brought into new existence.[129] (2 Corinthians 1:22) Our soul, on the other hand, is the place where either God's Life *can* manifest itself through us (if we are "clean") or "the flesh" will show forth (if there is sin and self-centeredness). Remember Ezekiel 36:27 talks about our new birth at which time we not only receive a new spirit but also a new heart. "I will put My Spirit within you, and cause you to walk in My statutes, and ye shall keep My judgments, and do them." This is the time that God "takes away our old stony heart" and gives us a new one. This is "Christ in us, our hope of glory."[130] This new heart is now the hidden core of our being and upon which everything else will be built. So, if we are born again, *our "new heart" is the place where God's Life (His Agape Love, His Wisdom and His Power) dwells.*

An analogy that might help to distinguish the difference between "our heart" and "our soul" is: Our heart is like the *roots of a plant.* No one can see those roots; they are underground and yet essential to the growth aboveground. Our soul, on the other hand, is like the flowers (or the fruit) that grow aboveground and that all can see. Those aboveground plants, however, can either be "flowers" (if God's Life is showing forth through our soul) or they can be "weeds" (if God's Life has been quenched and self-life is showing forth instead).

Hopefully, this little summary helps to clarify the difference between our heart, our soul and our spirit.

## LIFE COMES ONLY FROM THE CROSS

As you can see, God is not only desirous of making us holy by *removing all the sin* in our lives (our souls), He also wants to conform us into His image by *removing any character flaws, belief systems, habits or thought patterns* (in our spirit) that prevent His Life from flowing through us. God accomplished both of these purposes by the Cross. *Life comes only from the Cross.* The Cross is the heart of all Love, and Love is the heart of the Cross. The Cross is the only way to rise *above* all that imprisons our soul and spirit. The whole purpose of the Cross is to purge the soulish things in our lives (empty us out) so God can fill us up with His abundant Life.

The Cross must cut deeply in order to rid us of the things that prevent our fellowship and our life with Him. And this surgery hurts. If we don't "feel" the Cross, we really haven't suffered. Feeling pain is part of suffering, and suffering (barring our self from sin) is a major part of the sanctification and purification process. Without pain, there is no Cross; and without the Cross, there really is no exchange of life.

In the middle of our night seasons, we must learn to love the Cross, because this is the way God accomplishes our sanctification. *Abandonment to God's will and the Cross go hand in hand.* Sometimes we can bear the Cross in His strength and proceed the way God desires. But at other times, when we're weak, we must bear the Cross by *faith.* Either way, *we must bear the Cross* and allow God to do whatever He must do. Throughout the Bible, the principle that "life only comes through death" is very apparent.

Remember John 12:24: "Verily, verily, I say unto you, Except a corn of wheat fall into the ground and die, it abideth alone: but if it die, it bringeth forth much fruit. He that loveth [hangs on to] his life shall lose it; and he that hateth [is willing to surrender it] his life in this world shall keep it unto life eternal."

Just as Christ was raised from the dead after the Cross, we too can "walk in newness of Life" after being conformed to His death. As we allow God to deal not only with our *sinful acts* but also our *self-centered ways,* we too can experience His resurrection Life. God's desired outcome is that after the death of our self-life, we might "serve Him in newness of spirit."

The Cross that cleanses us from *sin* is very different from the Cross that deals with our *self.* Jesus made atonement for our sins by shedding His blood for us on that Cross 2,000 years ago. He paid the complete price, and there is nothing else needed for our salvation. But in order to be sanctified body, soul and spirit, we must also allow God to

In the middle of our night seasons,

we must learn to LOVE THE CROSS,

*because this is the way God*

*accomplishes our sanctification.*

daily, moment-by-moment, expose our self and then we must nail it to the Cross (crucify it).

## THE BIG QUESTION

The question becomes, are we really willing to be sanctified body, soul and spirit? Are we prepared for what that really means? A dear friend of mine, a missionary in New Zealand, wrote me a very provocative letter about this subject a few months ago that I would like to share with you:

"I read 1 Thessalonians 5:23 in my daily devotions this morning, and it really spoke to my heart. 'And the very God of peace sanctify you wholly; and I pray your whole spirit and soul and body be preserved blameless unto the coming of our Lord Jesus Christ.'

"When we pray to be sanctified, are we really prepared to face the standard of these verses? All of us take the term sanctification much too lightly. Are we really prepared for what sanctification will cost us? *It will cost an intense narrowing of all our interests on earth, and an immense broadening of all our interests in God.* Sanctification means an intense concentration on God's point of view. It means every part of our body, soul and spirit must be chained and kept for God's purposes only. Are we prepared for God to do that in each of our lives? Are we prepared to separate ourselves to God, even as Jesus did?

"Sanctification means 'being made one' with Jesus so that the disposition that ruled Him (God's Spirit) can also rule and reign in us. Are we prepared for what that will cost us? *It will cost us everything that is not of God!"*

When our hope is fixed upon Him, it embraces our sight, our expectation and our trust all at the same time.[131] Hope is the only way we won't be tossed about, the only way we won't be turned around and the only way we won't be driven by the winds of change as we patiently wait for God's promises to come to pass.[132] You can see now why God calls hope the "anchor of our soul." It simply means we have "sure confidence" in God, His Love and faithfulness no matter what He allows.[133] That's easy for me "to say"; now I have to "walk it out."

Romans 8:24–25 tells us that we won't necessarily always be "hoping" for things that we can see, but "hoping against hope" for things that are totally controlled by God.[134]

# CHAPTER FIVE: CAN WE TAKE GOD'S PROMISES LITERALLY?

1. Memorize Galatians 2:20.

2. Can we take God's promises in the Word personally and literally? Give some examples in your own life.

3. Define "faithfulness" as it relates to the Lord. Why is this so important to understand?

4. So it's our faith in His faithfulness that is going to give us "hope" for the future. Is this what Habakkuk 2:4 is really saying? What do you think?

5. Seeing God's Hand (His faithfulness) in the midst of our trials is what will help us persevere to the end. Can you give a personal example of this in your life?

6. There are a couple of conditions to claiming God's promises personally and literally. What are they? (Acts 2:38)

7. Speaking of receiving God's Spirit, what exactly is our spirit? What are the functions of our spirit? And why is it so important we let God sanctify our spirit?

8. What does it mean that we "become a dual man" when we are born again?

9. Why does our spirit need to be purified? (2 Corinthians 7:1)

10. What then is our soul? "Hope" is what holds our soul in place. What does this mean?

11. Why is it so important that our soul be divided from our spirit?

12. What exactly is our heart?

13. What does "sanctification" mean?

"Brethren, I count not myself to have apprehended;

but this one thing I do,

FORGETTING those things which are behind,

and REACHING forth unto those things

which are before,

I press toward the mark for the prize

of the high calling of God in Christ Jesus."

PHILIPPIANS 3:13–14

# WHAT IS
# GOD'S PLAN?
# HOW DO WE
# IMPLEMENT IT?

What, then, is God's overall plan? Why did He call us in the first place? What is our purpose here and now? And what are we working toward as Christians?

Is our goal simply to get saved? Is that all earthly life is about? Is there nothing more? What, then, does Philippians 3:14 mean when it talks about the "prize of the high calling of God in Christ Jesus"? What exactly is the prize? What is the "mark" for that prize?

In a nutshell, I believe God's overall plan is for us to have intimate and continuous fellowship with Him. He loves us and, amazingly, He wants to communicate that to us. This is the reason He calls us in the first place. But there is much more than that. "The prize of the high calling," in my opinion, is that God wants us to have an active part or role in His future Millennial and heavenly Kingdom. He wants all of us to rule and reign alongside Him.[135] But in order to accomplish this He must first "prepare" us, which simply means we must be "conformed into His image" of Love and holiness.[136] Then we not only can have personal fellowship with Him here and now, but we also learn to become overcomers (go from strength to strength) and thus are equipped to hold positions of responsibility in His coming kingdom. This life is simply the "training period."

This is exactly what Hebrews 12:1 means when it talks about "running the race." In a race, there's always something we are running toward—either a "goal" or a "prize."

God's goal for us here and now is not only to get saved but also to prepare us for positions of authority and great responsibility in His coming kingdom. This kingdom was declared by God from the beginning of time. Genesis 1:26 tells us that God created man in His image *so that we might have "dominion over all the earth"* and so that we might rule and reign alongside of Him. Can you imagine what that will be like? Psalm 8:3–6 expresses it this way: "When I consider Thy heavens, the work of Thy fingers, the moon and the stars, which Thou hast ordained: what is man, that Thou art mindful of him? and the son of man that Thou visited him? For Thou hast made him a little lower than the angels, and hast crowned him with glory and honour. *Thou madest him to have dominion over the works of Thy hands; Thou hast put all things under his feet.*" Matthew 25:34 confirms that this future kingdom was "***prepared for [us] from the foundation of the world.***"

This is God's purpose for calling us, saving us and sanctifying us. This is also the "prize of the

> Ruling and reigning with Christ in His future kingdom is *why* God has called us, *what* we are being trained for and *why* having hope is so very important.

high calling" that is waiting for us at the end of the race. This prize becomes the motivation we need in order to press forward, especially during the difficult times. It's the goal on which we are to fix our eyes. It's God's promise and our future hope. Unfortunately, very few Christians really understand this. Consequently, in their tribulation, they lose their hope and, rather than overcome, they forfeit their endurance as they let their trust slip.

Ruling and reigning with Christ in His future kingdom is *why* God has called us, *what* we are being trained for and *why* having hope is so very important.

I am praying that this book might encourage others and help them clarify the importance of "enduring" hope. This kind of hope can make the difference between "life" and "death." Once we personally know God's Love and faithfulness, we'll be able to find new courage and new confidence to "keep on keeping on" even in the middle of the darkest times.[137]

## He Wants to Conform Us into His Image

So the *"mark"* for the prize of the high calling of Christ is being conformed into His image of Love. This means getting rid of the "fleshly things" in us that hinder His Spirit and His Life from flowing out of our hearts and into our lives.

Alan Redpath, the notable English writer, tells us that God has brought us to this experience simply because "He wants to replace us with Himself." I love that! God uses our trials and tribulations to simply "replace us with Himself." This is the whole Christian life in a nutshell! This is God's will: to empty us of *ourselves* so that He can then fill us with *Himself*. When we willingly lay our lives down to Him and freely allow Him to do whatever is necessary, He can accomplish His will. However, if we are unwilling to allow Him to rearrange our lives, and we continue to hold tight to our selves, He then takes matters into His own hands (because He loves us). His way of turning us around and gently encouraging us to do His will is to allow more and more trials and difficulties into our lives so He can get our attention.

Therefore, the sanctification of our soul and the purification of our spirit is simply *the process of becoming holy.* It's the process by which Christ's Life can be freely reproduced in us. And God uses all of our life experiences in order to accomplish this. By the way, the word "sanctify" comes from the root word *hagion*, which actually means "holy place." This is particularly fascinating to me since the verb *hagiazo* (to sanctify) is used to describe the gold that adorns the actual Holy Place of the temple (which we will talk about briefly in Chapter Nine). And gold symbolizes the divine nature.

## God Wants to Separate the Impurities

Throughout Scripture, "gold" is always tested and refined by fire.[138] "Behold, I have created the smith that *bloweth the coals in the fire, and that bringeth forth an instrument for His work...*" (Isaiah 54:16)[139]

Gold is purified through a process of high temperature heating that includes three major steps:

- MELTING: For high-grade ore the metal is sent to a grinding mill and made into a powder. Then it is heated to over 1000°F, which removes the sulfide and the carbon.
- BINDING: Next, it is laced with cyanide and the gold is collected. It is then put into a vessel where the gold is removed chemically.
- SEPARATING: Finally, the gold is melted into bars and sent to an external refinery to make them 99 percent pure. (Taken from an article by Joseph Nicholson of the University of Phoenix.)

Interesting wording, when we compare this process to how God refines and purifies us. Mark 9:49 states that everyone shall be "salted with fire." This means, at one time or another, we all will undergo testing.

We begin our own course of gold purification when we first become believers, but we don't finish this cleansing process until we are sanctified *wholly*—body, soul and spirit. (I don't believe any of us have reached this stage yet; only Jesus did, because He is God. All of us are still at some point in the process.)[140]

The purification of our spirit simply means a spirit that is freed from all soulish influence. The only way, however, our spirit can ever be freed from soulish entanglements is by cutting, separating and dividing away anything that contaminates it, just like the process of gold purification.

Self-justification, self-defense and self-orientation only betray an *unbroken and unpurified spirit*. Until our spirit is purified, we will be "full of ourselves"—full of our own plans, our own ambitions, our own values, our own judgments, our own rationalizations, our own ideals and so on. Many of these things (even though they are not sin in themselves) can prevent God's perfect will from being accomplished. Thus, our greatest problem is *impurity*. Remember, we are still human and we still have a human spirit. In other words, we are a "dual" man. Our outward man (our soul) continually affects our inward man (our spirit), and this cannot be. There can be no mingling of our soul and spirit. Our inward man needs to be released in order to direct our outward man. And the only way this is possible is to divide and separate the two.

Psalm 105:19 tells us that it's the Word of God that is going to test us! The deeper God is allowed to go with His sword, the deeper the Cross can do its work. He must be allowed to expose even our most private and secret thoughts and intentions.

In contrast to our soul being cleansed from sin, which can be accomplished in an *instant* (through our faith choice to appropriate what Christ has already done), *spirit purification can last for months, depending upon our willingness or our unwillingness to unconditionally surrender our lives.* Every thought, emotion and desire must be governed by the spirit's control. When this happens, God's Spirit will be able to communicate directly with our spirit, show us His will and lead us into the intimacy we all so desire.

## HE WANTS TO EXPOSE OUR ROOT SYSTEMS
When God cleanses and purifies our spirit, He goes after our "human nature" itself. In other words, He exposes our "root systems." (If you are confused as to where this occurs, refer to Chapter Five—the purification of our spirit.)

Some examples of "root systems" are:

*Presumption.* Presumption is a preconceived belief about certain things, events or people. Presumption is taking something for granted or assuming something is true in the absence of proof to the contrary. In itself, this is obviously not sin. It's a behavior common to all of us. However, presumption can often be based on falsehoods that, if not dealt with, can lead us to disillusionment and bitterness, which *is* sin and *will* separate us from God.

*Expectation.* This is a big one! We pray and then we expect, but when we don't see the fulfillment of our prayers, we often give up. Expectation is very closely related to presumption. Expectation is a future hope in either "things," "events" or "people." We all have expectations; it's characteristic of our own self-centered human nature. This, in itself, is not sin. However, if our expectations are not fulfilled in the way we think they should be, they can lead to disappointment and doubt, which can end up quenching God's Spirit.

*Disappointment.* Disappointment is the failure to satisfy our own self-centered presumptions and expectations. Disappointment in itself is not sin, but if disappointment is not caught and taken care of (given over to God), it can lead to bitterness, resentment and depression, which *will* block God's Spirit in us.

*Comparing.* Another characteristic of our human self-centered nature is making comparisons. This, too, is one of man's inbred, natural ways and, in itself, not sin. However, if not caught and given over to God, it can open our senses (our soul) up to hurt, envy and jealousy. And these *will* quench God's Spirit in us.

*Loneliness.* It's certainly not a sin to be lonely. God has created every one of us with the need for companionship. As the Bible says, we were created for fellowship not only with God but with others. But if we allow loneliness to consume us and rule our thoughts and emotions, it can lead to soulish manipulation and control, which will quench God's Spirit in us.

*Even though some of the above things might not be considered sin, they must nevertheless be exposed and rooted out. Unless they are, these underlying belief systems will continue to direct our lives and prevent us from having the union with Christ that we so long for.*

These "root systems" can actually control us without our knowledge. Our ambitions, hopes, dreams, goals, desires, expectations and presumptions are beliefs, values and habits that

*If our expectations are not fulfilled in the way we think they should be, they can lead to disappointment and doubt, which can end up quenching God's Spirit.*

sometimes we are not even aware of. However, because they are also the programmed responses upon which we build our lives, it's vital that God exposes them so we can then surrender them to Him.

"Search me, O God, and know my heart; try me, and know my

thoughts; and see if there be any wicked way in me, and [then] lead me in the way everlasting." (Psalm 139:23–24)

And Lamentations 3:40 encourages us: "...search and try our ways, and turn again to the LORD."

We might be able to fool others into thinking we are doing Godly "good works," but if our spirit is tainted with any self-centeredness or any *self-love*, it's going to be "wood, hay [and] stubble" in God's eyes. "Every way of a man is right in his own eyes, but [only] the LORD weighs the hearts [the motives of our hearts]." (Proverbs 21:2) Only He knows the truth.

Second Timothy 3:2 tells us we are naturally "lovers of self." Consequently, we must be delivered from these things. And the way this is done is by the purification of our spirit.

God wants us to *know* Him, not just in our souls (where we experience His Life) but also in our spirits (where we can experience His presence). He wants us to willingly allow Him to burn up all that He knows is unnecessary in our souls and spirits so that we can *boldly* make our approach to Him in the ***Holy Place of our hearts.***

## GOD DOES NOT CAUSE OUR "NIGHT SEASONS"

Obviously, the purifying of our spirits can be very painful, to say the least. This is the time God uses the difficult times in our lives to do more of His refining.

It's important to understand, however, that while ***God uses our difficult life situations for His purposes, He does not cause them.*** Life is hard on its own. We have accidents, experience illness, go through divorces, face death, etc. ***God does not create or cause these situations; they are part of life itself. God simply uses these times in our lives for His purposes.***

In my case, I believe the malignant melanoma in the mucosal area of my nose might originally have been caused by my using and breathing in hair dye chemicals every three weeks for the past sixty years of my life. Being in a small bathroom and breathing in toxic chemicals could have very easily resulted in cancer of the nose. It's just a guess, but it's something I did, and the result could be something I caused. It's a part of the dangers of life. God did not cause it; I might have, but He wants to use it not only to conform me more into His image but also to show me how to trust Him more and how to glorify Him in all of it.

Consider the example that Paul gives us in Philippians 3:10: "That I may know Him, and the power of His resurrection, and the fellow-ship of His sufferings, being made conformable unto His death..." It's interesting that most of us want to *know Him* and *the power of His resurrection*, but in no way do we want to experience *the fellowship of His suffering.* However, this Scripture says knowing Him, know-ing His power and experiencing suffering are all somehow linked to-gether, and God is exhorting us (through Paul) to know (to intimately experience) all three.

When our son Chip died fifteen years ago, it wasn't something God did but something He allowed. Chip was out running on a hot August afternoon and physically his heart just couldn't take the pres-sure. He died of heat stroke. Yes, it was crippling for all of us to bear, but one of the results of that horrible accident is that it has allowed us to identify with, comfort and minister to others who have also lost children. Another result of Chip's death is that five members of our family came to know Christ. Again, the Lord didn't cause Chip's death, but He did use it in our lives to teach us not only how to know Him better and the power of His resurrection but also to know the fellowship of His suffering.

Somehow God is mysteriously working out His eternal plan in all of our lives. Take Job for an example. In his case, God was proving

Job's faith to all the heavenly angels. Did Job know that? Of course not! But we now, with 20/20 hindsight, can see God's plan very clearly. Only God knows what He is doing in each of our lives and how He will use each of our situations for our best and for His glory.

One believer recently sent me this: "There are moments where I am completely stunned by what God has put in front of me. My mind cannot comprehend it, and I am certain that I cannot endure it. But I think that is exactly the point He is trying to make to me. I can imagine Him smiling so sweetly and saying to me, 'Of course you can't on your own, *but I am with you...*' Some days that is the only peace I know, but it is sufficient."

Through dark times, God not only wants to show us things about Himself, He also wants to show us things about ourselves. Many of the qualities that we possess in the "natural" are really contrary to what God would have for us and must be changed and possibly eradicated from our souls. In order to accomplish this, God must uncover things that we desperately want hidden and covered. He wants us to see *for ourselves* our own self-centeredness and our own selfishness. *Until we actually see these things through God's eyes, we won't believe they are true.*

So one of the reasons God allows difficult times in our lives is to accomplish a much larger degree of self-renunciation, crucifixion and abandonment to Him. He wants to take us from a position of self-reliance to a place of complete reliance upon Him—from self-centeredness to God-centeredness. He wants each of us to learn to detach ourselves from *all* other supports so we can enjoy complete faith and trust in Him. When all other security measures are finally taken away, our lives can become completely His. And that's His purpose.

Romans 11:33 tells us that God's ways are past finding out (the whole book of Job certainly proves that).[141]

## THE FELLOWSHIP OF SUFFERING

Philippians 3:10 talks about "the fellowship of His suffering." What exactly does this mean?

It means that not only do we have the privilege of believing on Christ Jesus, but we also have the privilege of suffering as He did.[142] Hebrews 2:10 tells us He is our example and we must follow Him: "For it became Him, for whom are all things, and by whom are all things, in bringing many sons unto glory, to make the captain of their salvation *perfect through suffering*."[143]

First Peter 2:21 states: "For even hereunto were ye called; because Christ also suffered for us, leaving us an example that ye should follow His steps."

"O my Father, if it be possible, let this cup pass from me: nevertheless NOT AS I WILL, BUT AS YOU WILL." (Matthew 26:39) Even in

*Through dark times,*

God not only wants to show us

things about Himself,

He also wants to show us

THINGS ABOUT OURSELVES.

His agony in the garden, Jesus says: "My soul is exceedingly sorrowful, even unto death."[144]

Paul tells us we are to follow Jesus' example:

"Let this mind be in you, which was also in Christ Jesus: Who, being in the form of God, thought it not robbery to be equal with God: but made Himself of no reputation, and took upon Him the form of a servant, and was made in the likeness of men: and being found in fashion as a man, He humbled Himself, and *became obedient unto death, even the death of the cross.*" (Philippians 2:5–8)

And finally, 1 Thessalonians 3:3: "That no man should be moved by these afflictions: for yourselves know that *we are appointed thereunto.*"

As I mentioned, when Chip died, we experienced our own "fellowship of suffering." We were able to identify with so many other moms and dads who had lost children. It's a horrible thing to lose a child, and it causes unimaginable suffering. Losing a child is probably one of the most awful experiences a person can know, but there are other kinds of suffering that I was not familiar with…i.e., the suffering of pain.

Philippians 3:10 tells us, however, suffering is something the Lord wants us to "know" and be able to get through.

For some reason the past few weeks have been even more painful than the beginning of my ordeal. The physical suffering has been so intense. There have been times where I just laid on the bed weeping and begging God for mercy. The burns and effects of radiation are horrible. Over three-quarters of my face has been burned, resulting in over fifty boils, blisters, sores and then scabs and crusting. The boils turn to blisters, then they bleed and scab over. I can't eat, smile, talk, breath, wash my face, cough, blow my nose or taste. This cycle happens over and over again. Boy, do I identify with Job: "My flesh is clothed with worms and clods of dust; my skin is broken, and become loathsome." (Job 7:5)

God has been merciful, and He knew exactly what I could take.

I'm on the mend now (the burn and crusting has finally receded down to just my nose). I can make it through.

First Peter 4: 1–2, 13 tells us: "Forasmuch then as Christ hath suffered for us in the flesh, arm yourselves likewise with the same mind: for he that hath suffered in the flesh has ceased from sin; that he no longer should live the rest of his time in the flesh to the lusts of men, but to the will of God."

Our own feelings will be screaming, as Job's did: "Why have You forsaken me?"[145] The Word says however: "He will never leave us nor forsake us."[146] Which will we believe?

God is teaching us the "fellowship of His sufferings." This is how we go from strength to strength; this is how He renews us, and this is how we grow more into His image. "To suffer" simply means *to bar ourselves from sin*, to refuse to give in to the flesh and to choose by faith to go God's way whether we feel like it or not. Scripture is saying we are "called" to suffer. Only as we suffer, will we cease from sin (and the control of our "flesh") and be able to live the rest of our lives to the will of God.

Why do we never hear about this in church? It means, as Christians, suffering will come into our lives, just as it did the Lord's.

The Valley of Baca and the Secret Place of Thunder are our own Calvary, the place we must carry our own crosses. So "suffering" doesn't just mean a time we are thrown into prison or we suffer some sort of torture. Suffering means consistently "barring ourselves from following what **we** want, what **we** feel and what **we** desire," and choosing instead to follow what **Christ** is asking us to do. "Not my will, but Thine." In many cases, this brings tremendous suffering.

Under all other circumstances, our human nature can hide, but in the dark night it all comes out in blazing color. God wants us to see our true inner motives and see just how far we have fallen from what

He desires for us. He wants us to see through our night season that we <u>don't</u> have that persistent, ongoing faith that we thought we had, and that we actually have run to other things besides Him to fill our needs. *The more God enables us to "see" the truth about ourselves, the more we'll realize we cannot live without Him.* The truth is we must see our own nothingness next to His everything. In other words, our soul needs to be completely undone in order for us to be willing to "pick up our cross" and follow Him.

*The Valley of Baca and the Secret Place of Thunder are our own Calvary, the place we must carry our own crosses.*

*Scripture tells us that Jesus was made perfect (or complete) through suffering.*[147] The good news is that "as the sufferings of Christ abound in us, so our consolation also aboundeth by Christ."[148] We'll talk more about this later, but it's saying that the more we allow the Lord to put to death our "self," the more He will encompass us about with His Love.

I certainly have found this to be true in my own present trial! As 1 Peter 4:13 says, "But rejoice, inasmuch as ye are partakers of Christ's suffering..."

Someone dear to me recently wrote: "Nancy, you are going through this for all of us. Interesting, the Lord's face was also disfigured when He died on the Cross for us."

## GOD IS TEACHING US TO TRUST HIM

God allows trials and storms and confusion into our lives so that we will learn more about His Love and His faithfulness, and so that in the future we'll be able to unconditionally trust Him no matter what we see or what we feel or what we think. We must remember the stories of

Abraham, David, Joseph, and Mary and Martha. As was true for them, God will "work all things together for His purposes and His plans" in the end. He does love us and He will be faithful to His promises, even though in the middle of the trials, we won't be able to see where we are going or what God is doing. Most importantly, we mustn't let our hope get deferred.[149]

First Peter 1:13 warns us to "gird up the loins of our minds and be sober and *hope to the end* for the grace that is to be brought unto you at the revelation of Jesus Christ." This is exhorting us to be ready for the battle to which we have been appointed. Hope requires us to hold fast our confession of faith without wavering[150] and to be ready to give an answer to anyone who asks us a reason for the hope that is in us.[151]

Hope does *not* depend upon what a man possesses or upon what he may be able to do for himself or even upon what any other human being may do for him. Hope's fulfillment rests only upon God, His promises for the future and how that individual appropriates these.

God is using all our suffering and horrible circumstances of life to teach us how to overcome and how to trust Him more. This is part of His plan. He certainly is doing that in my life right now. The doctor called last night and said since I am having headaches, nose bleeds and so much congestion, I need to have a brain scan. If it has gone to my brain, there is nothing they can do. Do I trust God right now? You bet I do *by faith*. I trust Him because He knows what He is doing and how He is going to do it. I don't. I'm just a passenger on this wild ride.

God wants to instill an unconditional *spirit of trust* and a deep sense of hope in us—hope in His faithfulness. His goal is for us to be able to walk in the darkness no matter what—without seeing Him or feeling Him, yet unconditionally trusting Him. So that no matter what happens to us or how horrific the circumstances become, we'll be able to trust Him regardless. *When all around us is falling apart, if we can sit before Him without questions and without doubts, the test of our commitment will be established.* It's called "overcoming."

Only after every support is shaken in some way does our journey to real faith and hope begin. God wants *nothing before Him* in our lives. Now, don't let this make you afraid. I remember years ago there were some young moms who were so afraid when I said that God wants nothing before Him in our lives. They thought God would test them by taking away their children. Why would God do that? He is not a mean God. He loves us, and we are never to be afraid of Him.

Fear is not God's will. *If we willingly release to Him all the things that are precious to us (people, things, health, wealth, etc.,), He'll have no need to test us about them.* Right? However, if we hold on tight to them, it shows Him that we <u>don't</u> fully trust Him and that we <u>do</u> have other "gods" before Him.

Here's the question: When everything around us is in disarray, will we still believe and trust Him? Or will we collapse in utter agony and disbelief and immediately turn the other direction? God wants us to get to a place where we will *never* challenge His character or His nature again. God wants to build in us an *unshakable trust* and *resolve* so that no matter what happens we'll know that He will <u>never</u> leave us nor forsake us.

The further removed we can get from our faith relying upon our sight and our feelings, the more deeply we will enter into real intimacy with God. He wants us to get to the point where we can truly say and mean, "None of these things move me."[152] In other words, we won't allow any of the difficult things we are experiencing to "move us" away from the intimacy we have with Him. This attitude will only come about when we realize that everything He allows in our lives is "Father-filtered." Then, and only then, we'll be able to say with Job: "Though [You] slay me, yet will I trust [You]..." (Job 13:15) "[because I know You are always] at my right hand." (Psalm 16:8) And I shall not be moved.

## "Hoping" and "Trusting" in the Lord Defeats the Enemy

Notice another interesting thing about going through the "valley of weeping," the "shadow of death" and the "place of thunder" or "place of testing." These are the places where the enemy is defeated. Psalm 23:4–5 explains this: "I will fear no evil: for Thou art with me; Thy rod [His Word] and Thy staff [His Spirit] they comfort me. Thou preparest a table before me in the presence of mine enemies: Thou anointest my head with oil; my cup runneth over."

The enemy is out not only to destroy our witness but to keep us from crossing over that bridge of hope toward the "mark of the prize" that awaits us on the other side. If the enemy can cause us to become confused, disheartened and hopeless in the middle of our trials, he'll win "hands down." We'll become immobilized, regress or, even worse, turn back as Job said: "Where is now my hope?" (Job 17:15) We'll continue to make emotional choices, reflect our own image to others (not God's) and the Gospel will be hindered. Rather than overcome the situation and the enemy, we will be overcome by the same.

*God wants to build in us an unshakable trust and resolve so that no matter what happens we'll know that He will never leave us nor forsake us.*

Jesus even warns us in John 5:31 by saying, "If I bear witness of Myself, my witness is not true." Wow! If Jesus says this of Himself, how much more it must be true of us!

I am totally convinced that genuinely reflecting the Lord in all that we think, say and do is the "key" to revival and God's plan. Seeing "living examples" of Christ is what will bring our sons and daughters, our husbands and wives, our friends and our acquaintances to the Lord. When they see Christ's real Love and hear His words, even in our darkest times, they'll know that *yes, Jesus is real. He is alive. And He cares!* Nothing will bring others to a saving knowledge of Christ faster than seeing genuine "living" examples. Conversely, nothing will turn them away faster than phoniness and hypocrisy. Therefore, glorifying, manifesting and reflecting Christ in everything we do (even though it's not always perfect) is our highest attainment in this life.[153] This is the reason we were called, the purpose of our lives and God's test or barometer to see if we are prepared to hold positions of authority in the coming kingdom.

And thus, this is what the enemy is out to prevent, to deter, to halt and to hinder in any way he can. Luke 13:11–16 is an example of how the enemy deceives us and can keep us "bound up" for years! He does these things to defeat us, discourage us and to null our witness. When we allow our sin and self to grow, we give the enemy "grounds" to deceive us and to send "strong delusions" that we should believe a "lie." (We will continue our discussion of exactly how we defeat the enemy in Chapter Eight.)

Psalm 149:6–9 tells us one of the honors we have as Christians is that we can fight the enemy by praising God, by holding a two-edged sword in our hands and by binding the enemy in Jesus' Name and loosing his strongholds. Christ has given us the authority to do just that, by faith. "Let the high praises of God be in their mouth, and a two-edged sword in their hand; to execute vengeance upon the heathen and *to bind their kings with chains* and to execute upon them the judgment written..."

## WHAT ELSE CAN WE DO TO FURTHER GOD'S PLAN? LEARN TO LOVE HIM

Besides learning to trust the Lord unconditionally, what is another crucial thing we must learn to do in order to help fulfill His plan for our lives?

The first thing, I believe, that God would have us do after we have accepted Him into our lives is simply *learn to love Him.* Now, I don't mean "emotionally" love Him. That's easy. Most Christians do that quite naturally. No, I mean to learn to love Him as the First Commandment tells us: "Thou shalt love (*agapao*) the Lord thy God with all thy heart, and with all thy soul, and with all thy mind." (Matthew 22:37)

The Greek word for the verb "to love" used in the above great commandment is **agapao,** which means *to totally give ourselves over to something,* to be totally consumed with it, and totally committed to it. What we *agapao* is what we put first in our lives. All our intentions and abilities are focused and consumed with this one thing. In other words, it's a commitment or a binding of ourselves to something, so that we become "one" with it.

*Loving God is totally giving ourselves over to Him, with all our heart, will and soul.*

Loving God is continually giving Him anything in our lives that's "not of faith." It's staying clean and open (not letting the soulish things or the self-centered things in our lives get in the way) so that our spirit can continue to direct our lives. Then God's Life can freely flow from our hearts out into our souls and be seen through us. If we are not clean, however, we won't be able to hear God's voice or know the Spirit's leading and His Life in us will be quenched and blocked from coming forth.

If I asked you, "Do you love [*agapao*] God?" you would probably automatically respond, "Yes, of course I do!" But if you are really honest with yourself, how often do you seek to put His will and His desires above your own? How often are you consumed with what He wants for your life and not what you want out of life?

*Can you honestly say that you desire God's will above your own happiness?*

This question puts it right into perspective, doesn't it? People everywhere are seeking happiness and contentment as their ultimate goal. Is this your goal? Or is it to set yourself aside and please God? You can't do both at the same time.

## To Love God Means

In Scripture, to love (*agapao*) God means three specific things. I compiled these from Jesus Christ's three responses to Satan on the mountain of temptation in Matthew 4:1–10. When Satan questions Jesus about loving God (about totally giving himself over to God), Jesus answers:

1) To choose continually to <u>obey God's Word</u> (His Will), not our own thoughts, emotions, and desires that are usually prompting us to go the opposite way.
2) To choose continually to <u>trust God's Power</u> (His Ability) to perform His Will in our lives, and not our own natural ability and power.
3) And to love God means to choose continually to <u>worship and serve Him</u> only by binding ourselves with Him that we become one.

Matthew 16:24 sums this up: "If any man will come after Me, let him *deny himself* [choose to obey God's Will], and *take up his cross* [trust God to perform His Will], and *follow Me* [worship and serve God only]."

Loving God is how we "acknowledge Him" in all that happens to us. Remember Proverbs 3:5–6, which we said was one of the most important Scriptures of all: "Trust in the LORD with all thine heart; and lean not unto thine own understanding. In all thy ways *acknowledge Him* [love Him], and He shall direct thy paths."

Loving God is the only way we can "see" Him who is invisible and free Him to direct our paths. If we are not loving Him, *we* won't see Him nor will *He* be able to guide our footsteps.

The whole Bible is summed up in the First and Second Commandments: We are to love (*agapao—totally give ourselves over to*) God and then *He* will enable us to love (*agapao—totally give ourselves over to*) others as ourselves.[154]

It's completely impossible to love our spouses, our family, our friends and our enemies as God desires unless we have first learned to

# LOVING GOD

is the only way we can "see" Him who is invisible

*and free Him to direct our paths.*

love Him. The two commandments are inseparable and must go in the order they were given. In other words, we must first learn to love God with all our heart, mind and soul—become that open and cleansed vessel—*then*, and only then, God will be able to love others through us. It only works this one way.

Be careful, however, to not get this verb *agapao* mixed up with the noun *Agape* (that we talked about in Chapter Three), because they mean two totally different things. *Agape* is God's pure unconditional Love, and it's always used as such in the Bible. There is *never* a negative usage of the word *Agape* in the Scriptures, whereas *agapao* (what we are exploring here) is what we give ourselves over to. It's a commitment love. We can give ourselves over to something that is good (such as God and others), or we can give ourselves over to something that is bad (such as things of the world—money, materialism, pleasure or sex).

One of the prime examples of "things" we all love (*agapao*) before God is our *self*. Most Christians (me included) love ourselves first. In other words, we automatically and naturally think about what *we* want, what *we* feel and what *we* think rather than what *God* wants or what others want.

That's why we must constantly remember what Matthew 16:24 exhorts: we are to deny self (set self aside and *obey God*), pick up our cross (don't trust self, *trust Him*) and follow Him (*worship Him only*).

Loving Him is how we will be conformed into His image of Love. And Love is the *reason* we have been called, the *goal* that God desires from each of us and the *end* of all salvation.

The question to ask yourself is:

"Do I really LOVE God?"

If yes, then "how often do I seek to put HIS will before my own?"

# Chapter Six—What Is God's Plan?

1. Memorize Philippians 3:13–14.
2. Is our goal as Christians simply to get saved? Is that all there is to life here on earth? Share from your heart what you think God's overall plan is.
3. Why does Hebrews 12:1 tell us the Christian life is like "a race"?
4. How does God accomplish "conforming us into His image" so that we might be able to rule and reign with Him in the coming kingdom?
5. In Mark 9:49, it says that everyone will be "salted with fire." This simply means we will all be tested by fire just like when gold is refined. What are the three steps in the process of gold refinement? In your own words, how does this relate to what God is doing in our own lives?
6. Just like the gold process, God wants to separate the dross (impurities) in our lives (in our souls) and from His Spirit (in our hearts). How does He do this with us? What is the "self" that He wants to expose?
7. What are some of the "root systems" in our human nature that He wants to expose?
8. Does God cause our "Night Seasons"? Explain.
9. Philippians 3:10 tells us that God wants us to know "the fellowship of His suffering." What exactly is the "fellowship of His suffering"? What does this mean? Have you ever experienced it? (Philippians 1:29; Romans 8:13; Hebrews 2:10)
10. Through the fellowship of suffering, the dark times and the trials, what is God teaching us?
11. What is it that defeats the enemy more than anything else? (Psalm 23:4–5)
12. What more can we do to help further God's plan?

"THE THIEF COMETH NOT,
*but for to steal,
and to kill
and to destroy;*

*that*

I [Jesus] am come

that they might have Life,

and that they might have it

more abundantly."

JOHN 10:10

*ou might have life*

# What Is the Enemy's Plan? How Do We Stop Him?

God's plan for calling us is to conform us into His image of Love that we might be prepared to rule and reign with Him in His coming kingdom. He uses our "night seasons" here on earth in order to accomplish this purpose. He doesn't cause these night seasons; they usually are of our own doing. He simply allows them into our lives and then uses them to achieve His will.

In light of this, what is the enemy's plan?

Obviously, the enemy's plan is to make life miserable for us so we will stop trusting in the Lord, stop hoping in Him, be overtaken, lose our faith, give up and die.

John 10:10a confirms that this is the enemy's exact plan. It says the devil comes to *"steal, kill and destroy."*

STEAL—our hopes

KILL—our dreams, visions and desires

And DESTROY—our faith

The enemy wants control of our soul—our thoughts, emotions and desires. And, unfortunately, he is doing a very good job of that in many of our lives. He wants *to devastate us through our situations* so He can *steal our hopes* and *destroy our faith.* If he can get us confused, discouraged and ready to give up because we have not seen the Hand of the Lord in our situation, he's got us. So that's his goal! Thus, it's essential we understand his tactics and his schemes. And we do this by: 1) being aware of his ways; 2) walking by faith, not our feelings; and 3) speaking forth God's Word (binding the enemy and loosing his strongholds).

As we have continually said, "hope" is the only thing that allows us to "see" the Lord in the midst of the fire. To "see" doesn't necessarily mean to see Him visually, but simply to experience (to know) that He is there. Seeing Him in the fire is the only thing that will allow us to endure the trial. Consequently, the enemy's game plan is to quench our hope in any way he can. (Proverbs 13:12) If he can get us to give up our hope, he's got us.

I wrote a book a few years ago called *Never Give Up*, but I didn't realize the importance of hope in this process. If the enemy can *kill* our vision, our dreams and our expectations, he can *steal* our hope and eventually *destroy* our faith.

Hope, therefore, is like our main artery—it's our ventricular artery and **the enemy's target.**

When the enemy can "defer our hope," we become brokenhearted. By doing so, we give him control of our lives. And "control" is exactly what he is after.

My own personal trial has made me realize the huge spiritual battle that we are all in and the importance of "hope" in that battle. In my own case, if I gave up "hoping" now (either temporally or eternally), I would not only die spiritually but I would die physically. Hope is what keeps me going.

"Hope" must be the anchor of our soul; otherwise, we will drown for sure.

## THE SPIRIT OF CONTROL

In Revelation 2, God talks to the church of Thyatira and mentions that in the end times the spirit of Jezebel will again reappear. Jezebel was a queen in the Old Testament book of 1 Kings who was a seducer, a controller and a very evil woman. She first shows up in 1 Kings 18, where she cuts off the prophets and the Word of God (vv. 4, 13). Then she threatens Elijah in 1 Kings 19:1–2, and she has her encounter with Naboth over his vineyard in 1 Kings 21:5–7. Just like the enemy did to Jesus, Jezebel did her evil work and got Naboth killed.[155] In the end, because of Jezebel's witchcraft, God saw to it that dogs actually ate her body.[156]

Jezebel symbolically represents the enemy's spirit of control.

In the "broad sense," I believe the spirit of Jezebel is alive and working in these end times. And it's not just women that this spirit attacks. It's a spirit that permeates, usurps, and defiles an individual or a whole system. It brings with it a spirit of disunity, anxiety, insensitiveness. It's the exact opposite of the "fruit of the Spirit." It's the fruit of the "flesh" in all its living color. And it's rampant in the Body of Christ.

The spirit of Jezebel uses unaware vessels and instruments to do its dirty work. Once we let our guard down and begin to doubt, the spiritual battle of our lives begins. Who is in control? Is it the Spirit of God (through our own spirit) or is it "the flesh," i.e., the enemy (through our own soul).

One way the enemy keeps us under his control is by trying to evaporate our vision, our dreams and our hopes. As I mentioned before with my ordeal, I really had thought huge miracles would occur at the hospital and with the doctors. But they didn't. In fact, my time there turned out to be just the opposite. Yes, the big miracle was that they thought they got all the cancer at the time, but in all the little things, everything went haywire. Rather than witnessing to the doctors, I somehow impressed them the wrong way. It was a total disaster.

One example I mentioned earlier was, as I laid on the ER table for eight hours, bleeding to death while waiting for someone to help me, the assistants came in and ripped out the metal supports holding my nose up. They kept saying, "It's okay, we know what you are going through..." They were young interns and had no way of knowing what I was going through. They had no way of knowing what it was like to have your nose ripped off and the supports holding it up taken out *without* any anesthesia. I almost smashed their faces in. I think I must

## One way the enemy

keeps us under his control is by trying to

### EVAPORATE OUR VISION,

### OUR DREAMS

### *and* OUR HOPES.

have made quite a scene. My Chuck was there, and I'm afraid he let them know in no uncertain terms that what had happened was not okay with him. After that, they kept their distance from us.

Another time, the head reconstruction surgeon berated me for being a "sissy" and having to stay overnight in the hospital. He kept saying "none of my other patients have had to do that." When I asked him, however, "How many other patients have you had that had a complete nose removal?" his answer was "none." (All of his other patients had skin cancers of some sort.) After that, he too kept his distance from me.

I was devastated. "God, it was going to be such an opportunity for a witness. What happened?"

So there are times when, for whatever reason, God allows the enemy into our space to defeat, discourage and try to kill us spiritually. We know "he is the father of lies." This is just another area, however, where God is testing us to see what our reaction will be. Will we hold on "by faith" or be defeated "by the flesh"? Here again, our hope needs to be based upon the Word of God. Remember, Jesus was tested by the devil, just as we are.[157]

In Matthew 4:3, the devil says: "If thou be the son of God, command these stones to be made bread" (i.e., tempting him to do His own will). Jesus responds (v. 4): "Man shall not live by bread alone [our physical needs], but by every Word of God" (i.e., we must learn what God's will is).

The devil says (v. 6): "If thou be the Son of God, cast thyself down for it is written, He shall give his angels charge concerning them" (i.e., tempting Him to trust in His own power). Jesus responds (v. 7): "Don't tempt the Lord" (we must learn to trust only in God's power).

Finally, the devil says (v. 9): "Worship me and I will give you all the kingdoms of the world." Jesus responds (v. 10): "Get thee hence [be gone Satan], for it is written, thou shalt worship the Lord thy God and Him only shalt thou serve" (in every situation, we must learn to totally give ourselves over to the Lord).

Hope is the testing ground, the game plan and the enemy's target.

The Bible tells us that Jezebel not only killed God's servants and His prophets,[158] but that she was also full of witchcraft and sorcery.[159] She was a cursed woman[160] and a seducer[161] who never repented of her evil deeds. The Bible says that those who follow her ways in the end times will be cast into the "Great Tribulation."

This is why Jezebel is known today as such an evil schemer and

*Hope is the testing ground, the game plan and the enemy's target.*

the epitome of the enemy's spirit of control. This is exactly what Satan wants to do in our own lives. He wants to destroy our hope so that he can get full control of our lives. Then we won't be conformed to Christ's image and we won't be prepared to rule and reign with Him in the coming kingdom. That's Satan's plan.

Hope, again, is the connection and the link between our faith and God's Love. When our hope is wiped out by the enemy, confusion and devastation remain. That's exactly what the enemy is after. That's his plan for us—the cycle of defeat.

## THE CYCLE OF TRUST VERSUS THE CYCLE OF DEFEAT

So the enemy continually challenges us in the areas of control. He wants us to slip down the "Cycle of Defeat."

In my book *Never Give Up*, I mention two different kinds of cycles—the Cycle of Trust and the Cycle of Defeat. See if you can identify with either of these. (I've changed them a little as I have grown in more understanding.)

The <u>Cycle of Trust</u> goes something like this:

1) If we know that God loves us and that His plan is to conform us into His image so we might rule and reign with Him in the future,
2) Then we will have the confidence to make the appropriate "faith choices" (to do His will regardless of how we feel or what is going on in our lives),
3) Which means laying our wills and our lives down to Him (and loving Him),
4) Which enables us to walk by "faith" and not by sight,
5) Which then allows Him to show us His Handprint of Love in the little things,
6) Which allows us to "see" Him and thus hope in Him even more.
7) The end result being—we will be able to overcome the trial and endure to the end.

If, however, we don't know the above things, the enemy pushes his way in with his <u>Cycle of Defeat</u>:

1) If we doubt God's love for us and don't know His plan for our lives in the future,
2) Then it causes us to make emotional choices (to do our own will, not God's),
3) Which prevents us from laying our lives down to Him (and loving Him),
4) Which pushes us to walk by "sight" and not by faith,
5) Which then prevents Him from revealing His Handprint in all the little things,
6) Making us unable to see His Hand in our lives (causing hopelessness).
7) The end result being—we are overcome and left with the feeling of confusion, disorientation and wanting to give up.

## THINGS THE ENEMY USES

Some of the things the enemy uses that cause us to lose hope are unanswered prayer, continual physical pain, lack of finances, mind-altering medications, bitter disagreements and arguments with spouses, children, friends or family (even the church) and, of course, lack of change in our circumstances or in our relationships.

The first night I was in the hospital (after the initial operation where they removed my nose septum), Satan's messengers did their best to get me down with fear, worry, anxiety, dread, etc., but what they did was actually push me to my knees and closer to the Lord. Battling the enemy for my physical "life" itself is something new for me. I've always been healthy. But that night I was so miserable that the enemy did everything he could to make me give up and let go. And at times I certainly felt like it. The Lord, however, sustained me, and I heard His voice so clearly in that dark hour. He showed me that the battle that was raging around me was really a spiritual battle being fought in the heavenlies over much bigger things than just me. He showed me that the spirit of Jezebel (the spirit of control) is still around and causing untold confusion, strife and division in the Body of Christ. I was just one of the "pawns" he was attacking. The enemy wanted me dead and would do anything he could to accomplish that. I was excited because I knew that the "word" was from the Lord. It's as if *I saw Him* who is invisible in my darkest hour. That revelation was so real to me that night that it gave me the will to go on.

It also made me realize the huge spiritual battle that we are all in and how important "hope" is in that battle. The enemy wants to STEAL OUR HOPE; he wants us to GIVE UP in the middle to our night seasons; he wants us to DIE spiritually, and in doing so, HE WINS because he gains control.

## WHAT ARE WE CONTROLLED BY?

The question we must then ask ourselves is: "Who are *we* controlled by? Are we allowing God to work out His plans in our lives (using all the circumstances of our lives to conform us into His image and prepare us for the future), or are we allowing the enemy to control us through our circumstances, our emotions and own desires and making us even more fleshly, self-centered and devoid of a Christian witness?

Here's a simple chart that might help you answer the question: *Who are you controlled by?*

| *The Flesh* | *The Spirit* |
|---|---|
| Spirit of Jezebel—Spirit of Self | Spirit of God—Spirit of Love |
| Pain | Joy, peace, etc. |
| Adultery | Longsuffering |
| Fornication | Gentleness, goodness |
| Uncleanness | Faith |
| Idolatry, hatred, strife | Meekness, self-control |

Are we a minister of God's Love or are we a minister of the enemy, causing confusion, defeat, hypocrisy, discouragement, complaining, murmuring, etc. (just the opposite of the "fruit of the Spirit")?

A person who is unloving, insensitive, insincere, and uncompassionate, who also speaks discouragement or gossip about others, not only *brings division and disunity* but also despair and hopelessness. Second Corinthians 11:13–15 says these supposedly believers "transform themselves into the apostles of Christ…[but] whose end shall be according to their works." Scary stuff!

How do we survive the battle against the enemy?

## BINDING AND LOOSING

In Chapter Four we discussed the incredible authority Christ has given the church *to bind* the enemy in Jesus' Name and *to loose* the strongholds that the enemy controls. This is one of the ways we can resist the enemy, speak forth the Word of God and defeat the enemy's devious plans.

Matthew 16:19 tells us this authority holds "the keys of the kingdom."[162] In other words, it's what connects the two worlds—our earthly realm and the kingdom to come. Remember, "control" is the objective—Spirit control or fleshly enemy control. Yes, our hearts belong to the Lord, but our souls are up for grabs, even as believers. This is exactly what God is trying to accomplish by conforming us (our souls) into His image (becoming "spirit filled"). Remember, the "flesh," which includes our souls and our bodies, needs to be daily submitted and controlled by God's Spirit or else the enemy will be in control.

What then is our defense against the enemy? We must renounce him and stand firm against him. How do we do that? By "binding him" and telling him to leave *in Jesus' Name.* Telling him to back off and be gone. As we said earlier, ***"to bind" means to break control because of Jesus' authority***. To loose means *in Jesus' Name* to free the "strongholds" the enemy has used to keep us captive.

God allows the enemy into our space for His own reasons (remember Job); our responsibility is to be ready to fight the evil one any way we can. One of the best ways is to speak forth God's Word, depend upon the Holy Spirit to implement that Word in His timing and way and plead the Blood of Christ over us. Once we have done these three things, it's critical we put on the whole Armor of God.[163]

It's interesting that Psalm 149:8–9 talks about the importance of binding the evil kings. And it tells us that this is an honor that all the saints have.

The only authority that Satan and all his hordes have in us is what we give him and what the Lord allows. Job 1:12 is an example. "The LORD said unto Satan, Behold, all that he hath is in thy power; only upon himself put not forth thine hand."

The enemy's plan is to get control of our lives in any way he can. Then he can destroy our witness and counteract any sort of authority we might have in the coming kingdom. Our responsibility is to recognize the devil's schemes, speak forth the Word, and continue to hope and trust in the Lord.

# GOD ALLOWS THE ENEMY INTO OUR SPACE

*for His own reasons (remember Job);*

our responsibility is to

BE READY TO FIGHT THE EVIL ONE

*any way we can.*

## ANOTHER PERSONAL EXAMPLE

Over the last year, many of you have heard my prayer request to be able to "see" physically. At first, I had no nose, so obviously I could not wear glasses. (Unfortunately, I have trifocals. Thus I am not a candidate for contacts. That would have solved everything.) Then my reconstructed nose was so sore I couldn't stand anything touching it.

My intense desire to wear glasses was mainly so I could finish this book. How frustrating it was to just be able to hold a pair of glasses to my eyes but not be able to type or write anything alongside. Finally, my nose healed enough to be able to support my glasses, and I was so excited.

But just when I thought I was through with that trial, the melanoma came back on the top of my new nose and once again, because of the aggressive radiation therapy, I couldn't support my glasses without extreme pain. Now, I was in the middle of the book and you can imagine how frustrated I was. My precious daughter, Lisa, creatively came up with a great idea. She found a visor and rigged it up so that my glasses hung from its rim. You should have seen me driving home from my radiation appointments. What a scene! My face blackened by radiation, and my glasses hanging down from my visor so that I could see.

I was aware then that my being able to see or not was obviously one of the ways the enemy wanted to control the situation, steal my hopes of finishing the book and get me to put the whole thing aside.

But recently he has gone even further, if you can believe it. About two weeks ago, the cement mask from radiation finally fell off, and I've been able to once again wear decent glasses with a cotton pad over my nose. But yesterday, one of the most important "input" days for the book, the enemy took a new tack. The tops of my fingers started to bleed. I have a heart condition called AFib (my heart beats irregularly), so I am and have been on blood thinners for years. Because of the steroid medicine, however, my blood must have gotten extremely thin, and my fingers (two or three on each hand) began bleeding from the fingernail down. So I had to wear huge bandages to keep the blood from oozing all over the place.

Have you ever tried to type with huge bandages on your fingers? It's totally impossible. I made more mistakes than I made corrections.

The point of this example is that I recognized the extremes to which the enemy will go to keep us bound. Since I knew where the attack was coming from, I was able to bind the enemy in Jesus' Name and loose the strongholds the enemy held in order to keep me in his control.

Today my fingers are better and not bleeding, so I'm going gung ho on the book. My simple prayer nine months ago was that I would just be able to "see," and I meant "physically." The irony I believe is that God has not only allowed me "to see" physically (the answer to my prayer), but He has allowed me *through hope* to "see the Lord who is invisible" in all things. How crazy is that!

The enemy's plan is to get control of our lives in any way he can. But know that God is always ten steps ahead of him, preparing to use all these things and work them together for good and in a much greater capacity, not only physically but also spiritually.

## Our Responsibility

Second Corinthians 4:8–12 tells us that it's okay for us to be troubled, but not in distress; it's okay to be perplexed, but not in despair; okay to be persecuted, but not forsaken, and okay to be cast down, but not destroyed.

This is really funny because I just got off the phone with my oncology doctor and he told me there really are no other options for me right now, except for further radiation. It will not cure the cancer, but hopefully it can control it. Otherwise it will be fatal. I had just typed the above Scripture so, when I got off the phone, this Scripture was the first thing I saw. Boy, as I told you, I am living this book. Then my eyes fell on the next Scripture that says:

*I am to be "exceedingly joyful in all my tribulation."* (2 Corinthians 7:4)

Again, it comes down to our eternal hope against our temporal hope. Next chapter we'll talk exclusively as to how we are to do this on a daily basis.

On a final note, a precious brother in the Lord just wrote me this: "We won't give up, give in or give over to the one who comes to steal, kill and destroy. Our God is faithful and will show you grand and mighty things that will surpass what He has already done. Hope will conquer the unknown darkness, and light will not fail to radiate and heal your body. Agape conquers all...."

# CHAPTER SEVEN— WHAT IS THE ENEMY'S PLAN?

1. Memorize John 10:10.
2. In your own words, what is the enemy's game plan, and how does he use our loss of "hope" to accomplish it?
3. Why is hope so important in the scheme of things?
4. The spirit of Jezebel is mentioned quite often throughout the Bible. (1 Kings 18—19:21; Revelation 2) What does she represent, and why is it important for us to understand?
5. What are some of the things the enemy uses to steal our hope? Share from your heart.
6. Did you see yourself in the Cycle of Trust or the Cycle of Defeat? Share from your heart.
7. What exactly is the "spirit of control"? Why is the enemy so intent upon having control?
8. Satan wants to destroy our "hope." Why? (Proverbs 13:12)
9. How do we know if we are controlled by the "flesh" or by the "spirit"?
10. What does Scripture say is our defense against the enemy?
11. Second Corinthians 4:8 tells us that we can be troubled, perplexed, persecuted and cast down, but not distressed, not in despair, not forsaken or destroyed. How is this possible? Have you ever been here?

"Trust [hope] in the Lord with *all* thine heart;

and lean not to

thine own understanding.

In *all* thy ways acknowledge Him,

and [then] He shall

direct thy paths."

PROVERBS 3:5–6

CHAPTER EIGHT

# What Is the Answer to Restoring Our Hope?

God's plan for choosing us in the first place is intimate fellowship—He desires to restore us into His image so we'll not only be able to intimately fellowship with Him here and now but also hold positions of authority in His coming kingdom. Of course, the enemy wants to stop that plan in any way he can. Thus he tries to attack and destroy our hope. Hope is the link to our future. Consequently, if the enemy can wipe out our hope, he's got us.

So what do we do to restore our "hope" that has somehow been lost? How do we have enough faith to see the Lord in the middle of our trial, especially when all the circumstances, events and physical pain push us in the opposite direction? This becomes our choice point. We either succumb to the situation and let the enemy win control, or we, *by faith,* make choices to follow God no matter how we feel or where He leads.

I'm at this crossroads now. At the moment, I am undergoing my third week of radiation on my face. I can't eat because the pain medications make me nauseous, yet I have to take the pills because, as you can imagine, the discomfort is intolerable. Also, the radiation has produced sores in my mouth so I can't eat anything solid. However, I can't lose any more weight because I've already lost close to 25 pounds. Here again, I could just collapse by feeling sorry for myself and let the enemy in, or I can use this opportunity to somehow glorify the Lord, knowing He can perform a miracle at any time.

Second Corinthians 6:7 tells me exactly what I am to continue to do:

Speak forth the Word of God—the Word of Truth

Put on the Armor of Righteousness

And rely upon the Power of God

That's my answer, but first I must confess and repent of any lack of faith on my part, any fear, anxiety, doubt, etc., give it to the Lord, read the Word and then replace those things with "the truth" (the Word of God).

So when circumstances, other people or the flesh (pain) triggers discouragement, despair and depression, we must choose (by faith) to depend upon what the Word of God says, not our feelings. Our faith choices, moment-by-moment, determine WHO is in control of our lives (the enemy through the flesh or the Lord through the Spirit).

Remember what Job said in Job 13:15, "Though You slay [kill] me, I will trust You." That must be our continual response also.

God cannot use us unless we are "clean" vessels. This means we not only need to confess our sin and self, but we also need to confess, sever and break whatever control the enemy has had in the past (through our natural thoughts, emotions and desires). And we do this by binding him and loosing his stronghold in us. I don't think I ever have been in so much of the enemy's control as I was the first thirteen months after my operation, what with the pain, the meds and my "flesh." I neglected to put on the Armor of God daily, especially the Shield of Faith (faith not only to believe, but faith to keep on believing, no matter what occurred), thus I lacked hope "to see Him in the fire." I never lost my "eternal hope," but that daily "temporal hope" waned. I've repeated the Scripture: "Though You slay me, yet will I trust You," a million times over the past fifty or so years that I've been a Christian, but I've never had to live it out as I have in the last twelve months.

We must learn to recognize when the enemy has control of our lives. Murmuring about our circumstances or the pain we are in or our failing relationships allows the enemy more of an entrance or a hole into our souls. This is how he gains control. However, when we confess our sin and self, repent of it and give it to God, we close the door on the enemy and he no longer has influence in our souls.[164]

Furthermore, speaking forth (not just reading) the Word of God and pleading the Blood of Christ over us are two more ways we can change WHO is in control. Then it's important to walk in that freedom, no matter how difficult.

Remember, it was Paul who said in 2 Corinthians 4:8–9: "we are troubled on every side, *but not distressed*; we are perplexed, *but not in despair*; persecuted, *but not forsaken*; cast down, *but not destroyed*." Paul was beaten, stoned, shipwrecked in the deep and experienced many perils, weariness, painfulness, hunger, thirst, cold and nakedness.[165] If he could say and believe these things in the middle of all his horrific trials, we can learn to trust the Lord in ours. We must trust that God knows what He is doing and that somehow He will bring "good" out of everything. If we don't choose to believe this, we'll fall back into the enemy's clutches and end up, once again, "murmuring, discouraged and defeated." And he'll be back in control....

## WHEN HOPE IS LOST, HOW DO WE REGAIN IT?

What then are some of the actual steps we can take in order to make the weeping in the Valley of Baca and the discouragement of the Valley of the Shadow of Death into a well of blessing and a time of praise? How do we go from strength to strength? How do we make our difficult seasons a time where we fear no evil and where we can stand strong against the enemy?

In other words: How do we restore our hope?[166] How do we soar on the wings of eagles? How do we run and not grow weary? And how do we walk and not faint during these horrible times?[167] As we have "laid among the pots" (the horse stalls), how do we now fly "as a silver dove"?

There are three essential steps to restoring our hope that we will cover, but first, let's talk about the three critical foundational truths that we must not only know but apply in order to have our hope restored.

### THE IMPORTANCE OF KNOWING GOD LOVES US

The absolute "core" foundation of our faith and the only way our hope will be restored is the knowledge that God loves us and that He will be faithful to us no matter what. This is the bottom line and the footing that our entire spiritual house must be built upon. Please see page 338 for Scriptures on "Knowing God Loves Me."

This sounds so simple and so trite. We've all heard "God loves you" a million times, but what I am talking about here is actually seeing His Handprint of Love in everything—not just thinking in your head that He loves you, but actually seeing it with your own eyes. Because it's impossible for us to lay our lives down to Him and trust Him unless we first know without a doubt that He loves us and will be faithful to us. Unless we really know this, we won't be able to go a step farther.

His Love becomes the basis of our hope and the foundation of our faith. Without this knowledge, we'll <u>never</u> be able to move forward. In other words, we won't be able to surrender our wills or our lives to Him, especially if we don't think He cares. It's a given then that we will stay in that dark place. This is true no matter how long we have been Christians, no matter how many people we have led to the Lord, no matter how many Scriptures we know or the number of Bible studies we have led. If we don't know that God loves us personally and will be faithful, we'll be unable to walk ahead because we won't be able to "see" Him in the darkness.

*Love is the basis of our trust!* Yes, we receive His Love into our hearts as a "gift" when we are first born again, but until we actually experience that Love in our everyday lives, it will be difficult to make "faith choices" to constantly rely upon Him and do His will.

The absolute "core" foundation

of our faith and the only way

our hope will be restored

## *is the knowledge that God loves us*

### *and that He will be faithful to us*

# NO MATTER WHAT.

If we know that God loves us, however, we'll have the confidence to continually lay ourselves down to Him, which will give Him an opportunity to show us more of His faithfulness, which in turn will revive our hope in His promises for the future.[168] Conversely, if we doubt His personal Love, we won't have the confidence to trust Him, which will limit our ability to experience His faithfulness and ultimately quench our hope in His promises for the future.

To help you recall His personal Love for you, make your own notebook and write down all the things He has done for you in the past, even the little things. Describe them in detail if you can. Pray and ask God to bring them all back to your memory. By writing them down you can keep remembering them. Then choose by faith (not feelings) to believe in His personal Love for you. You might also want to see the "Knowing God Loves Me" Scriptural promises at the end of this book. Then recite the Scriptures that speak of His Love for you. Finally, choose by faith to believe in His faithfulness to perform these things in your life.

Remember Habakkuk 2:4: "the just shall live by **HIS** FAITHFUL-NESS [to do the things He promises]." It's His faithfulness, not ours! Without this, we might as well give up and die spiritually.

So one of the first things we must do in order to have our hope restored is to know God's personal Love. It's the initial stepping-stone. Only then will we be able to totally relinquish our lives back to Him and trust Him as we walk across that "bridge of hope" toward the unseen future. Without knowing His Love and faithfulness today, there really is no hope for tomorrow.[169]

## The Importance of Making Faith Choices

A second thing that we must know and apply in order to have our hope restored is how to make daily "faith choices." After almost sixty years as a believer, I've found that making "faith choices" is the key to my whole Christian walk.

Faith choices are simply "choices" we make to follow God's will, *regardless of our own negative thoughts or emotions.* They are choices we often don't feel, choices we don't think will work and, much of the time, choices we don't want to make. God, however, has given us *His authority* and *His power* to make these kind of non-feeling choices, and then He promises to align our natural feelings with our choices. In other words, He will make us "genuine." This is exactly what Jesus models for us in Matthew 26:39: "Not as I will, but as Thou wilt." In other words, God wants *us* to make the choice to obey and to follow Him by faith; *He* then will implement His will in our lives.

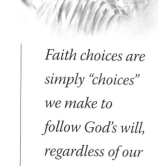

*Faith choices are simply "choices" we make to follow God's will, regardless of our own negative thoughts or emotions.*

So faith choices are "key." God gives us His *authority* (His Word) to make these kinds of choices, and then He gives us His *power* (His Spirit) to perform them.

Non-believers can make all the non-feeling choices they want to, but it will never do them any good, because they don't have the power of God in them to perform *anything different* than what they feel, what they think or what they want. Christians, however, do! Because we have Christ's divine nature—His Life in us—we not only have His authority to choose His will (regardless of how we feel) but also His power to perform that will in our lives.[170]

A few months ago, a precious gentleman in prison wrote me a letter about making "faith choices." Here's what he had to say:

"I am currently incarcerated in the Texas Department of Corrections where I may very well spend the rest of my life. I am fifty-five years old with a fifty-year prison sentence. I've lived most of my life on my own terms, without any regard to God or the spiritual realm whatsoever. However, three years ago God got my attention and I chose to become His. He then began to teach me about 'faith choices', choices to do God's will regardless of our feelings or our own thoughts. This has been some really good food, and I've made some key changes deep inside that have indeed produced rewards, one being 'patience' (believe it or not). Now, rather than act out of my own feelings, I am able to stop and reflect on the outcome. And that's another huge step in growth for me since I used to rarely care about what the outcome may be. And though I am in prison and some days are very lonely, I trust God. I keep 'walking all of this out' because I know, feeling it or not, Jesus is walking it out with me."

Hope is also implemented by making "faith choices." We choose by faith to trust the Lord to perform His promises, even though we often can't see how He is going to do it or when He is going to do it. It's always His timing and in His way. Then He will align our feelings with our faith choice and we'll experience real and genuine hope.

## THE IMPORTANCE OF BEING SANCTIFIED

And a third basic foundational truth in order to restore our hope is that we must understand the importance of being daily sanctified. Sanctification is how God conforms us into His image. Faith choices are the key to being sanctified. Only by presenting our bodies as a living sacrifice and being cleansed by the washing of the water of the Word can we advance into the presence of the Lord.

The word "sanctification" is the Greek term *hagiomos*, which means not only purification and holiness but also consecration and to be set apart. First Thessalonians 5:23 says this another way: "And I pray God your whole *spirit* and *soul* and *body* be preserved blameless [having no spot or blemish] unto the coming of our Lord Jesus Christ." First Thessalonians 4:3 tells us that "sanctification is the will of God."

Therefore, before hope can be fully restored to our lives, we must learn to be sanctified, cleansed and open vessels so that God *can* make Himself visible. Sanctification is simply *the process of becoming holy, purified* and *consecrated.* It's the means by which anything in our lives that is unrighteous, unholy or not of God is removed. **Sanctification, however, is really a three-stage operation.** There's a sanctification of our body that is an ongoing process and depends upon our daily choices (our physical body, however, will never make it to heaven). **Then there's the sanctification of our soul, which is an ongoing process and what we are mainly talking about in this chapter. And, finally, there's the sanctification of our spirit that we will cover next chapter.** God not only wants us conformed into His image in this lifetime, He is also preparing us to be able to rule and reign with Him in His future kingdom. We begin our course of sanctification when we first become believers, but we don't finish this cleansing and purifying process until we are sanctified *wholly*—body, soul and spirit. *Sanctification is simply God's method of separating the sinful and selfish things in our lives from the spiritual.*

God is the only One who can sanctify us, because He is the only One who knows *what is spiritual* and *what is soulish.* We could <u>never</u> accomplish this separation in our own strength or by our own wisdom. Only God can! And the way He implements this division in our lives and spirits is by literally applying Hebrews 4:12: "For the Word of God is quick, and powerful, and sharper than any two-edged sword, piercing even to the *dividing asunder of soul and spirit, and of the joints and marrow,* and is a *discerner of the thoughts and intents of the heart."*

What this is saying is that God, by His Word, is the One who separates, divides and cuts away anything in our souls and spirits that is not of Him. He does so in order to produce the "fruit of the Spirit" through us—the "works" that will glorify Him here and now and the ones that will qualify us for future responsibilities.

## SANCTIFICATION STEPS

The following sanctification steps are not ones that I have "made up" or found in some psychology book or a self-help book. These are the actual steps that the priests took in the Inner Court of Solomon's Temple in order to deal with their sin and be reconciled to God. I have simply taken these same steps and made them personal, so we too can approach the Lord in holiness.

First Peter 2:5, 9 says: "*Ye* also, as lively stones, are built up a spiritual house, *a holy priesthood,* to offer up spiritual sacrifices, acceptable to God by Jesus Christ.... But *ye are a* chosen generation, a *royal priesthood*..."

Briefly, the priests first entered the Inner Court of the temple and went to the Lavers of Bronze, where they confessed and repented of sin; then they went to the Brazen Altar where they sacrificed their offerings, and finally, they went to the Molten Sea where they bodily were cleansed of all sin. (We will discuss this whole "Inner Court Ritual"—the actual steps of the priests—in detail in Chapter Nine.)

I recommend putting these steps on 3 x 5 cards and keeping the cards with you at all times. Things will occur when you are away from your Bible and notes, and if you haven't memorized the steps, you'll be lost. So keep these cards handy—in your purse, briefcase or in your car (some people have put them on their iPhones and iPads)—until they become first nature to you.

Even after being a Christian for over fifty years, I still do these steps every day, especially NOW in my trial! Maturity in Christ is not knowing a bunch of Scriptures, going to church regularly, attending prayer meetings, leading Bible studies, writing books or even being on TV, but simply knowing how, moment-by-moment, to make the proper faith choices to cleanse our souls so that God's Life will be able to shine forth and His Spirit lead us.

Going through these four necessary steps every time we are confronted with a hurtful remark, a painful situation, pride, fear, resentment, bitterness, and so on is the *only* way we can stay prepared vessels for what God might call us to do next. Doing these steps is our own responsibility. Nobody can do them for us. They are also the only way to restore our hope, our joy and our peace. In fact, John 13:10 tells us that if we don't *cleanse our feet* (meaning our souls), we'll *not have any part of Him* and we'll end up contaminating everyone we come in contact with (i.e., "making a stink" as Isaiah 3:24a says). And it's true; we'll be showing off our own "self-life" and not God's Life at all.

## STEP ONE: TAKE EVERY THOUGHT CAPTIVE

One of the very first things we must learn to do in order to have our soul sanctified is to "take every thought captive." Second Corinthians 10:5–6 exhorts us to do this very thing: "Casting down imaginations, and every high thing that exalteth itself against the knowledge of God and **bringing into captivity every thought to the obedience of Christ**; and having in a readiness to revenge all disobedience, when your obedience is fulfilled."

How many of us really do this? Most of us, even after we've been Christians for a long time, still react naturally or emotionally in difficult circumstances. Very few of us stop and think before we respond.

Now, when God says take every thought captive, He doesn't mean examine every single thought that we have. That would be overwhelming. He simply means stop and take a good hard look at the anxious thoughts, the hurtful ones, the doubtful ones, the frustrations, the anger, the pride, and all the other "emotional" and self-centered thoughts that take away our peace. "Lack of peace" is a good barometer to see which thoughts are not of God and which thoughts must be dealt with. Romans 14:23 teaches us that "whatsoever is <u>not</u> of faith is sin." This is huge. How much of our own thinking is not of faith. Wow! This is saying that any thought that is not of faith will quench God's Life and thus must be looked at and put away in order for us to be sanctified.

The reason our thoughts are so important to God is that our thoughts are the first to be triggered in the chain reaction of our souls. Our thoughts stir up our emotions; our emotions then cause our desires, and our desires produce our actions. Therefore, if we can catch our negative thoughts when they first occur, we'll stop the whole chain reaction before it even gets started, and God's Life can continue to flow. What happens, however, when we don't take every thought captive is that we'll end up being carried away by the tide of emotion (that chain reaction), quenching God's Spirit, and then His Life in our hearts will be blocked from coming forth and we'll end up in the "pits."

Therefore, our efforts to change should not be solely focused on our wrong actions but on our wrong thinking. If we can change our thinking, new life actions will follow.

When you realize what you are thinking or feeling is not of God, if at all possible try to get alone with the Lord so you can go through these cleansing steps and deal with your sin the proper way. Try not to put this off. Remember, Jesus is the <u>only</u> One who can expose and cleanse our sin, and He is the only One who can heal us completely. The times that I have "put off" going through these steps are the times I seem to "contaminate" everyone I come in contact with.

Also, in a crisis situation, it's important that we are cleansed in order to respond the way God would have us. Don't ever take a stand

Dear Margaret, I pray the reading of Nancy Missler's Book touch your heart with God's love for you.

Nancy was a great Bible teacher. I had the blessing of taking her studies and visit her seminar on "Agape Love".

She has recently gone home to be with the Lord after much suffering for three years with cancer that took away her nose and part of her face. Her story is on the internet. She was amazing.

This was her last book written by her

Lovingly, Jill Moon

2002
423-00306

with someone unless you are a cleansed vessel! If you're not clean, it will be "self-life" coming forth from you and not God's Life at all. The other person will immediately sense your judgmental attitude and react from his defenses—not his heart. The truth will then be hidden. As a result, you'll sink even further into the pit than you were before and the situation will be perpetuated. If you can get clean first and respond in God's Love and His wisdom, that other person will sense your acceptance and respond from his heart. The truth will then have a chance to be exposed and the situation righted.

The reason our thoughts are so important to God is that our thoughts are the first to be triggered in the chain reaction of our souls.

Even if the current circumstances will only allow you to go through these steps "mentally," still do so. By mentally, I mean that if you are unable to pull away from the situation and be alone with the Lord, *still go through these steps in your mind*. By faith, at least, say the words. Later, you can go to the Lord and go through the steps properly. But no matter what the situation is, don't let sin and "self" accumulate. Don't let the enemy get a handle in you. By faith, deal with the situation as best you can at the moment.

## RECOGNIZE AND ACKNOWLEDGE SINFUL AND SELF-CENTERED THOUGHTS

As a result of taking every thought captive, we must also recognize and acknowledge our negative thoughts, emotions and desires (our self-life).

Going back to the ceremony that the priests did in the Inner Court of Solomon's Temple, it's interesting to me that the priests at the La-vers of Bronze asked God to expose what needed to be repented of. And because the Lavers were made of women's looking glass, as the priests bent over to wash themselves, what they saw was their own reflection. And this is exactly what the Spirit does with us. As we ask Him to expose the sin in our lives, He will show us the truth.

*Taking every thought captive and acknowledging how we feel is the first step to restoring our hope.*

When we have time to actually be with the Lord, ask Him not only to bring to light what's going on in our conscious thoughts, emotions and desires, but also ask Him to shed light on the hidden things in our soul (the "root causes"—the things we are unaware of). In other words, are there any root causes for the self-centered thoughts and emotions we are experiencing. Often, the conscious, surface emotions are really just the symptoms of a much deeper cause. If the real root cause can be exposed and gotten rid of, the surface emotions will go away also. (See "root causes" in Chapter Six.)

It's critical that we not "vent" how we feel or "push down" our emotions, but simply ask God to expose what's really going on inside of us. At this point, it's impor-tant not only to be honest with ourselves and acknowledge the pride, fears, insecurities and doubts that we are experiencing, but also to be honest and truthful with God. He knows all of it anyway. He just wants us to see it and acknowledge it.

Remember, too, we cannot give something over to God if we don't know what it is. This is why describing and naming what we're feel-ing and what we are thinking is so very important. Call your feelings for what they are: "I am angry. I am resentful. I feel betrayed. I am fearful." Experience your thoughts and feelings. Cry, scream, or yell if you want to or have to. (Remember, we're doing this only to the Lord alone.) This will not only help us understand what we are feeling, it will also help us to recognize exactly what we are to give over to God. Experiencing our emotions, I believe, is part of dealing with our sin and part of the healing process. We're all human, and we <u>all</u> experience negative, self-centered thoughts and emotions. Now, I <u>don't</u> mean going back and reliving the actual experiences of the past or putting Jesus in the middle of them or visualizing them; I just mean acknowledging what God has just revealed to us as the root cause of what is affecting our choices today.

Taking every thought captive and acknowledging how we feel is the first step to restoring our hope.

## STEP TWO: CONFESS AND REPENT OF THEM

The second step of the sanctification process is that we must now, by faith (not feelings), <u>confess and repent of all that the Holy Spirit has shown us</u>.

If we can catch the negative or ungodly thought before we entertain it or before we vent it, we can skip this step of confession and repentance because no sin or disobedience has actually occurred. In other words, *the initial negative thought or emotion is not sin.* We are human and we are all going to have bad thoughts at one time or another. The sin comes in when we chose to mull that negative thought over and over again and then choose to follow what it is telling us to do. This is what quenches God's Spirit in us and this is what we need to repent of.

Repenting is simply saying "by faith" (not feelings): "I don't want to follow this feeling, this thought, desire, etc., any more. I want to follow what You, Lord, want me to do."

This step of confession and repentance is our own responsibility. As 1 John 1:9 teaches, "If *we confess* our sins, [then] *He is faithful and just to forgive* us our sins."

### Unconditionally Forgive

A part of this second step of confessing and repenting of our own sin is that we must also unconditionally *forgive others* of theirs. This is where we choose by faith to forgive because most of the time we certainly don't "feel" like forgiving. But we must choose to do so, because it's God's will. "For *if* ye forgive men their trespasses, your heavenly Father will also forgive you: but *if* ye forgive not men their trespasses, neither will your Father forgive your trespasses." (Matthew 6:14–15)

God is hindered from working *in us as well as in the other person* until we have "released" them. And *we release them by unconditionally forgiving them*, whether they have asked for it or not!

Jesus gave us His own example. In Luke 23:34, as He was being crucified, He said, "Father, forgive them; for they know not what they do."

The process of forgiveness works like a *triangle*. <u>We</u> choose to forgive because God tells us to do so; <u>He</u> then gives us the Love and the forgiveness we need for that other person, and this then releases that <u>other person</u> to respond as God would have them. We must realize that we will only "heal" *after* we have made the choice by faith to unconditionally forgive those who have hurt, betrayed, gossiped, etc. about us. It's imperative we do this, regardless if they ever ask for our forgiveness or not.

### Step Three: Give All to God

The next essential step of the sanctification process is that we must <u>give everything that God has shown us that is "not of faith" over to Him</u>. Romans 12:1 tells us we must offer ourselves as a "living sacrifice": "I beseech you therefore, brethren, by the mercies of God, that ye present your bodies a living sacrifice, holy, acceptable unto God, which is your reasonable service."

God will not violate our free will by forcibly taking these things from us; we must willingly choose to hand them over to Him.

He wants us to give Him—to sacrifice to Him—everything that is "sin," so it can be purged and cleansed by His Blood. As we willingly give these things over to Him, He promises to take them from us: "As far as the east is from the west." (Psalm 103:12)

## STEP FOUR: READ GOD'S WORD

The final step in dealing with our sin is that we must read God's Word. God is the only One who, by His Word, can cleanse, sanctify and heal our souls completely. He is the only One who can replace the lies we have believed with the truth and give us that hope.

It was at the Molten Sea (a 20,000-gallon pool of water) where the priests actually allowed the water to flow over them in order to receive a total cleansing. Since they had gotten all "blood splattered" at the Brazen Altar, they now needed a complete bathing in order to be completely cleansed and able to enter the Holy Place and worship the Lord. In like manner, after we have confessed, repented and sacrificed all to God, we too are "bloody" and "torn apart" and in desperate need of God's complete healing power. Only God's Word can totally restore us and give us that hope again. God is the One who washes us "with the washing of water by the Word."[171]

As I read God's Word, I literally picture myself being bathed in God's Love. One of my favorite Scriptures to read at this time is Psalm 18: "In my distress I called upon the LORD...He heard my voice out of His temple...He bowed the heavens also, and came down..." (v. 6, 9) (This verse has become particularly special to me over the last six months.)

Another suggestion: Memorize appropriate Scriptures. Often, we must go through these steps when we are away from home and don't have our Bibles or our notes at hand. If we have memorized Scriptures, we can bathe in His Word anywhere, anytime.

Now we can step out in faith, knowing that God will be faithful to align our feelings with our faith choices, give us the Love and the Wisdom we need, and perform His Will through us.

### OTHER ACTIONS WE CAN TAKE TO RESTORE OUR HOPE

So knowing God loves us, making faith choices, and the criticalness of daily being sanctified are basic to having our hope restored. Knowing and doing these things by faith will help us begin to trust Him in all our circumstances and begin to once again see His faithfulness.

God is the only One who,
# BY HIS WORD,
*can cleanse, sanctify and heal
our souls completely.*

Even if we never understand "why" God has allowed these difficult times in our lives, we must "by faith" keep on walking, keep on hoping and keep on trusting Him. Just as we made "faith choices" to believe, we must also make "faith choices" to trust.

Psalm 81:7 tells us: "You called in trouble, and I delivered you; I answered you in the secret place of thunder: I proved you at the waters of Meribah." Notice this Scripture says that *He answers the one who is in trouble and the one crying out to Him...by testing him! Wow!*

Here are a few other things we can do to restore our hope in the Lord:

## BE FAITHFUL TO HIM

We've talked a lot about the importance of God's faithfulness to us. What about our faithfulness to Him? *It's critical that we are just as faithful to Him as we expect Him to be to us.* Why should He remain faithful to us if we can't at least do the same to Him? It works both ways.

Remember Proverbs 3:5–6: "Trust in the LORD with all thine heart; and lean not unto thine own understanding. In all thy ways acknowledge Him, and He shall direct thy paths." What this is saying is that if we remain faithful to Him, He can work in our lives. Being faithful to Him is simply making "faith choices" to continually follow Him, no matter how we feel or what we want. It's being still, knowing that He is God and will "work all things together for our good." We have heard this so often that it's become almost like a cliché. But it's so true. The part that's difficult is that He does it in His timing and in His way. And often we don't understand either. We must be content to stay in and endure the darkness until He brings the light.

It's only by our willingness and our faithfulness to be sanctified daily that allows Him to conform us more into His image.

Galatians 2:20 tells us: "I live by the faithfulness of the Son of God." Galatians 3:11 states: "The just shall live by faith" (our faithfulness to Him). And Revelation 17:14 says: "...they that are with Him [the Lord of lords] are **called,** and **chosen**, and *faithful*."

Wow! Are we faithful to Him?

## HAVE PERSEVERANCE AND ENDURANCE

Another thing we can do in order to restore our hope is to have endurance and perseverance to finish the race. It's called being an overcomer. It's going from strength in the Lord to more strength in the Lord.

In a practical sense, this means we are to cease striving and trying to understand what is going on. We must lie still and let God accomplish all He needs to *in us* and *through us.* Our response should always be, "let it come." Because if we can *face it, accept it and rejoice in it*, we will make it through. Even though our feelings are raging and our understanding is darkened, we must choose to remain submissive to God and know that He has it all under control. His perfect will is somehow being accomplished. (This hits home to me right now! Because allowing the cancer to return is mind-boggling to me. Why would He heal me only to put me through it all over again? Only He knows the answer; I certainly don't. But because I trust Him and I personally know His faithfulness, He has the freedom to do what He wants with my life. I know He will somehow bring "beauty out of ashes.")

Most important of all, we must choose to **rely upon God's faithfulness and His Love** in the midst of the fire and in spite of everything that is happening all around us.[172] We must learn to trust His plan for our lives and remember that there is <u>no</u> other remedy, no other cure and no other way out except to have complete confidence in Him. Remember Moses, who endured (persevered) only by "seeing Him who is invisible" in the midst of his trial.[173] But also note Abraham in Hebrews 6:15, who only "after he had patiently endured, he obtained the promise."

God promises to work "all things together for good" to those who love (*agapao*) Him.[174] It takes incredible effort on our part (at this difficult time) to stay abandoned to His will. And, unfortunately, this is not just a onetime choice; it's a continual choice.

## "See" the Lord in the Little Things

In Chapter Five, we spoke about the importance of seeing God's faithfulness in the little things. I want to stress that again. This is one of the basic ways we can restore our hope. Remember Job 42:5: "I have heard of Thee by the hearing of the ear: but now mine eye seeth Thee."

*Most important of all, we must choose to rely upon God's faithfulness and His Love in the midst of the fire and in spite of everything that is happening all around us.*

Another small incident (but huge to me) of seeing God's Hand in my circumstances is that when they told me that the melanoma had come back to my nose in October, the tip of my new nose had sunken down about a quarter of an inch. When they first reconstructed it in March, sideways it looked like a straight nose. Now in October, sideways it looked awful, not only hooked but stair-stepped.

The oncology surgeon said that wouldn't matter because they would simply remove the whole thing. However, as you know, we opted for radiation rather than removal. Radiation, we understood, would not cure the cancer but could control it.

What I want to acknowledge here is that after the four weeks of radiation and the horrible four weeks of aftereffects (the boils and blisters), when the rock mask came off my face, the nose was straight again.

How did He do that? My nose is not stair-stepped anymore; it's not perfectly straight, but it's a different nose than went into the radiation.

Another touch of the Lord's Hand...I experienced it...and I want to acknowledge it!

One more huge, huge, huge sign of the Lord's Hand in my circumstances is our phenomenal insurance. You can only imagine what my bills have been. First, three huge reconstructive operations, six weeks of radiation, doctors' visits and hospital stays. Probably hundreds of thousands of dollars!

God picked our perfect insurance agent and company years ago, and neither Chuck nor I have hardly ever used it until now.

A couple of nights ago, I received four bills (I have a stack of bills probably six-inches tall that have been already taken care of), but for some reason these four really scared me. I prayed and decided to open them the next day, in case they were overwhelming and I wouldn't be able to sleep. God, however, gave me a "peace," and I decided to open them then.

Do you know how much I owed on those four huge bills (one was a CT scan; one an MRI; one a spinal tap, and I forgot what the fourth one was)?

The bill was $15 for all four!!!!

I really fell to the ground in utter thanksgiving and praise. This, obviously, was not a "little thing," but a huge blessing from the Lord. But in spite of all the other hard things that are going on, I saw and recognized His Hand. My hope restored. God is involved and watching over everything.

Seeing God in the little things will allow you to take the next needed step—to endure and to overcome. It's the hope from God we need.

These are just some of the recent incidents of seeing God's Hand in the little things. But I can't talk about seeing God's Hand in our everyday lives without mentioning one of my most *favorite examples that happened many, many years ago in Newport Beach, California.* It has nothing at all to do with my current situation (and it's way off the subject), but I just have to tell you about it because it's a miracle. Here's what happened:

I had a carpool of four girls, and we were headed out of town to go horseback riding. I was coming down a steep incline on a four-lane highway toward a stoplight at the bottom of the hill. The light had been green for quite a while, and I was probably driving a little too fast (which I have a tendency to do as I am an L.A. born and raised freeway driver). All of a sudden the light turned red, and the cars in both the two lanes in front of us stopped. There was no way I could stop or avoid hitting them as I was in the center lane, there still was oncoming traffic going the other direction, and thus nowhere else for me to go.

I yelled at the girls to "duck down...we're going to hit the car in front of us!" when lo and behold those two stopped cars parted sideways from each other (I'm not kidding), which allowed our car to squeeze right between them and pass through. Fortunately, there were no cars at the intersection coming from the other direction, so I could get through the red light without being hit. When we got to the other side of the crossroads, I pulled the car over to the side, stopped and all of us turned around and looked back at the two cars still waiting for the red light to turn green.

In all honesty, there was no room for a car to go between them as we had just done. The cars were only two-feet apart. It was a total miracle. Even to this day, my girls and I talk about that incident and how we know God moved those cars so we could pass through them without being killed.

Remember this little incident and look for God's Hand even in the little things.

## Praise the Lord

Another thing that we can do to help restore our hope when we go through a Valley of Baca experience is try to praise the Lord in everything. No matter what is occurring, we need to try to find something to praise Him for. Hebrews 13:15 tells us that praise is the "fruit" of our lips.

Remember Psalm 92:2, which tells us we should praise His loving kindness in the morning and His faithfulness at night. Like the priests of Solomon's Temple, *after* we have been personally sanctified (soul and spirit) and are abiding in God's presence, we too can carry His Love to the whole congregation and tell them about His faithfulness. *And, like the priests did, we need to continually praise and thank the Lord for all that He has done for us in the past, all that He is doing for us in the present and all He will do for us in the future.* By praising God for these things, we will pierce the darkness and the evil spirits will flee away. The enemy hates the Name of Jesus and despises the praises of God. So if we want the enemy to flee, try praising and thanking the Lord continually.[175]

Now, before I begin to pray at all, I praise Him for everything I can think of: my precious husband, my children, our ministries, our friends and families, our home, etc. Hebrews 13 calls this a "sacrifice of praise." That's praise that is given at a time when everything in our life is dark and we don't "feel" like praising Him. Thus, at the time it is given, it's a sacrifice. The Bible also speaks about a sacrifice of joy in Psalm 27:6 and a sacrifice of thanksgiving.[176]

Philippians and 1 Thessalonians tells us to sing, rejoice, be glad by faith and give thanks to the Lord.[177] This is what the priests did in the Outer Court of the temple after they had worshiped the Lord in the Holy Place.

## Do Warfare

Alongside of perseverance and endurance is the importance of doing battle against the enemy. As we learned last chapter, the authority and power that the Lord has given us is our own "rod" and "staff" as symbolized in Psalm 23 and also Exodus 17:5–11 with Moses. God's Word (our rod) is His authority and God's Spirit (our staff) is His power.

"Rod" in Psalm 23 is the Hebrew word *shebet*, which means a branch or a stick for punishing, fighting or ruling. It was a tool used by shepherds and is a *symbol of authority.* It's an instrument of warfare. The Lord says in Psalm 89:31–34: "If they break My statutes, and keep not My commandments; then I will visit their transgression with the ROD, and their iniquity with stripes. Nevertheless My lovingkindness will I not utterly take from him, nor suffer my faithfulness to fail."

"Staff" is the Hebrew word *mishenah* and means to support or to help walk, which is exactly what God's Spirit does in our lives—it gives us support and helps us to walk.

So doing warfare (binding and loosing) is another way of restoring our hope. Revelation tells us we fight the enemy by God's Word and by "dying to self." Then God's Spirit can come forth.

Another thing that we can do to help restore our hope when we go through a Valley of Baca experience is try to praise the Lord in everything.

## Worship the Lord

Finally, no matter what is happening in our life or how we really "feel," we must choose *by faith* to worship the Lord. Worship is simply *a divine encounter with God.* Psalm 16:11 tells us: "...in His presence is fullness of joy." It doesn't say only "by feelings" is there joy. *It says in His presence is fullness of joy.* So it's our responsibility to come before His presence; He then will give us that "fullness of joy."

Worship is the means by which real Love can flow between a believer and his Lord. *It means bringing the Love that Christ originally put in our hearts when we were first born again full circle back to Him in adoration and exaltation.*

Worship is what makes us one. Picture the priests of Solomon's Temple offering incense and how it intertwined with the cloud of fire and became one. Our spiritual praise and worship rise up toward heaven and intertwine with God's Spirit (the cloud), and they become one. In other words, it's a two-way communication. We come into His presence by loving (totally giving ourselves over to Him), adoring and exalting Him. He then makes Himself known to us by communicating His Love in a deeper and more meaningful way. And this intimate knowledge between us results in unutterable joy!

The Greek word for worship is *proskuneo,* which means to bow down, stoop down, fall down, adore, show absolute reverence, homage or submission.[178] It means to *kiss, to prostrate oneself* or touch one's nose to the ground. Throughout Scripture you can see how the believers, when they worshiped the Lord, always fell on their faces, bowed down and prostrated themselves before Him.[179] *Proskuneo* is something that is done on the "inside"—"in our spirit." It's prostrating and bowing down our inner man before the Lord, asking nothing of Him, but losing ourselves in adoration, reverence and homage.

The definition of worship that I really like is that worship means *to catch fire* with the Love of God. Again, you can see the symbolism here. This is exactly what happened when the priests put those "hot coals of fire" on the Incense Altar. It sparked a fire that burned even brighter and stronger. When something catches on fire, it is literally *consumed by it.* This is exactly what happens in worship. We become consumed in our love for the Lord and *one* in spirit with Him. It's a uniting or the becoming one of two separate spirits. It's a binding of oneself or a joining of oneself to the object of our love. In other words, we catch fire with the love of God.

God is a Spirit, and the Bible tells us that only that which is spirit can abide in His presence. Thus, worshiping the Lord in the spirit means adoring, praising and loving Him *in the same nature as He is*— in the Spirit, not in the flesh. Again, this highlights John 4:23–24: "But the hour cometh, and now is, when the true worshipers shall worship the Father *in spirit and in truth*: for the Father seeketh such to worship Him. God is a Spirit: and they that worship Him <u>must</u> worship Him *in spirit and in truth.*"[180]

Being one with God is being willing, as Mark 8:34–35 and Luke 9:22–24 indicate, not only to *suffer* as Jesus did, be *rejected* as He was and also willing *to die* as He did. It's being continually willing to lay down our life and our body so Jesus can pour His Life and His Love through us to others. Peter tells us: "Forasmuch, then, as Christ hath suffered for us in the flesh, arm yourselves likewise with the same mind [attitude]: for he that hath suffered [barred himself from sin] in the flesh hath ceased from sin." (1 Peter 4:1) And also Ephesians 5:1–2 states: "Be ye therefore *followers of God*, as dear children: and walk in love, as Christ also hath loved us, and hath given Himself for us an offering and a sacrifice to God for a sweet smelling savour."

As you will see in the coming chapters, we **learn to obey Christ** in the Inner Court of our temple (our soul), where God teaches us how to walk by faith. We **learn to trust Him** in the Holy Place of our temple (our heart), **where God teaches us how to endure and wait** *for His promises to be fulfilled.* And finally, *we learn to worship Him* at the Incense Altar of our hearts (our spirit), where we become one spirit with Him.

The bottom line is that in order to restore our hope in the Lord, we must choose to love (*agapao*) Him not by our feelings but by faith. Loving Him means totally giving ourselves over to Him no matter what our circumstances are, no matter how we feel and no matter what we want. He, then, will give us the Love and the hope that we need to endure and to walk out His plan.

This sounds so simple, and yet is so difficult to do. It's relying upon His promises even though they make no sense to us at the time. *This is what "hope against hope" is all about.* It's knowing (by faith, not feelings) that He is on our right hand, that He loves us and that He will never leave us. Thus we will not be moved.[181]

# Chapter Eight—What Is the Answer to Restoring Our Hope?

1. Can you quote Proverbs 3:5–6? This is one of the most important Scriptures of all to memorize.

2. When our circumstances, other people in our lives, pain, or the flesh triggers discouragement, despair, or depression, what must we choose "by faith" to depend upon? Why is this so important?

3. What must "we" do in order for God to direct our paths? (Proverbs 3:5–6)

4. Once we are in the enemy's grip, how do we get out of it?

5. There are three essential steps to restoring our hope. What are they?

6. Sanctification is critical. What exactly is it, and why is it so important in restoring our hope?

7. What are some of the other things we can do to restore our hope?

8. What does worshiping the Lord really mean to you?

9. The definition of worship that I really like is to "catch fire" with the Love of God. Has this happened to you? Explain. (Psalm 16:11)

"Know ye not that ye are

the temple of God,

*and that the* Spirit of God

dwelleth in you?

IF ANY MAN DEFILE THE TEMPLE OF GOD,

HIM SHALL GOD DESTROY;

*for the temple of God is holy,*

*which temple ye are."*

1 CORINTHIANS 3:16–17

CHAPTER NINE

# GOD'S PATTERN FOR
# OUR LIVES—
# THE
# TEMPLE MODEL

In many of my previous books, we've talked about Solomon's Temple and its various rooms and courts and rituals and how all of these relate to our own walk with the Lord. First Corinthians 10:11 tells us that "all these things happened unto them for examples; and they are written for our admonition [our advice, our counsel and our guidance]." In this chapter, let's delve into this area of Solomon's Temple a little deeper so you can see the incredible parallels that God has laid out for us there. It's an absolute treasure hunt!

What's fascinating to me is that there are over 52 chapters in the Old Testament that talk about *"the temple of God"* and its significance, and yet today we hear very little about these things. To the writers of the Bible and to the Jewish people, the temple of God was something that *was* very important, *is* very important and *will be* very important. Three places in Psalms, it talks about the Lord ruling the world from His temple.[182] The only temples ever mentioned in the Bible are the Jewish Temples (either Solomon's Temple or Nehemiah's in the Old Testament and Herod's in the New Testament).

Remember Hebrews 6:19 that tells us "hope" is not only the anchor of our soul, but it's also what enables us to penetrate "behind the veil of the temple" (referring to the Holy of Holies). This is telling us that "hope" is the bridge or the link or the connection that allows us to lay hold of God in the Holy of Holies. This is hugely important! Remember that an anchor has two parts: the anchor itself and the chain that holds it in place. Our spiritual anchor (hope), when it is firmly tied to the Lord "behind the veil," is the only thing that will hold our soul in place, especially during the hard times.

After seeing the connection between hope and God behind the veil, the Lord had me again review Solomon's Temple. The reason I've always used Solomon's Temple in my books is that Solomon's Temple was very special and unlike all the others in at least three special ways: 1) It was the only temple in which the plans of its structure were given to David by the Holy Spirit.[183] This is very important as it validates *divine instruction.* 2) It was the only temple in which the Spirit of God (the Shekinah) resided permanently, until the temple was actually destroyed. The Shekinah did not dwell in the other temples. Again, this is extremely important because it describes the *divine presence* was in Solomon's Temple! And finally, 3) it was the only temple in which the Ark of the Covenant resided (with its Mercy Seat covering), symbolizing *God's residence.* So Solomon's Temple was very special in the past, is very special to us now as Christians and will be very special in the future.[184]

To build our analogy, let's first take a look at the front view of Solomon's Temple:

## CHART 1—FRONT VIEW OF SOLOMON'S TEMPLE

**A** is the Holy of Holies; **B** is the Holy Place; **C** is the Porch; **D** is the Pillars on the Porch; **E** is the Hidden Chambers, and **F** is the Inner Court.

CHART 1 | **Front View of Solomon's Temple**

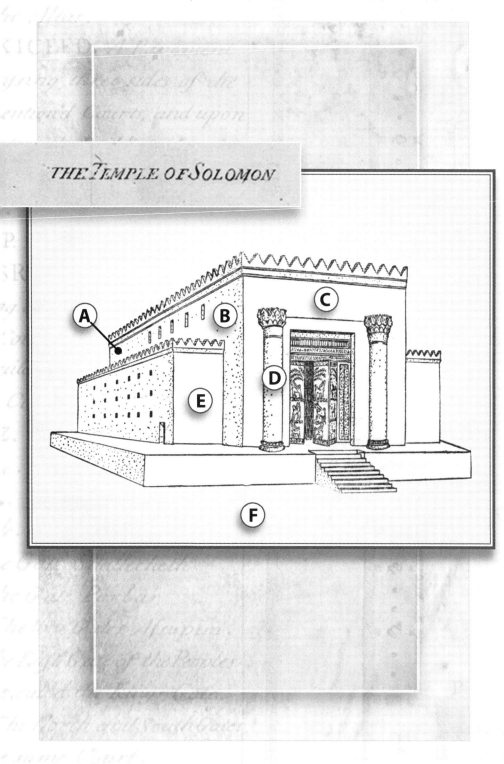

THE TEMPLE OF SOLOMON

Solomon's Temple took seven years to build. They used 70,000 bearers (whom I assume are builders) and 80,000 hewers.[185] This temple stood in Jerusalem for 420 years and was finally destroyed in 422 B.C. The Bible tells us that there will be another temple built in the Millennium,[186] and it is here that the Kingdom of Heaven will be revealed and all the world will come to serve the Lord.[187]

## CHART 2—THE FLOOR PLAN

Looking down upon the actual floor plan of the temple, we can see that the main sanctuary was made up of the Holy of Holies (A) in the rear, the Holy Place (B) in the middle, and the Porch (C) in the front. (Note: The Porch not only included the golden vestibule between the Holy Place and the Inner Court (C), but it also included the two bronze pillars on either side of the Porch (D).)

The temple sanctuary itself rested on a raised platform (G). Surrounding it were the secret hidden chambers (E), where the priests were supposed to store the worship items for the Holy Place and some of Israel's treasures and trophies to remind them of all that God had done for them. However, it was here that the priests actually stored their own personal idolatrous worship items, thinking that since they were out of sight, no one would see or know. (If you are at all interested in pursuing this area of the "hidden chambers" further, you might want to see the book *Be Ye Transformed* and how each of the areas of the temple relate to our own body, soul and spirit.)

Stepping down seven steps from the Porch, one would find the Inner Court (H) and on an even lower level the Outer Court (I).

As we said, many of the Bible's illustrations and examples, such as this temple, are "shadows and patterns of things to come."[188] And thus we must pay close attention to these pictures, types or patterns because they will give us a greater understanding of what God wants

## CHART 2 | The Floor Plan

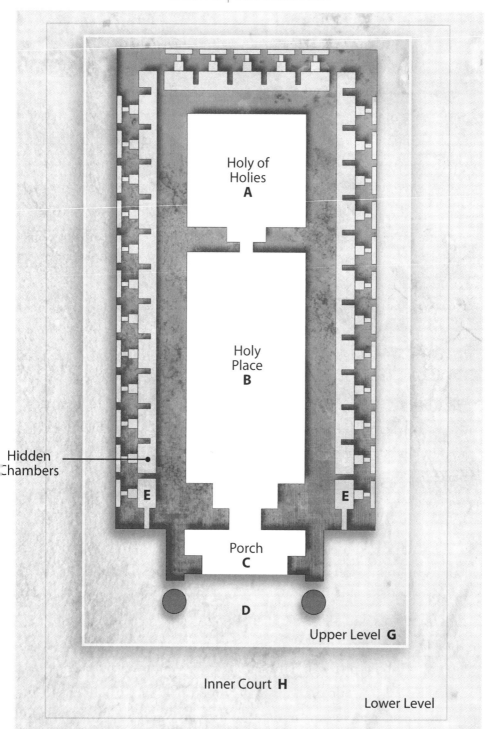

Holy of
Holies
**A**

Holy
Place
**B**

Hidden
Chambers

**E**          **E**

Porch
**C**

**D**

Upper Level **G**

Inner Court **H**

Lower Level

Outer Court **I**

of us and of what we will personally experience either in this lifetime or in the next. First Corinthians 13:9–13 even tells us: *"For [now] we know in part, and we prophesy in part. But when that which is perfect is come, then that which is in part shall be done away. When I was a child, I spake as a child, I understood as a child, I thought as a child: but when I became a man, I put away childish things. For now we see through a glass, darkly; but then face to face: now I know in part; but then shall I know even as also I am known."*

One of these examples (hints, clues, indicators) is that seven times in the New Testament, both Paul and Peter liken our bodies to *"the temple of God."*[189]

I believe Hebrews uses this Old Testament temple and what occurred there to illustrate Christian teaching. It's a pattern of what God desires for each of our own lives as we seek to be conformed to His image. Hebrews 9:11–28 and 10:7–23 tell us that Christ is our High Priest. His death made a new life-giving way for us to approach the Father through the sacred curtain to the Holy of Holies. We can go into His presence anytime we desire by appropriating His blood to make us clean.

## CHART 3—ARCHITECTURE OF MAN

The Lord showed me many, many years ago that there is so much we can learn architecturally about ourselves and our walk with the Lord by studying the actual layout of the physical temple itself. Thus, in most of my teachings and in most of my books, I have used Solomon's Temple as a Biblical model or a blueprint of the architecture of man, i.e., what is our spirit (1), our heart (2), our willpower (choice point) (3), our soul (4), our body (5) and the hidden part of our soul (6). Hundreds of people have written and told me that the comparison has been a tremendous help to them.

# CHART 3 | **The Architecture of Man**

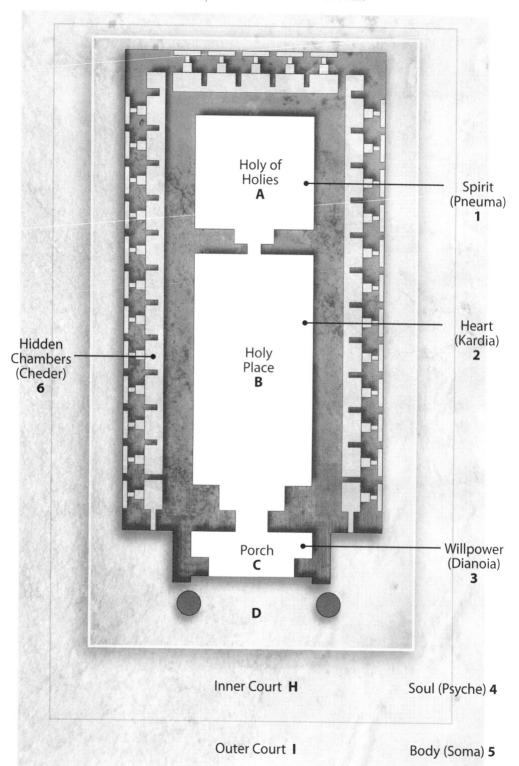

Holy of Holies
**A**

Spirit (Pneuma) **1**

Holy Place
**B**

Heart (Kardia) **2**

Hidden Chambers (Cheder) **6**

Porch
**C**

Willpower (Dianoia) **3**

**D**

Inner Court **H**

Soul (Psyche) **4**

Outer Court **I**

Body (Soma) **5**

In this book, however, God has turned my attention away from just seeing the temple as a model of man to the ritual that the priests went through in the Inner Court (in order to cleanse themselves) and the purifying ceremony they went through in the Holy Place at the Incense Altar where God would then meet with them. It's been an absolutely fascinating adventure, and the more I've discovered about these ancient rituals of the priests in Solomon's Temple, the more

I'm convinced they have some present-day significance. The specific areas of the temple and what the priests did in each of these areas line up exactly with what the Lord requires of each believer in his own moment-by-moment walk toward intimacy with the Him. In other words, what happens when we are born again (i.e., the Outer Court experience); how our soul is sanctified (i.e., what occurs in the Inner Court); how we must endure trials in order for our spirit to be purified (i.e., the dark night of the Holy Place), and finally, what happens when we enter the Lord's presence at the Incense Altar and for that moment become one with Him.

*The specific areas of the temple and what the priests did in each of these areas line up exactly with what the Lord requires of each believer in his own moment-by-moment walk toward intimacy with the Him.*

What particularly fascinated me and influenced me to research the temple ceremony on an even deeper level is why the priests (after they went through the Inner Court Ritual) had to then change their clothes and carry "hot coals of fire" from the *Brazen Altar* in the Inner Court back into the Holy Place and deposit them on the *Incense Altar* that sat before the Holy of Holies. This was part of the priest's purification process. What significance do these "hot coals of fire" have in our own lives? And how might this be connected to "hope" and going from "strength to strength"?

So let's first review the priest's entire sanctification ceremony in the temple, and then we'll come back and see how it all relates to our own sanctification process and where those "hot coals of fire" come in. I am more convinced than ever that this ritual is a shadow or a copy or a figure of things yet to come.

Interestingly, Hebrews 9:23 validates that this temple must be cleansed and purified in order to be a model, a pattern or an example of the future heavenly temple. It's interesting because the Bible continually emphasizes *the cleansing aspect of the temple*. And, of course, the cleansing and sanctifying of our earthly bodies (conforming us into His image) in preparation for ruling and reigning with Him is what the whole New Testament is all about.

The Jewish rabbis still hold to the idea that the "temple of God" is a very important part of the end-time's scenario. In his book *The Odyssey of the Third Temple*, Rabbi Chaim Richman says, "The origin of the temple can be traced back to the beginning of time—to the very dawn of creation—to the days of Adam and Eve.... It's the physical manifestation of a vast idea which existed even before the creation of the world.... [The temple] is at the center of global spirituality.... The reason God erected the temple in the first place was because He desires to *dwell among us. Thus, the temple has always been [and is] to the Jewish people, a 'symbol of hope.'"*[190]

Now, I'm obviously not Jewish nor is the above quote from the Bible, but I thought it very provocative nevertheless.

## CHART 4—THE PRIESTS' CLEANSING CEREMONIES
Now that you understand the basic layout of the temple, let's describe the cleansing and purifying ceremony that the priests went through as

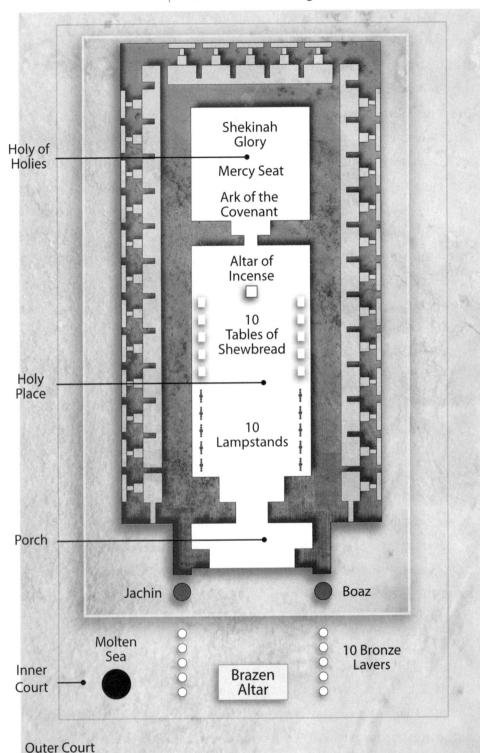

CHART 4 | **The Priests' Cleansing Ceremonies**

Holy of Holies

Shekinah Glory

Mercy Seat

Ark of the Covenant

Altar of Incense

Holy Place

10 Tables of Shewbread

10 Lampstands

Porch

Jachin

Boaz

Molten Sea

10 Bronze Lavers

Inner Court

Brazen Altar

Outer Court

they progressed from the Outer Court to the Inner Court and on to the Holy Place where they worshiped the Lord at the Incense Altar. Let's see if we can find any comparisons to our own walk with the Lord.

The first thing the priests did as they entered the **Outer Court** in the morning was to sing and praise God. In the Outer Court, the priests encountered people from all walks of life, and it was there that they sang and praised God. Note the songs they sang in the morning were ones giving thanks for God's mercy and His loving kindness (specifically Psalms 135 and 136).

After the Outer Court times of praise, the priests then entered the **Inner Court** where they had to wash their hands and feet in the Bronze Lavers, sacrifice their offerings on the Brazen Altar and then bodily wash in the Molten Sea.

Next, the priests changed their clothes in the **Holy Place** by "putting off" their old garments and "putting on" their new robes. Then they went back into the Inner Court where they picked up a golden censer[191] full of "hot coals of fire" from the Brazen Altar, reentered the Holy Place, walking slowly through the darkness, and put these hot coals of fire on the Incense Altar. After that, they crushed the incense and sprinkled it over the hot embers, prostrated themselves before this altar and worshiped the Lord.

The Incense Altar is a fascinating piece of furniture, and we will explore it in full detail in just a moment. (This altar is critically important because it represents the place in our hearts where God's Spirit is united with our own human spirit.) The altar actually sat in the Holy Place just in front of the veil to the Holy of Holies. However, in the Bible it's always spoken of as being in the Holy of Holies.[192] So note that the priests never actually went inside the Holy of Holies where God dwelt, except once a year on the Day of Atonement when only the High Priest was allowed to go in.

In the evening, after the priests finished ministering to the Lord in the Holy Place, they then went back to the ***Outer Court***, where they once again ministered to the "congregation" by joyfully singing songs of praise and thanksgiving (this time, specifically *Psalms 146—150 about God's faithfulness*).

Let's explore the Outer Court a little further, only this time as it relates to our own personal walk with the Lord.

## CHART 5 A—THE OUTER COURT (OUR BODY)

I believe the Outer Court represents or is analogous to our bodies and our natural and worldly lives. This is the place we take the step to give our lives to Christ—our salvation experience, our new birth. The Outer Court is also the place where we encounter various outside influences pulling us in many different directions. And it is also the place where (after we are cleansed) we can minister to others.

Remember, the Outer Court in the temple was where the general public was allowed and thus where the pull of the world was strong.

Morning and evening (twice a day), the priests used the opportunity to publicly praise the Lord and to thank Him for His loving kindness and His faithfulness. In the morning, remember, they sang songs praising His Love (specifically, Psalm 135 and 136): "Praise ye the LORD. Praise ye the Name of the LORD; praise Him, O ye servants of the LORD. Ye that stand in the house of the LORD, *in the courts of the house of our God*. Praise the LORD; for the LORD is good: sing praises unto His Name: for it is pleasant.... Give thanks unto the LORD: for He is good: for His mercy endureth forever." At night, however, they sang songs praising His faithfulness (specifically Psalms 145—150): "I will extol Thee, my God, O king; and I will bless Thy name for ever and ever. Great is the LORD, and greatly to be praised; and His greatness is unsearchable."

# CHART 5A | **The Outer Court (Our Body)**

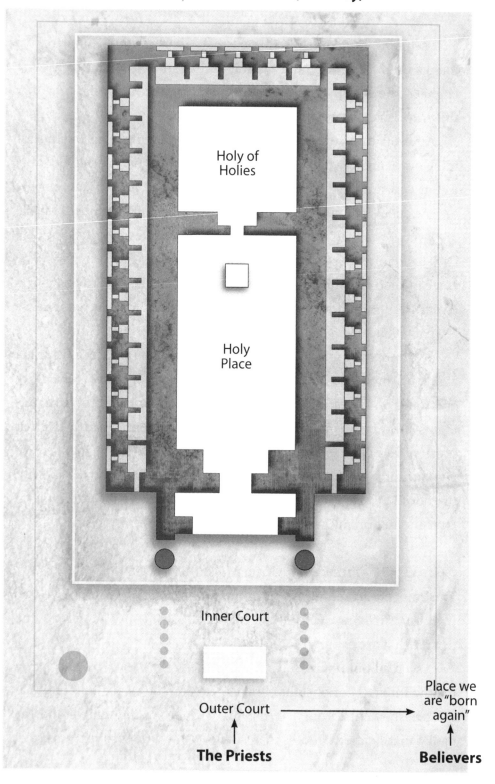

Holy of Holies

Holy Place

Inner Court

Outer Court ⟶ Place we are "born again"

**The Priests**

**Believers**

Psalm 92:1–2 confirms this custom: "It is a good thing to give thanks unto the LORD, and to sing praises unto Thy name, O Most High: *to* shew forth **Thy lovingkindness in the morning, and Thy faithfulness every night.**"

Applying this to ourselves, the first thing every morning and the last thing every night, we should remember not only how much God loves us but how faithful He is. If you are in a trial right now, try to remember the details of how you first came to know Him. Remember how He drew you. Recall the whole experience if you can. Describe it. Bring it all back to your memory. Praise Him for it! Write it down if you need to, so you can keep remembering it. Remembering His Love in saving you is critically important for your walk ahead. And recalling His faithfulness is what will help you endure the trials. Continually thank Him.

So one of the things we need to do every morning and the last thing at night is choose by faith (not feelings) to believe in His personal Love and stand on His faithfulness in spite of the circumstances surrounding us at the moment. Like the priests, recite Psalm 135 and 136 that speak of His Love for you. And recite Psalms 145—150 that speak of His faithfulness. This has made a huge difference in my own walk with the Lord because it daily reminds me and refocuses my attention on Him and not on my circumstances. It truly has been a blessing.

## CHART 5 B—THE INNER COURT (OUR SOUL)

The Inner Court represents our soul, which is the place where we deal with our sin—our own natural and fleshly thoughts, emotions and desires that are so often "not of faith."

As a result of years of searching of the Scriptures, God has shown me the intensely important parallel between the cleansing ritual that the priests went through in the Inner Court of the temple and the daily sanctification process that a believer must go through. As I said,

CHART 5B | **The Inner Court (Our Soul)**

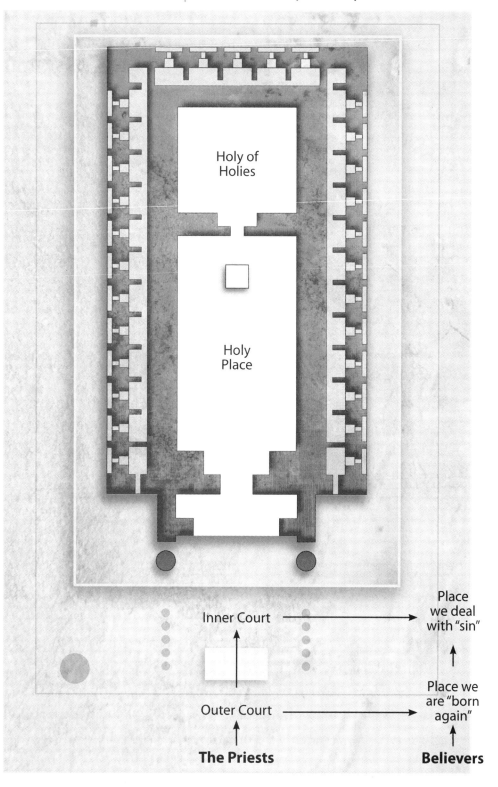

Holy of Holies

Holy Place

Inner Court → Place we deal with "sin"

Outer Court → Place we are "born again"

**The Priests**

**Believers**

I have shared "the Inner Court Ritual" in most of my teachings and in most of my books. In Chapter Eight, we learned what some of these sanctification steps are. I believe it's all a "shadow or a model or a pattern of things to come."

In the Inner Court, there were three cleansing and sanctifying pieces of furniture that the priests had to attend to—the ten Lavers of Bronze, the Brazen Altar and the Molten Sea. First, they went to the ten <u>Bronze Lavers</u>, five lavers on each side, which were used for the *continual washing of the priests' hands and feet*. This washing was mandatory because Exodus 30:18–21 says all things used in worship had to be cleansed and washed first, "lest they die."

Next, the priests went to the <u>Brazen Altar</u> *where they offered their sacrifices*. This was a huge altar 15-feet high and 31-feet square. It was often called the "mountain of God." This is where the blood of the animal sacrifice was shed in order to purge the offenders' sins and restore their fellowship with the Lord.

Finally, the priests went to the <u>Molten Sea</u> where they *allowed the water to flow over them bodily* in order to be completely cleansed. This was a huge basin of water that sat on 12 oxen and held enough water for 2,000 baths. Since the priests had gotten all "blood splattered" at the Brazen Altar, they had to completely bathe in this water in order to be totally cleansed.

One of the things we need to do every morning and the last thing at night is choose by faith (not feelings) to believe in His personal Love and stand on His faithfulness in spite of the circumstances surrounding us at the moment.

## CHART 5 C—THE HOLY PLACE (OUR HEART)

Leviticus 16:12 tells us that after the sacrifice had been presented on the Brazen Altar in the Inner Court and the priest had been bodily cleansed in the Molten Sea, he then would go into the Holy Place and change his clothes. After this, he returned back to the Brazen Altar in the Inner Court where he took a censer, filled it full of hot burning coals of fire and then carried those coals into the Holy Place where he laid them on the Incense Altar. Then he took some incense, ground it up small and scattered it over the hot coals. The fire and smoke then intertwined into a column and filled the entire Holy Place. As the fire cloud circled up toward the ceiling and spread out throughout the entire sanctuary, the priest then prostrated himself on the ground before the altar, worshiped the Lord and the glory of the Lord filled the house.[193] Only those priests who had been cleansed and sanctified in the Inner Court had access to the Holy Place. The priests who had defiled themselves in one way or another were separated and made to stand at the eastern Gate (of the Outer Court). That way, all who entered could see that these men were impure and that they were not allowed to serve in the temple at that time. (Page 29, *The Holy Temple of Jerusalem*, Chaim Richman)

Thus, in order to advance to the Holy Place and worship the Lord at the Incense Altar, the priests had to first go through their ritual at all three pieces of furniture in the Inner Court. Only then were they considered cleansed enough to go into the Holy Place. (Notice the emphasis in the temple on sanctification, purification, physical cleansing, personal cleansing and ceremonial cleansing.)

As an aside, the Inner Court vessels and furniture were all bronze (brass), just as were the two huge pillars on the porch. (Bronze in Scripture symbolizes that sin is still present and cleansing is needed, whereas the Holy Place and the Holy of Holies were the only rooms in the temple that were pure gold.[194]

Applying this Old Testament model to ourselves, the **Outer Court** is analogous to the place where we are born again; the **Inner Court** is analogous to our soul, where "sin" is sometimes present and must be dealt with, and the **Holy Place** is analogous to our heart, where God's Spirit

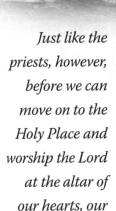

is united with our human spirit. It's also the place where we must often deal with our "self" on an even deeper level. As 2 Corinthians 7:1 says: "Having therefore these promises, dearly beloved, let us cleanse ourselves from all filthiness of the *flesh and spirit*, perfecting holiness in the fear of God." This is also the place where, if our spirit is purified, we will be able to "see God who is invisible."[195]

*Just like the priests, however, before we can move on to the Holy Place and worship the Lord at the altar of our hearts, our souls must be cleansed.*

Just like the priests, however, *before* we can move on to the Holy Place and worship the Lord at the altar of our hearts, our souls must be cleansed. As you just read, the priests "put off" their old garments in the Inner Court and "put on" new ones in the Holy Place. We too must daily go through the steps of putting off the old man and putting on the new, just as Colossians 3:8–12 tells us to do. This sanctification is accomplished by making constant "faith choices" to do what God has asked—recognizing our negative thoughts and emotions, confessing them and then giving them to Him.

Only those who are experientially sanctified (holy) will be allowed to enter the Holy Place sanctuary and experience intimacy with Him.[196]

"Follow peace with all men, *and holiness, without which no man shall see the Lord.*" (Hebrews 12:14)

Notice something interesting. When the incense was presented at the Incense Altar, the fire and smoke rose up and filled the entire

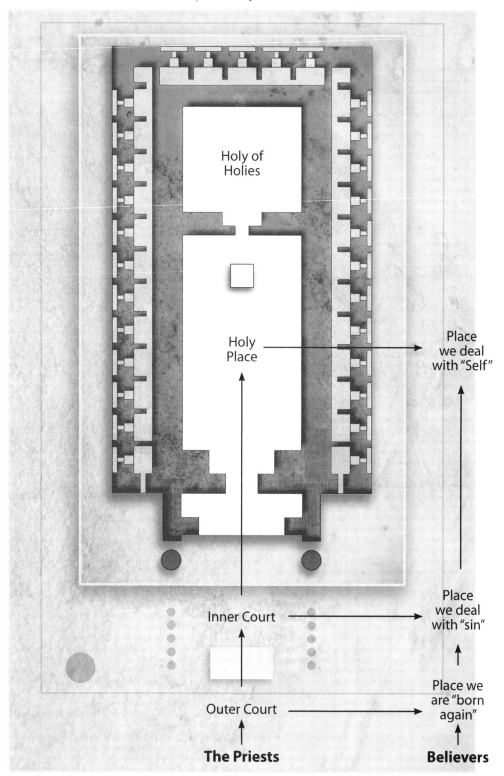

CHART 5C | **The Holy Place (Our Heart)**

Holy of Holies

Holy Place → Place we deal with "Self"

Inner Court → Place we deal with "sin"

Outer Court → Place we are "born again"

**The Priests**

**Believers**

sanctuary with a "the cloud of God's presence." So much so that 1 Kings 8 tells us "the priests could not stand to minister." In other words, the sanctuary was dark and filled with a cloud. Thus the priests had to find their way through the dark cloud of God's presence besides carrying the hot coals of fire. This will all be important as we begin to see the parallel between what the priests did in the Holy Place and what God requires us to do to.

(Remember, this altar, even though it physically sat in the Holy Place just outside the veil, was *always considered in the Bible to be a part of the Holy of Holies.* This again is very significant as you will see.)

So the service of sanctification for the priests *began* by presenting a sacrifice at the Brazen Altar in the Inner Court but *ended* with the cloud of fire and smoke rising up from the Incense Altar in the Holy Place. *It's a long dark walk between these two altars—it's like a "bridge" that goes from the seen to the unseen, from faith to intimacy and from belief to knowing.*

The same analogy can be applied to our lives. The sanctification of our "souls" *begins* with the offering of ourselves as a "living sacrifice" in the Inner Court,[197] but *ends* with the purification of our "spirits" as we carry "our own crosses" (the death of self) to the Incense Altar of our hearts.

"Who shall ascend into the hill of the LORD? or who shall stand in His Holy Place? He that hath *clean hands*, and a *pure heart*; who hath not lifted up his soul unto vanity, nor sworn deceitfully. He shall receive the blessing from the LORD, and righteousness from the God of his salvation."[198]

## THE PLACE THE WORD OF GOD TESTS US

Psalm 105:19 tells us that it's the Word of God that tests us in this deeper state. And this is exactly what happens in the Holy Place. Our trials and tribulations allow God to show us what is soulish and what is spiritual. It allows Him to divide asunder our joints and marrow, even to the discerning of the thoughts and intents of our heart.[199]

The only other pieces of furniture in the Holy Place, besides the Incense Altar, were the ten Golden Lampstands and the ten Golden Tables of Shewbread, both of which are described by the Septuagint as being solid gold.[200] The Tables of Shewbread are symbolic of the Word of God, which is where the thoughts and intents of our heart are read by Christ. And the Lampstands are symbolic of the fruit of the Holy Spirit. I almost see the TRINITY reaching out from the Holy of Holies here.

As we symbolically walk through the Holy Place of our hearts, the Word of God is what examines our lives and exposes anything that is not of the Lord. Together the Word and the Spirit are able to reveal and uncover the hidden motives of our hearts and test us on an even deeper level.

Therefore, I believe the Holy Place represents the area where we will encounter the cloud of God's presence. He will urge us on with His Love, but at the same time we might still be overwhelmed and confused by the "the hot coals of fire" (the life situations) that we are supposed to be carrying to the Altar. This is the time we might be "pressed out of measure, troubled on every side, perplexed, persecuted and cast down; but [if we know what to do—continue to walk toward Him] we won't be distressed, nor in despair, not forsaken nor destroyed."[201] This is the time that God teaches us how to unconditionally trust Him and keep on walking in the darkness. This is where He tests us. The act of bringing the hot coals of fire from the Inner Court into the Holy Place represents the death of self and trusting God to a greater extent.

## AN EXAMPLE: ISAIAH

There's an interesting example of the use of "hot coals of fire" in Isaiah 6:1–9. Isaiah had a vision in which he saw the Lord in the temple, "sitting upon a throne, high and lifted up." Note that Isaiah must have actually been in the Holy Place in order to have "seen" the Lord in the Holy of Holies because it's impossible to see the Holy of Holies from the Inner Court. Above the throne, Isaiah saw the seraphim crying out: "Holy, holy, holy is the LORD of hosts." (v. 3)

Isaiah is so overwhelmed by what he sees that he sobs: "Woe is me! For I am undone, because I am a man of unclean lips..." Then one of the seraphim flew to him with a *live coal of fire* that he had taken from off the altar and he laid it on Isaiah's mouth. He then said, "Thine iniquity (*Strong's* # 5771, meaning "self") is taken away." (vv. 6–7)

It's interesting that Isaiah, who obviously was a believer and who apparently was already sanctified, finds himself in the Holy Place of the temple, experiencing a deeper sense of his sin and self. No one could enter the Holy Place without passing by the ten Lavers, the Brazen Altar and the Molten Sea, which Isaiah had obviously already done. And yet here he is in the Holy Place, experiencing a deeper death to self.

## "HOT COALS OF FIRE"

"Hot coals of fire" represent a deeper inner cleansing, a purging, not of "sin" but of our very "self." Hot coals of fire represent the things in our own lives that we must let go of. In spite of the darkness, confusion and discouragement that we are experiencing, we must carry our hot coals of fire to the Incense Altar (just like the priests did).[202]

So, yes, "fire" is a symbol of God's Love, but He also uses it to correct, purify and cleanse us. Hebrews 12:29 tells us that "God is a consuming fire." God wants to purge from us "anything that is not of Him," and that includes things such as self-love, self-confidence, self-reliance,

self-will, self-interests, self-seeking, self-preservation and self-esteem. These things are not necessarily sin, but because they are "not of faith," they
can and will quench His Spirit in us. Remember
1 Thessalonians 5:23 and 2 Corinthians 7:1. Both
these Scriptures tell us that as *believers* we must
not only have our soul sanctified but also our spirit
must be purified.

Hot coals of fire then represent the difficult
situations that each of us face in our walk toward
God and being conformed to His image. We have
to carry these hot coals of fire into the Holy Place
and put them on the Incense Altar, in spite of the
darkness, in spite of the confusion and in spite
of the discouragement we might be experiencing.
We must know that God loves us, that He is surrounding us with His presence and urging us on.
We must "hope against hope," which means we
must "walk on in darkness" but nevertheless "see
the Light."

Because of Jesus and what He has done for
us, the way to the Holy of Holies has already been
opened and we are already "positionally" clothed
in His righteousness. The moment Christ died for
our sins, the veil to the Holy of Holies was torn
and from then on the way to the Holy of Holies
was opened for us. God reaches out and meets
us at the Incense Altar.[203] Hebrews 10:19 tells us
we have "boldness to enter into the holiest by the
blood of Jesus."

God wants to purge from us "anything that is not of Him," and that includes things such as self-love, self-confidence, self-reliance, self-will, self-interests, self-seeking, self-preser-vation and self-esteem.

But in order for us to daily *enter His presence*, we must be like those priests and carry those hot coals of fire (the death of self), wholly and completely burnt, right up to God's presence at the Golden Altar. There is <u>no</u> other access or pathway to God. *His death is the provision that opens the door for us, but only by personally appropriating His sacrifice are we allowed to enter the inner sanctuary where He now dwells.*

Therefore, our experiential union with God can only come about through the two altars! The fire that consumed the sacrifice at the Brazen Altar is the same holy fire that causes the perfume to ascend on the Incense Altar. There is no other pathway to intimacy. God makes us one with Himself only through the fire.

## THE INCENSE ALTAR

The Incense Altar in the Holy Place of Solomon's Temple was the place that God heard and answered the priests' prayers. As we said before, it actually sat in the Holy Place next to the veil. However, many places in Scripture hint that this altar actually was "within the veil in the Holiest of all." Exodus 30:6 tells us: "And thou shalt put it [the Incense Altar] before the veil." Also Revelation 8:3: "...there was given unto him much incense, that he should offer it with the prayers of all saints upon *the golden altar which was before the throne.*" And finally Hebrews 9:2–4: "For there was a tabernacle made; the first, wherein was the candlestick, and the table, and the shewbread; which is called the sanctuary (the Holy Place). And after the second veil, the tabernacle which is called *the Holiest of all; which had the golden censer.*"

The Bible presents the Incense Altar as if it were in the Holy of Holies, when it actually sat in the Holy Place. This, I believe, is analogous of our dual position as believers in Christ. "Positionally," we are at one with the Lord in the Holy of Holies, but "experientially," as long as we are human, we can only stand in the Holy Place (if we are cleansed). In other words, we are saved and positionally sanctified, but like the priests, we must continually deal with our sin and self.

So when you think of the Altar of Incense, always think of it as an extension or a part of the Holy of Holies. This Golden Altar, at the heart of the temple, was called "the Altar before the Lord" and was considered in God's eyes to be the most sacred part of the temple and the most holy piece of furniture (except for the Ark of the Covenant with its Mercy Seat covering in the Holy of Holies).[204] The inscription on the Incense Altar read, "He ever liveth to make intercession for us." The priests themselves yearned to do service at this altar, as it was the most beloved ministry in the temple. They believed that whoever did service there would be highly rewarded by God. Thus, the Incense Altar represented the high calling and the high standing of the priest. (*Holy Vessels and Furniture of the Tabernacle*, Samuel Bagster and Sons, London 1870)[205]

The Golden Incense Altar was a place of worship, communion and fellowship that opened the way to the Holy of Holies where God's glory dwelt. There were no sacrifices on this altar, only the offering of incense. *Incense was the result of a sacrifice already given on the Brazen Altar.* The incense used on this Golden Altar was *never* presented to the Lord without *first* being completely burnt[206] and then beaten small.[207] You can see the analogy here with our own walk with the Lord. Only death of self (where we are beaten small) allows us to meet with Him and become one.

Keeping the fire on this altar continually burning was also necessary in order to symbolize uninterrupted communion and worship of God. The priests offered this incense three times a day as a fragrant memorial of the presence of God—in the morning, when they trimmed the lamps, and at evening.

The Incense Altar is the place in our hearts where God's Spirit—His Life—and our spirit (if we are clean) become one, not only positionally but also experientially.

Making this analogy personal, entering God's presence at the Incense Altar of our hearts is contingent upon the sanctification of our soul and the purification of our spirit. Jesus' blood gives us the boldness to enter, but only *the sanctification of our soul (the Inner Court) and the purification of our spirit (the Holy Place) allows us to experience His presence.* The veil has already been rent, so there is no barrier hindering our approach to Him. Thus, the basis of our fellowship is completely dependent upon the cutting away of the soulish things in our lives and the cleansing of any defilement of our spirits. As Hebrews 10:19, 22 urges, "Let us draw near with a true heart [a cleansed and purified heart] in full assurance of faith...[with] boldness to enter into the holiest..."

*The Incense Altar is the place in our hearts where God's Spirit—His Life—and our spirit (if we are clean) become one, not only positionally but also experientially.* This is where we worship Him, where He hears our prayers and where we will see His Love as we never have before.

### HISTORY OF THE INCENSE ALTAR

Allow me to briefly go over the history of the Incense Altar, because it's so fascinating and so important that we understand its significance in our own walk toward the Lord. It also shows the extremes God has gone to convey its importance to us.[208]

First of all, keep in mind that the furniture in the Tabernacle in the wilderness and the furniture in Solomon's Temple were completely different. If you remember this, it will help with some of the confusion. We are studying Solomon's Temple as a model here, not the tabernacle.

If you recall, God chose King Solomon to build "a house for His Name." (1 Chronicles 28:3–21) King Solomon's father, David, had received "the pattern" for that temple directly from the Spirit of the Lord. (vv. 11–12)[209]

First Kings 7:48 tells us that Solomon made all the vessels special for his temple (in other words, they were different from the ones used in the tabernacle). First Chronicles 28:14 tells us that Solomon used "pure gold" for all the furniture, the lamps, the tables and all the other bowls and cups, *but for the Incense Altar he used only wood and "refined gold by weight"* (v. 18), which means he purged the gold, strained it and only took an extract of it. What this is saying is that the Incense Altar was not as pure as the golden Shewbread tables or the golden Lampstands. This little detail is very significant as you will see in just a moment.

So first understand that there was a difference in the making of the vessels for the temple. They were not all the same. The Incense Altar was made of gold and cedar wood. It was not pure gold as were the other pieces of furniture. The Septuagint version of the Bible validates this—"it was made from cedar wood covered with refined gold." So even though it was called the Golden Altar, it was still wood covered with gold.[210] In Ezekiel 41:22, speaking of Solomon's Temple, the Incense Altar is still called the Altar of Wood.

The significance of this is that, even in this small detail, God is confirming a very important fact. We have a "dual" spirit. We still have a human spirit (wood), and yet at the same time it is united with God's Spirit (gold). Even in the making of the Incense Altar, this fact is validated.

See how fascinating all of this is?

## INCENSE IS LIKE OUR PRAYERS

In Malachi 1:11, God says, "For from the rising of the sun even unto the going down of the same My Name shall be great among the Gentiles; *and in every place incense shall be offered unto My Name, and a pure offering: for My Name shall be great among the heathen, saith the* LORD *of hosts."*

The Incense Altar was a sacred space—the place that God made His presence known. The priests could see the smoke and cloud rise from the Altar and penetrate the veil to the Holy of Holies, but they themselves could not go in.

Psalm 141:2 tells us that incense is likened to our prayers.[211] Our prayers are like a sweet smelling savor to the Lord. But fire had to be applied to the incense in order to produce the right aroma. This Altar is always identified with Jesus and becoming one with Him. This is the place, if our spirit has been purified, that God can once again direct our souls.

Psalm 51:16–17 tells us that God is not looking for a sacrifice but a broken spirit and a contrite heart. "For thou desirest not sacrifice; else would I give it; thou delightest not in burnt offering. *The sacrifices of God are a broken spirit: a broken and contrite heart, O God, thou will not despise."*[212]

## SWEET AROMA OF LOVE

Incense in the Bible also symbolizes the *fragrance of a life*. A good savor means a holy and pure life; a bad savor means an unholy life or an impure life. That sweet fragrance "before the Lord" assures us of access to His throne.

In 2 Corinthians 2:14–16, Paul tells us that God manifests "the savor of His knowledge by us in every place." In other words, when we are before Him and loving Him as He desires, we will manifest

His Life and His fragrance wherever we go. Now, to some people this fragrance will be the "savor of Life," and they will be drawn toward Christ as they fellowship with us. To others, however, the fragrance in our life will be the "savor of death," and those people will be offended at us and often flee from our presence.

When sin and self no longer form a barrier and quench God's Spirit, a sweet aroma can come forth from our lives. That incense rises up to God as an acceptable offering. It's the result of the sanctification of our soul and spirit, i.e., *the crucifying of our flesh* and *the purifying of our spirit.* In other words, in order for us to *enter God's presence*, we must be like those hot coals of fire, wholly and completely burnt. There is <u>no</u> other access or pathway to God. *His death is the provision that opens the door for us, but only by our personally passing through the place of sacrifice and carried as hot burnt embers are we allowed to enter the inner sanctuary where God dwells.*

*When sin and self no longer form a barrier and quench God's Spirit, a sweet aroma can come forth from our lives.*

The wholly burnt offering on the Brazen Altar testified that sin had been eradicated and the believer was accepted, just as the live coal on the Incense Altar demonstrated a deeper death of "self." The resulting incense cloud and aroma that arose was pleasing to God. As Ephesians 5:2 exhorts us, "Walk in Love, as Christ also hath loved us, and hath given Himself for us an *offering* and a *sacrifice* to God for a sweet smelling savor."

*God wants us to be like those priests who did not stop at the Brazen Altar but carried those hot embers of a wholly burnt sacrifice right into the Holy Place and presented them there before God's presence as a sweet smelling aroma.* He wants us to willingly allow Him to burn up all that He knows is unnecessary in our lives, so that we can *boldly* make our approach to Him.

I read a very interesting article about the importance of incense and our sense of smell from a Mr. Grant Luton (www.bethtikkun. com). Listen to what he has to say:

"Incense is beaten fine and then burned on the Altar of Incense. It represents prayers, rising to the Lord. Incense is experienced via the sense of smell. This sense is unique amongst our five senses. Sight and hearing operate at a distance from the thing perceived. Touch and taste require direct contact with the thing experienced, and so might be understood as the fleshly senses, and vision and hearing as the spiritual. The sense of smell, however, is somewhere between; we do not require direct contact with the thing smelled, but perceive via the nostril particles of the thing sensed. The nostril is unique in Scripture; in Genesis 2:7, God breathed the soul of His life into Adam's **nose, the place where the spirit and the flesh come together** in Adam. God breathed air (physical) and His Neshama, His soul life (spiritual), into Adam. We need to keep breathing physical air for life, but we also need our soul and spirit to breathe; our spiritual air is the Scriptures. If we are cut off from the Word, we die through lack of spiritual oxygen."

I'm not sure that I agree with his theory here, but I found this article quite fascinating, since for the last year and a half I have dealt with the reconstruction of my own nostrils, a lack of the sense of smell and also not being able to read the Scriptures (because I wasn't able to see). I, too, just as he said, was dying from a lack of spiritual oxygen as my spirit was unable to breathe both physically and spiritually

## TURNING THE DARKNESS INTO LIGHT

When the light goes out in our own lives because of trials and adversities, that's when we need to depend upon the reliability of God's

Word. When walking through our own Valley of the Shadow of Death and our own Valley of Baca, we can turn the darkness into light, the crisis into a blessing and our weakness into more strength by continuing to "hope" in the Lord and His Word.[213]

But remember what we talked about in Chapter One, "the darkness from above." It means God's presence and is sometimes even called "the cloud of His presence." Here are some of the passages we reviewed: Psalm 97:2: "Clouds and darkness are round about Him..." Exodus 19:9: "I come to thee in a thick cloud..." Even 1 Kings 8:10 tells us that the Holy Place of Solomon's Temple was filled with the dark cloud of His presence and the priests were not even able to stand. Traversing the Holy Place was very difficult as only the ten Candlesticks gave some light. In our walk with the Lord, the same can be true. This is where we must depend upon the "chain of hope," knowing that Jesus is not only with us but is also directing us to the Incense Altar of our hearts.

The enemy and all his hordes are *not* able to enter the Holy Place (as they can in the Inner Court if we give them a hole), but when we hold on to our self-centered thoughts and our self-consumed ways, we give the enemy a handle to once again attack. Doubt, misunderstanding, confusion and a lack of hope allow the enemy an inroad.

So the Holy Place seems to be the place where we *hope against hope.* But it's also the place we can turn the darkness into light if we know what to do and how to do it.

## CHART 5 D—THE PLACE GOD MEETS WITH US

The Incense Altar, then, is symbolic of the place in our hearts where God meets with us. When sin and self no longer form a barrier preventing our approach to God, a sweet aroma can come up before Him. Because "self" has been wholly burnt, His Life can come forth as a sweet savor.[214]

CHART 5D | **The Place God Meets with Us**

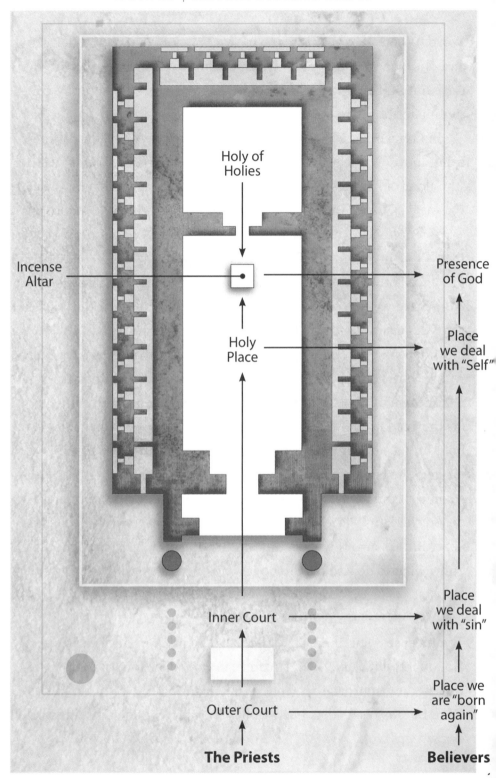

Holy of
Holies

Incense
Altar

Presence
of God

Place
we deal
with "Self"

Holy
Place

Inner Court

Place
we deal
with "sin"

Place we
are "born
again"

Outer Court

**The Priests**

**Believers**

One of the main reasons God has put us in the sanctification and purifying process is so that He might bring us near to Him (in order to fellowship). Numbers 16:9 validates this: "Seemeth it but a small thing unto you, that the God of Israel hath separated you [consecrated you] from the congregation of Israel, to bring you near to Himself...?" No veil now hinders our spiritual approach to God, but we must be holy and pure before we can come before the Throne of Grace. Our motives must be sifted and scrutinized. There can be no self-exultation or self-glorying. We cannot make our own incense. Self has no place in the Holy Place; we must glory only in Him.

In other words, He separates the holy from the profane and sets the purified apart. (Remember the purifying process of gold: first He melts it, then He binds it, and finally, He separates it.) All of this in order to bring us closer to Him. "Self" needs to be burned up on the Brazen Altar of our souls so that our spiritual union with the Lord can be deepened at the Incense Altar of our hearts.

## THE PLACE OUR PRAYERS ARE HEARD AND ANSWERED

The Incense Altar is not only where we meet with the Lord and worship Him; it's also the place that He hears our prayers. Throughout Scripture our prayers are said to ascend to God as sweet incense. Listen to Revelation 8:3: "And another angel came and stood at the altar, having a golden censer; and there was given unto him much incense, that he should offer it with the prayers of all saints upon the *Golden Altar which was before the throne.*"

"Let [our] prayer be set forth before Thee as incense; and the lifting up of [our] hands as the evening sacrifice." (Psalm 141:2)

The Incense Altar is where we make our requests known to the Lord.[215] But He will not be able to hear our prayers until we come all the way to this Golden Altar. Now, it's not that we must become "perfect"

The Incense
Altar is not
only where
we meet with
the Lord and
worship Him;
it's also the
place that
He hears our
prayers.

in order to approach this altar (only Jesus could do that), but simply continue to make those moment-by-moment "faith choices" to confess our sins and give them to Him. It all boils down to a second-by-second faith walk. Staying clean (not perfect) is what keeps us at this altar. Thus, one of the reasons why we don't get the results from praying that we expected or hoped for is that we have let doubt or unbelief or frustration to filter in and self-life has taken over. When we become experientially one with God's Spirit, however (even for just a few moments), He will hear our prayers and He promises to answer them. At that time, we can be assured that He not only will hear us but that He will also answer us in His timing and in His way.[216]

## A PERSONAL EXAMPLE: MY ANSWER TO PRAYER ON FEBRUARY 4, 2014

Healing is a huge theological subject, and I am not at all qualified to speak on it or teach it. I believe God's Word absolutely, which tells us over and over again that we are "healed by (Christ's) stripes" and that He will heal us of all our diseases. I believe this completely. The confusing part to all of us is *His* timing for that healing and how that healing will take place in each of our lives.

I have had thousands of people, plus my family and my close friends, praying for over a year for my total healing, but God has chosen His own way of healing for me. I've had three huge cancer operations, radical radiation, two return bouts with the cancer and some heart issues. My plan has always been to listen to His Spirit and not get in front of Him or behind Him.

About two months ago, I was particularly sick, but as usual I took my Bible to read before I went to bed. As I was face down on the floor worshiping the Lord, He very clearly led me to read Psalm 118.

Now my prayer all this past year has been "my total healing if possible" and that He would glorify Himself in doing so. I started reading in earnest when David says in verse 5: "I called upon the LORD in distress; the LORD answered me, and set me in a large place." I became even more interested when verse 14 talks about the Lord being my strength, because that had been my prayer all along.

But I became absolutely dissolved into tears when I read in verses 17–18: "I shall not die, but live, and declare the works of the LORD." Then, He confirms it again: "The LORD has chastened me sore: but He hath not given me over unto death." I knew those Scriptures were for me. I cried all night long, knowing in my heart that He had touched me.

Let me back up a little so you can understand what had gone on in the previous three weeks. Monday, January 13, I had a horrible setback and ended up in the hospital emergency room. They found two things: one, a small lesion (tumor) on the left frontal lobe of my brain and also some suspicious cancer cells in the brain fluid itself. I was having horrific headaches and vomiting. Then three weeks later, on February 4, I got the above Scriptures.

I didn't tell anyone until one week later. All three doctors called. They all told me the new scans showed that the tumor in the brain was absolutely gone and they could find no cancer cells in the brain fluid. They didn't go so far as to say it was a "medical miracle," but one did say he had heard of such a thing but never seen it.

I, of course, wanted to shout God's praise from the rooftops.

I've been given a temporal promise. The doctors have confirmed it. I believe the promise, and I trust Him to fully perform that promise in His timing and way.

Can everyone expect a miraculous healing? We see it happen in the Bible over and over again, but we also see that Job was not healed immediately nor was Paul. So, again, it's God's will whether we are instantly healed or whether we are healed over a period of time or whether we are healed in a way only God can do.

Why do some get healed instantly and others go through agony and suffering? I don't know. Romans 11:33 gives us a hint: "His ways are past finding out!" I don't pretend to understand it. I just know I believe it and I trust Him.

Our prayer should always simply be "not my will, but Thine." (Matthew 26:39)

## WAITING ON GOD

So some prayers are answered immediately and miraculously at the Incense Altar, but other prayers seem to take a lifetime to be answered.[217] The Holy Place is where we "wait on the Lord" and His timing.

The Hebrew word for "wait" is *qavah* (*Strong's #6960*), which means "**to literally bind together by twisting**." It means to be coiled. How cool is that, because that is exactly what happens at the Incense Altar. We bind together with the Lord by the twisting and the coiling of the Incense cloud and our prayers. It is synonymous with the word "hope." It simply means that while we are waiting for all God's promises to be fulfilled, we have bound ourselves together with Him so we have become "one."

To those who love God, *hope is promised* and *is demonstrated by a new strength*. "They that *wait* upon [hope in] the LORD shall renew their strength; they shall mount up with wings as eagles; they shall run, and not be weary; and they shall walk, and not faint." (Isaiah 40:31)

Psalm 40:1 tells us: "I waited patiently for the LORD; and He inclined unto me, and heard my cry."

Another Hebrew word for "wait" is *chabah* (*Strong's #2442*), which means to adhere to, to await, to long for. Psalm 33:20 tells us: "Our soul waiteth for the LORD: He is our help and our shield." Waiting for the Lord and His answers is part of our responsibility and a big part of restoring our hope.[218]

## The Climax of our Relationship with Him (Becoming One)

I find it interesting that all of Israel had access to the Outer Courts of Solomon's Temple, but only the sanctified priests had access to the Incense Altar in the Holy Place. And it's the same with us. The whole redeemed Church of God has access to the Outer Courts, but only the sanctified and consecrated believers have access to the Incense Altar where God now dwells and answers our prayers.

Sacrificing ourselves as a wholly burnt offering on the Brazen Altar, carrying those hot coals of fire as a symbol of our burnt and crucified life, placing them on the Incense Altar, and watching as the perfume and the fire become one is a graphic picture of what it means to truly love Him.

Ephesians 5:1–2 tells us: "Be ye followers of God, as dear children; and walk in Love, as Christ also hath loved us, and *hath given Himself for us* an offering and a sacrifice to God for a sweet smelling savor."

Our soul's natural strength is broken and dealt with on the Brazen Altar, but it's not until we reach the Incense Altar that God can truly rule and reign in our lives. *The Incense Altar represents our spiritual union with God.* It represents our oneness and our communion with

Him. It simply means our spirit has been purified and strengthened so that it is now able to freely direct our soul in all things.

This spiritual union becomes the climax of our relationship with Him here on earth. We have finally become one (conformed to His image), *even if it's just for a moment.* This is the completion, the perfection and

the fullness of God that He has designed for every one of us. Everything on the *inside* and everything on the *outside* has finally become Christ's.

John 17 expresses it this way: "That they all may be one; as Thou, Father, art in Me, and I in Thee, that they also may be *one in us*...Father, I

*Worshiping the Lord "in the beauty of holiness" signifies that all known sin and self have been dealt with and Jesus' Life is freed to come forth.*

will that they also, whom Thou hast given Me, *be with Me where I am;* that they may behold My glory, which Thou hast given Me...that the Love wherewith Thou hast loved Me may be in them, and I in them." (vv. 21, 24, 26)

At this point, we are united like in marriage, fused and intermingled as the fire and the incense cloud. **We are loving Him and in return He is loving us.** We have become enveloped and possessed by Him.

God uses *marriage* throughout Scripture to convey His most intimate truths. Marriage is one of His "word pictures." Therefore, I don't believe that it's an accident that the different aspects of the marriage "act" perfectly exemplify the difference between having a *beginning knowledge of God* through salvation and *knowing Him intimately* through the sanctification of our soul and the purification of our spirit.

Now, please don't misunderstand me. I don't believe we will ever experience a complete or a permanent union of our spirits while we are in our physical bodies here on earth. There will always be more sin and self for us to deal with. Only Jesus could enjoy a perfect and permanent union with the Father because He was and is God. *Full, eternal and incorruptible union happens only when we reach heaven and are glorified.* (But this Incense Altar is significant because it represents not only our humanity here and now but also our position in Christ in the coming kingdom.)

## The Beauty of Holiness

When we become "one" with God through the sanctification and purification of our soul and spirit, we not only will radiate the fragrance of His Life but also the "beauty of His holiness."[219]

What does "the beauty of holiness" really mean?

Worshiping the Lord "in the beauty of holiness" signifies that all known sin and self have been dealt with and Jesus' Life is freed to come forth. Just as God's supernatural Love is not our own love and His supernatural Power is not our own power, so this kind of holiness is <u>not</u> our own holiness. Jesus is the only One who is holy, and He is the only One who makes holiness beautiful. But when we are clean and open vessels, the Lord is able to shine forth <u>His</u> holiness through us.[220] In other words, as Hebrews 12:10 says, we are *"partakers of <u>His</u> holiness."* Consequently, we don't have to work at being holy, but simply relinquish ourselves to Him and allow Him to be holy through us.

Again, this does <u>not</u> mean that we will *always* stay cleansed, pure and holy. Even though "positionally" this is an accomplished fact, the reality is that none of us in this lifetime will be able to stay holy or pure on a permanent basis! Romans 3:10 confirms this: "There is none righteous, no not one." Only Jesus was consistently holy, because He is God. However, moment-by-moment, we *can* go before the Lord and surrender the things in our lives that are not of faith. Then we can be assured of being filled with the beauty of <u>His</u> holiness.

There is an infinite gap between the highest in us and the lowest in God. It's unbridgeable from our side, but He has made a way for us on His side. He is the One who is holy and set apart in absolute righteousness and goodness. He can have nothing to do with sin. If we are to approach Him at all, we must do so on His terms. We, too, must be made holy, otherwise we cannot stand in His presence. In other words, we must daily appropriate God's gift of holiness, which is required not only for worship but also for our inheritance in the coming kingdom.

## SECOND VISIT TO THE OUTER COURT

Finally, after the priests worshiped the Lord in the Holy Place, they returned to the Outer Court where they again ministered to the needs of the "congregation" and to share their joy. The priests first held up the vessels they had used during the service in the sanctuary, then laid them down and extended their hands over the congregation in love, reciting a priestly blessing.[221]

If you look closely, you will see that the songs of praise and thanksgiving that the priests sang in the morning before they had gone through the Inner Court Ritual[222] were all about **God's loving kindness** and that "His Love (His Mercy) endures forever." (Thirty-three times it says this in Psalm 136.) The psalms the priests sang in the evening, however, were all about **God's faithfulness** and His trustworthiness.[223] It's interesting to notice that their morning praise and thanksgiving prayers were somewhat private, whereas their evening prayers, praise, singing and dancing were "in front of the whole congregation of saints." In other words, they were public.

Upon leaving the temple sanctuary, the head priest stood upon the steps facing the congregation in the Outer Court. The rest of the priests then joined him there, and all extended their hands toward heaven and called upon the unutterable Name of God. The head priest then blessed the people and recited Scriptures. At this reading, the rest of the priests and all the people, again, fell on their faces and worshiped God. After this, the priests who were appointed as singers sang.

Then the real fun began. The priests began to sing, and oh did they sing. They used trumpets and harps and stringed instruments and organs and cymbals. The congregation would "praise the Lord,"[224] and they would dance. At three points in their song, the priestly signers would pause, sound their silver trumpets and all the people in the courtyard would prostrate themselves before God.

In Chaim Richman's book *The Holy Temple of Jerusalem*, it says: "the priestly or Levitical songs were just as important a temple function as the priestly service of sacrifice. In other words, one cannot function without the other." (p. 98)

I loved hearing this because the same thing is true for us. Experiencing God's Love and comfort and seeing His faithfulness in our lives during the hard times makes us want to sing with joy, dance and shout! It makes us want to share with others from the depths of our soul. This is where the "fruit of the Spirit" is truly shown forth.

## PATTERN OF THINGS TO COME

Let's go back to the temple for just a moment and look at Psalm 92:13–15. This psalm tells us that the saints who remain, endure and persevere in the Holy Place are the ones who will thrive, bloom and bring forth "fruit" in the Outer Court festivities.

It says: "Those that be planted in the house of the LORD [i.e., in the Holy Sanctuary) shall flourish in the [in the Outer] courts of our God [in front of the congregation]. They shall still bring forth fruit in old age; they shall be fat and flourishing; to show that the LORD is upright; He is my rock [faithful], and there is no unrighteousness in Him." *"Planted"* (*Strong's* #8362) means transplanted or moved or relocated (from our original, natural station in life to our supernatural location). *"In the House of the Lord"* means in the sanctuary of the temple of God. *"Shall flourish"* (*Strong's* #6524) means to break forth, to bloom, to flower, to spread, to thrive and to grow. *"In the courts of our God"* means in front of the congregation. And *"to bring forth fruit"* (*Strong's* #5107) means to germinate, bring forth and make an increase in harvest. "To show that" is the Hebrew word *nagod* (*Strong's* #5046), which means to stand boldly out, to manifest, to announce, declare and to inform. It means to reveal something that one previously did

# EXPERIENCING GOD'S LOVE AND COMFORT
### and seeing His faithfulness in our lives during the hard times

makes us want to sing with joy,
### *dance and shout!*

It makes us want to share with others

from the depths of our soul.

*This is where the "fruit of the Spirit"
is truly shown forth.*

not know or understand. Simply, to be a living example of the Lord and to glorify Him (reflect Him), not ourselves.

And this is exactly God's purpose in every circumstance of our lives—to show forth His Life, His Love and His Strength rather than our own.

"Now the end [goal, purpose] of the commandment is *Love* [Agape] out of a pure heart, and of a good conscience, and of faith unfeigned." (1 Timothy 1:5)

So it's important that we pay close attention to even some of these small details and patterns and examples because, as Hebrews tells us, they will all become important later. They are the hints and the clues and the "shadows of things to come." Even though there are over a thousand references to this Old Testament temple and its services, many of us simply overlook them. And we should not. (1 Corinthians 13:12) I believe this ancient priestly cleansing ceremony somehow refers to the Biblical pattern that God has laid out for us in order to reach our "goal"—"*the mark* for the prize of the high calling of God"—being conformed to His image so we can be prepared to rule and reign alongside of Him in the coming kingdom.

"...forgetting those things which are behind, and reaching forth unto those things which are before, [we are to] press toward the mark for the prize of the high calling of God in Christ Jesus." (Philippians 3:13–14)

# CHAPTER NINE—GOD'S PATTERN FOR OUR LIVES

1. Quote 1 Corinthians 3:16–18. What does it mean that our "body" is a temple?

2. 1 Corinthians 10:11 tells us that all that is written in the Bible is for our learning. "Now all these things happened unto them for examples and they are written for our admonition, upon which the ends of the world are come." Are you beginning to see the connection between the temple of God, our bodies and our walk with the Lord?

3. What does Hebrews 6:19 tell us is the only thing in our lives that will penetrate "behind the veil"? In other words, see God's Handprint in our lives during the difficult times.

4. As simply as you can, explain the ritual the priests went through, first in the Inner Court to cleanse sin, and then the purifying ceremony at the Incense Altar in the Holy Place for a deeper cleansing. What's the difference between these two places?

5. What then does the Outer Court represent in our own walk with the Lord? How about the Inner Court, what does it represent? And the Holy Place?

6. Explain as best you can what the priests did in the Inner Court? What pieces of furniture did they encounter? How does that apply to what we must do in our own sanctification process?

7. I think the Holy Place is the most exciting and most intriguing place in all the temple. What did the priests do here, and how does that correlate with what we must do in order to see God's Handprint in our lives?

8. What is the significance of the "hot coals of fire" in the Holy Place? What is meant by the priests having to "change clothes"? (2 Samuel 22:13; Psalm 18:12)

9. The Incense Altar is one of the major themes of this book. Tell what you now know about this interesting altar. What is its significance? Where did it sit?

10. As briefly as you can, give a little history about this fascinating altar. (Exodus 30:1–10; 1 Kings 6:22; 1 Chronicles 28:18)

11. What is this telling us we must do when we face the confusion of our own storms and valleys? Explain.

12. Why has God's presence always been portrayed in a cloud of darkness? What is the significance here? Is this true in the Holy Place also?

13. Give an example in your own life of where you had to walk in the darkness and confusion, but knew that God's Hand was there guiding you.

14. Explain how "hope against hope" comes into play in the Holy Place.

15. The Incense Altar represents "what" special place in our own walk with the Lord?

16. Some prayers are answered right away, others we have to "wait" for. "To wait for" has an unusual meaning; what is it? What does this mean to you personally?

17. Becoming one with God's Spirit is the ultimate goal. Only Jesus has done this perfectly, because He is God and He, Himself, is perfect. Have you ever experienced special moments like this— where you really felt God's presence? Share from your heart.

"...by faith (Moses) forsook Egypt,

*not fearing the wrath of the king;*

FOR HE ENDURED,

AS SEEING HIM

WHO IS INVISIBLE."

HEBREWS 11:27

# THE SUM OF
# IT ALL

God has called all of us to be His own, and He has a wonderful plan for each of our lives in the future. In order to participate in that plan, however, there are certain things we must learn to do here on earth. One of them is that we must allow the Lord to conform us into His image— i.e., empty us of ourselves and fill us with Himself. We must also learn to love as He desires, share His wisdom when He desires and always depend upon His power. Unfortunately, this total change of character comes at a great cost to us and is usually accomplished in the darkest times of our lives. These are the times when we are pushed to give up our own natural strength, pressed to yield our own self-centered thoughts and persuaded to surrender our own desires.

That's what the dark night of the spirit (or the purifying of spirit) is all about. This can occur at the height of our spiritual experience with the Lord as we finally reach the point where we can "see Him who is invisible." Or it can happen in one of the hardest times of our lives when everything around us is in complete disarray and the enemy is right on our heels ready to pounce.

As we learned in the last chapter, we symbolically go from the Outer Court to the Inner Court (where the Lord cleanses our soul), to the Holy Place (where the Lord purifies our spirit), and to worshiping with the Lord at the Incense Altar (where the Lord meets with us). Hope is what carries us through this whole process. If we lose our hope, we'll flounder and lose our way.

The whole point of being at the Incense Altar is that we might come *to know* the Lord intimately—to see Him who is invisible. This means not just having a "beginning knowledge" of Him, but having an "intimate and personal knowledge" of Him; a constant, continuous communion and fellowship with the Holy Spirit leading and guiding us *in the bad times as well as the good.*

## A Renewed Spirit

One of the major results of meeting the Lord at the Incense Altar of our heart is that our spirit will be instantly purified. This means that we will now have a clear conscience, a supernatural intuition and intimate fellowship with the Lord. It means that our spirit will have been renewed.

To be renewed simply means to "stand back up again" or to "reset to zero." It means a spirit that has been restored back to its original image. As Psalm 103:5 declares, "...thy *youth* is renewed like the eagle's." What makes this Scripture so interesting is that after an eagle molts and loses its feathers, it literally regains new physical strength as its new feathers come in. It reminds me of the saints in the Valley of Baca who went from "strength to strength."[225]

In review, our spirit is *quickened* or made alive when God's Spirit unites with our human spirit and we are "born anew." A *purified spirit* is one that has been cleansed and all soulish entanglements have been separated. A *renewed spirit* is simply a purified spirit that is not only cleansed but now freed to serve God.

Paul notes in 2 Corinthians 4:16: "...though our outward man [our body] perish, yet the inward man [our spirit] is renewed day by day."

As we unconditionally surrender ourselves to God, we can expect a similar experience. Once our soulish powers are deflated, our spirit can once again be renewed, strengthened and endowed with power by God's Holy Spirit.

Remember, however, our spirit can only be released according to the degree of brokenness in our lives. Consequently, the more we are broken, the more God can release our spirit, and the more sensitive we can become, not only to the Lord Himself but also to others. Unless we have been truly broken and our spirit released, not only will our communication with God be hindered but also our spiritual fellowship with others will be mixed. Our conversations will simply be "soulish communication." The Spirit is what makes people "come alive."

To have a renewed spirit means our *conscience* has become cleansed, our *intuition* heightened and our *communion deepened*. Thus we *can* freely now "serve God with our spirit."[226]

## A Clear Conscience

A renewed spirit means that our conscience (the inner voice of God) is once again opened and cleansed. Our conscience is what enables God to teach us, to guide us and to communicate with

> Unless we have been truly broken and our spirit released, not only will our communication with God be hindered but also our spiritual fellowship with others will be mixed.

us. In other words, if our conscience is defiled, we won't be able to discern either His voice or His will. Consequently, the purer our conscience becomes, the clearer we will hear Him and the freer He will be to lead us.

Romans 8 tells us that the Spirit of God alone knows the mind of Christ, and He alone can make intercession for us according to the will of God. (vv. 26–27) When we're not sure how to pray, what to pray or what God's will is, the Spirit will intercede for us.

This is why it's so very important to deal with even the slightest accusation in our conscience; otherwise, our spirit will be quenched. Our conscience needs to be totally pure, both in order to hear God correctly and in order to know right from wrong.

## A Supernatural Intuition

When our spirit is renewed, our spiritual intuition becomes heightened. Remember that our conscience and our intuition work hand in hand. Our conscience advises us what is right and wrong, and our intuition leads and guides us in God's way.

Remember Proverbs 3:5–6: "Trust in the LORD with all thine heart, and lean not unto thine own understanding. In all thy ways **acknowledge Him**, and *He shall direct thy paths.*" Only a renewed spirit can give us discernment of what those paths are.

Scripture tells us: "There is a way which seemeth right unto a man, but the end thereof are *the ways of death.*" (Proverbs 14:12) This means that to the "natural man," his own self-centered intuitive ways are fine. He has no understanding that down the road, his pleasure-seeking life will eventually take its toll. This is why it's critical for believers to continually renew their spirit and to listen to their spiritual intuition to lead and guide them. Only God knows the "right way" for us to walk, and only He can guide us along that path. The moment

God's Spirit says "stop," we must be sensitive enough to stop. When He says "be careful," "watch out" or "something is amiss here," we must heed His nudging. In my own life, the times I have overlooked God's "red flag" and His gentle touch on my shoulder, I have gone down the wrong path.

## Restored Communion and Fellowship—a "Friend of God"

One of the greatest blessings of a renewed spirit is the communion, fellowship and friendship with God that results. *Friendship simply means a union of two wills.* Friendship begets intimacy, and intimacy comes from abiding and sharing common ideals, goals, objectives and secrets. Friendship with God, like human friendship, means not allowing anything to hinder our face-to-face relationship. It's being governed and constrained purely by our love for each other. A friend of God is one in whom God confides and shares secret things. It's not only experiencing His company but also conversing with Him and doing all that He asks.

Jesus declares in John 15:14–15: "Ye are my friends, if you do whatever I command you. Henceforth I call you not servants; for the servant knoweth not what his lord doeth; but I have called you friends; for all things that I have heard of my Father I have made known unto you."

Some great Biblical examples of those who had an intimate friendship with God are: *Abraham* in Genesis 17:1–10, where he talks with God and also in James 2:23 where he is called "a friend of God." And *Moses* in Deuteronomy 5:4 and Exodus 33:11, where he, too, sees God's face. As a result, Moses' own face began to shine with the glory of God. These anointed men had the privilege of "seeing" God face-to-face and being His "friend."

Our face, too, will shine as we dwell in God's presence. An unusual serenity and peacefulness will spread over our souls as it becomes apparent that the God of the universe is continually at our side.

## SECRET REVELATIONS

A friend of God is one to whom the Lord often reveals His secret will. And He does so both through His Word and through His Spirit, not through our own reason or our own thoughts. This is a hard concept for many very intelligent people, but the Bible tells us that it's

*A friend of God is one to whom the Lord often reveals His secret will.*

"not by might [or our own strength], but by God's Spirit [a heightened intuition]" that things are made known to us.[227] According to 1 Corinthians 2:10–12: "God hath revealed them [identified them] unto us by His Spirit: for the Spirit searcheth all things, yea, the deep things of God.... Now we have received, not the spirit of the world, but the Spirit who is of God; that we might know the things that are freely given to us of God."

Therefore, the more abandoned and surrendered we can become to God's Spirit, the more insight and revelation we will have. Everyone who walks intimately with God will enjoy His secret communication and the bestowing of His revelations. This is often called God's anointing or "His presence to give light."

The Old Testament word for "anoint" means *oil producing light.* And this is exactly what God means here. God anoints us with His presence (and His oil producing light) and gives us His supernatural revelation—supernatural wisdom and understanding.

This book has been an exercise in "revelation" for me as God has consistently revealed new and wonderful spiritual insights. Scriptures that I have read for years are popping off the page with new meaning. Sometimes the Lord wakes me up in the middle of the night to pour out page upon page of specifically worded sentences, thoughts and ideas. Other nights I'm unable to sleep because I'm so excited to see what He is going to reveal the next day. That may sound silly, but it's the truth. Constantly, if I am faithful to wait upon Him with a pure and renewed spirit and ask for revelation, God fills in the "gaps" for me. He teaches me deep things I don't understand with my natural mind. I often think of revelation as God simply "turning the lights on" for me. In other words, only God's Spirit knows what God's thoughts are. Man in his natural state can never comprehend the "deep things of God," as they require special spiritual enlightenment. Only through our renewed spirit can we perceive the wondrous things of God. And only through our spirit can He lead and guide us as He intends.

As we have seen in the last few chapters, God's Word and His Spirit work alongside of each other. God's Spirit works alongside God's Word to give us supernatural revelation not only about God's will but also about ourselves. In other words, God's Spirit enables us to see our own selves as we truly are. Only by His Word and His Spirit working together can our lives begin to change *from the inside out.*

*Repentance and the Cross* are the ways God has laid out in Scripture for us to deal with our sin. *Revelation and the Cross* are the ways God has chosen for us to deal with our self. Through our renewed spirit, God will reveal what part of our self needs to be dealt with. Then it's our responsibility to bring that self to the Cross and surrender it to God.

## INTIMATE KNOWLEDGE OF GOD

A renewed spirit is what allows us to enjoy an intimate relationship with the Lord. It means dwelling in His presence no matter what our circumstances are and enjoying a peace and a joy that passes all human understanding. This is the type of "knowledge" that becomes the basis of our hope and the climax of our Christian walk. This is what allows us to experience His Love and what enables us to see His faithfulness. This is what allows us to "see Him who is invisible."

As Acts 2:25 says, "I foresaw the Lord always before my face, for He is on my right hand, ***that I should not be moved.***" This Scripture says it all. Seeing Him who is invisible is the answer to the hopelessness so many of us are experiencing right now in our walk with the Lord and also the answer as to how we endure our night seasons.

### An Example: Richard Wurmbrand

The most important principle of this whole book is knowing that God is faithful. When we know that, we'll be able to "see Him" in all the little things as we pass through the darkness and the confusion of our night seasons. Acknowledging Him in the darkness is the only thing that will open our eyes to the truth—that *He is with us, that He loves us and that we can endure.*

*A renewed spirit is what allows us to enjoy an intimate relationship with the Lord.*

An incredible example of this was Richard Wurmbrand, a Romanian pastor back in the 1940's who spent fourteen years in a Communist prison. He is an amazing example of hope in the night seasons and of one who saw "Him who is invisible."

Pastor Wurmbrand was involved in the Christian Romanian underground movement. He met with groups of Christians in homes, basements, army barracks, and in woods, knowing full well what the cost of his actions could be. The Communists were determined to stamp out the Christians so that they could control the churches for their own purposes. Eventually the pastor and his Christian brothers and sisters were exposed and captured.

Taken from his wife and son in 1948, Pastor Wurmbrand spent three years in a slave labor camp, three years in solitary confinement, and five more years in a mass cell. He was finally released after many years, only to be arrested two years later and sentenced to another twenty-five years. He was released for good in 1964. His wife was also arrested and confined to another prison where the women were repeatedly raped, made to work at hard labor, forced to eat grass and rats and snakes, and required to stand alone for hours at a time. At the time of their arrest, their son was only nine years old. He was left to roam the streets of their city.

Many of the Christians who were arrested at the same time lost their faith as they were brainwashed by the Communists. Some even joined the party and denounced their own brothers and sisters. It was a tragic and horrendous time. The human torture was beyond anything one could ever imagine or describe. One prisoner said, "All the Biblical descriptions of hell and the pain of *Dante's Inferno* are nothing compared with the torture in the Communist prisons."

Loving God with his whole being, Pastor Wurmbrand would not let any circumstance or any emotion separate him from his beloved Lord. Someone asked him, "How did you resist the brainwashing?" The pastor replied, "If your heart is truly cleansed by the Love of Christ and your heart loves Him back, you can resist any torture.... *God will judge us, not on how much we had to endure but on how much we loved.*"

Wurmbrand said he was not frustrated by all the years that he lost in prison because he also saw beautiful things happen there. He saw great saints and heroes of all kinds, much like the first-century church. "Christians could be happy even there," he said. The reason they could be happy was that "*they saw the Savior in the midst of everything.*"

The lesson here is that if the Spirit is truly the *master* of the body, God is always with us, no matter what is occurring in our lives. And there is always "hope." The enemy, of course, wants to discourage us with all the things that happen in our lives, but as we can see in this example, God wants to use our circumstances, no matter how difficult they are, for our learning, our growing and for His glory.

After his release from prison, Wurmbrand wrote numerous books and became the head of an international ministry called The Voice of the Martyrs, serving the persecuted church.

### WITHOUT "INTIMACY," THE ENEMY WILL OVERTAKE US

Isaiah 5:13 tells us that God's people will "go into *captivity*" if they don't know God intimately. "Captivity" simply means bondage. It means that the soulish things in our lives will prevent us from experiencing the full union with Christ that God desires and, because of that, we'll be "destroyed." Hosea 4:6 validates this also: "My people are destroyed for lack of knowledge..."

This is so true at the present time. *Rather than being overcomers, many of us are being overcome, and this is why we are crumbling in our night seasons and losing hope.*

Knowing Christ intimately is of vital importance. Philippians 3:10 tells us God wants us to "know" Him so personally that we know the power of His resurrection and the fellowship of His suffering and are being made conformable unto His death.

Consider what Matthew 25:11–12 says about the different ways we can "know" the Lord. "Afterward came also the other virgins [believers], saying, Lord, Lord, open to us. But He answered and said, Verily I say unto you, *I know you not*." The Greek word here for "know" is *oida*, which means "to know intimately." *Oida* comes from the root word *eido*, which means "to see." *These virgins had no intimate relationship with the Lord.* They did not see Him or really know Him.

On the other hand, remember Job, who acknowledged after all his trials, "I [had] heard of Thee by the hearing of the *ear* [beginning knowledge of God], but *now mine eye seeth* Thee." ("Now I have intimate, experiential knowledge of You." Job 42:5)

The fire of God's Love can push us to see and know Him *as we never have before.* Matthew 5:8 states it perfectly: the "pure in heart [and spirit] shall *see* God." In other words, the more our soul is stripped away from our spirit (the more we are conformed into His image), the clearer we will be able to see Him. ***Purity is a prerequisite for seeing Him.*** Only when our soul and spirit are cleansed can God's light shine forth and we see Him clearly.

Therefore, because God loves us so much, He often uses our difficult situations to push us toward "intimacy" with Him. He wants to commune and fellowship with us in the innermost part of our being where He dwells. He doesn't save us only to show us how much He loves us; He saves us so that we can have an intimate relationship with Him that will last forever.

# THE FIRE OF GOD'S LOVE
*can push us to see and know Him*

## *as we never have before.*

## CHART 6—THE CHAIN OF HOPE

Remember our pivotal Scripture, Hebrews 6:18–19, which says: "That by two immutable things, in which it was impossible for God to lie, we might have a strong consolation, who have fled for refuge [shelter] to lay hold upon the hope set before us: which hope we have as *an anchor of the soul*, both sure and steadfast, and *which entereth into that within the veil*."

Hope is like that. It's really two parts. It's not only the heavy "anchor" itself that holds us in place and keeps us from straying and floating away in storms; it's also the chain or the connecting "tie" or "bridge" that allows us to cross over the crevasses and the gorges and experience God's presence.

*But that anchor must first be "secured within the veil" through intimacy with the Lord in the Holy of Holies or we will float aimlessly down the river*. Securing ourselves is what will allow us to endure the dark times so we *can* continue to walk toward the unseen. Thus, *we* are the ones who determine the degree of intimacy we will have with the Lord. *Once we are sanctified—body, soul and spirit—heaven will simply be a continuation of the intimacy with Christ that we have already begun here on earth.*

Because it's costly, the question is: Are we willing to pay the price for it?

As Jesus tells us in Luke 9:62, "No man, having put his hand to the plough, and looking back, is fit for the kingdom of God."

## FOUR DEGREES OF INTIMACY

Intimacy comes from two different actions on our part: an increased cleansing of our soul from sin and a deeper relinquishment of our self-centered ways. God's Love is the only means by which we are drawn to this kind of intimacy, and His faithfulness is what will keep us there.

CHART 6 | **The Chain of Hope**

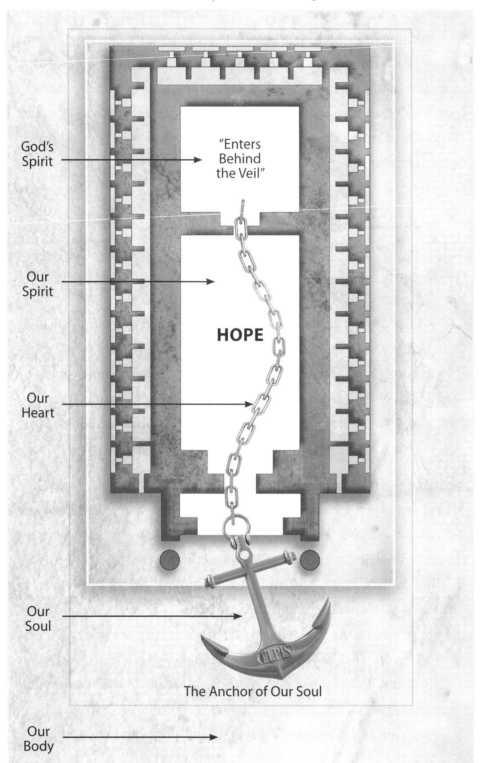

God's
Spirit

"Enters
Behind
the Veil"

Our
Spirit

**HOPE**

Our
Heart

Our
Soul

The Anchor of Our Soul

Our
Body

Nothing in life will ever give us the identity, the meaning and the purpose we need to be fulfilled as will intimacy with the Creator of the universe. Everyone else and everything else in our life fades in comparison to this. Only God can be that "perfect" Father, Provider, Protector, Companion, Lover, Spouse, who will <u>never</u> let us down, never leave us nor forsake us. (Psalm 146:3–10)

"Intimacy" seems to have four degrees:

1) Approaching the mountain (the Lord's presence) but *unable to ascend* (Exodus 19:11–12);

2) Having an intimate *vision of God*, but nothing else (many believers dwell here) (Exodus 24:9–11);

3) Proceeding *halfway up* the mountain, then stopping (because of trials) (Exodus 24:13–14);

4) *Seeing God face-to-face* at the top of the mountain (Exodus 33:11). This is what we are talking about here with intimate knowledge of God—**"seeing God face-to-face" means talking to a friend.**

Many Christians know they are "positionally" united with God. They have experienced some enjoyment with Him and have born some "fruit" in their lives. But very few of them have any idea as to what an intimate knowledge of God really means or how they go about finding it. They know *about* Christ and they possess His Name, but they have little idea as to what becoming one with Him really means on a practical day-to-day basis. As Ezekiel 33:31 declares, "...they come unto Thee... they sit before Thee as [Your] people...and they hear [Your] words, but they will not <u>do</u> them: *for with their mouth they show much love, but their heart goeth after their covetousness."*

Many of us *talk* about "intimacy" and pray earnestly for it and even exhort others to it, but how many of us *really* have that daily, personal, intimate union with God that the Bible talks about?

***How many of us are willing to be burned up with Love for God?***

## ABIDING IN HIS PRESENCE

Now, it's one thing to enter God's presence, commune there for a while and then fall away (we probably have all done this at one time or another). But being able to stay in God's presence by continually confessing and repenting of our sin and self is a whole other thing. This is what *abiding* in Him is all about. John 15 is a chapter devoted completely to abiding in the Lord. "Abide in Me, and I in you. As the branch cannot bear fruit of itself, except it abide in the vine; no more can ye, except ye abide in Me. I am the Vine, ye are the branches; he that abideth in Me, and I in him, the same bringeth forth much fruit for without Me ye can do nothing. If a man abide not in Me, he is cast forth as a branch, and is withered; and men gather them, and cast them into the fire, and they are burned." (vv. 4–6)

*Nothing in life will ever give us the identity, the meaning and the purpose we need to be fulfilled as will intimacy with the Creator of the universe.*

Abiding is important to the Lord. Abiding is not only staying in a continual intimate relationship with the Lord, it's also the key to bearing "fruit." Only as we abide in Him can we bear the "fruit" He desires.

"Abide" (*Strong's* #3306) is the Greek word *meno*, which means to stay in a given place, to remain, to dwell, to continue and *to endure*. Abiding is staying in that close relationship with the Lord at the Incense Altar. Abiding not only allows us to "see" Him but is the means by which we can endure whatever He allows in our lives. (John 15:4)

Again, entering God's presence for a moment is one thing, but remaining there through the ups and the downs of life is another. Abiding is where we learn to truly stand in His Love (John 15:10), stay in the ship regardless of the storms (Acts 27:31), and choose to *follow Him no matter where He leads*. (1 John 2:28)

So the secret to abiding, I believe, is simple. It's not only intimately knowing (*oida*) His Love; it's also seeing His faithfulness in everything that happens in our life. These are the two things that give us the unconditional "trust" that we need for endurance. Remember, it's hope that connects us to God's presence "within the veil." But it's God's Love and His faithfulness that keeps us there and that becomes the basis of our hope.

Debbie, my dear friend and co-laborer at the ministry, has just gone through a very difficult period in her life, a classic "hot coals of fire" experience in the Holy Place. She said her "faith" remained strong, but her hope totally evaporated. She felt as if there was "no light at the end of the tunnel." But when she began to make *faith choices* to praise the Lord in spite of everything, to hope in His Love and faithfulness regardless of her feelings and to take a stand against the enemy, "within minutes" she said peace began to flood her soul and she knew God had heard her. "Peace and hope," she said, "go together." They are keys to abiding.

The problem is that most of us have not been taught how to be cleansed and sanctified in the Inner Court. Thus, we're unable to even enter the Holy Place, let alone abide or remain in God's presence at the Incense Altar. Consequently, because God's Spirit has been quenched in our hearts, we're unable to experience His Love or see His faithfulness. This is how it works. If we are clean, we'll experience God's Love not only for others but also for ourselves. If, however, we are defiled by sin and self, we won't have His Love for others or experience it for ourselves. God's Love will be quenched and blocked in our hearts.[228]

This place of "abiding" is new for me. I've always been so busy, it was hard for me to stay in one place, but over the last few months I've gotten to where I love the Holy Place, its safety, its quietness, its darkness, its rest, its peace, joy, comfort...etc. I truly experience God holding me as I kneel down and prostrate myself before Him at the Incense Altar. His Love is as real as anything I will ever experience in this lifetime.

## GOD'S SECRET PLACE

In studying more about the Holy Place and the Incense Altar, I kept running into Scriptures that talked about God's "secret place" and the believers that abide there.

Could the Incense Altar of the Holy Place be God's secret place?

Listen to Psalm 91: "He that dwelleth [abideth] in the *secret place* of the most High shall abide under the shadow of the Almighty.... He shall cover thee with His feathers, and under His wings shalt thou trust... Thou shalt not be afraid for the terror by *night*...because thou hast made the LORD, which is my refuge, even the most High, thy habitation...because he hath set his love upon Me, therefore I will deliver him...because he hath known My Name...I will answer him; I will be with him in trouble." (vv. 1–15)

"Secret place" (*Strong's* #5643) means a *hiding place* or a shelter.

Psalm 31:20 speaks of it as hiding us in the secret of His presence, the place that is "nearest to Him." And Psalm 27:5 talks about being hidden "in His pavilion: in the secret of His tabernacle." And, of course, we already spoke about the "secret place of thunder" where Moses called on God and was tested. (Psalm 81:7)

Are these all connected? You decide.

## RESULTS OF INTIMACY

Let's explore what some of the other results of intimacy (becoming one with the Lord at the Incense Altar) might be:

God desires to break our outward man so that our spirit can once again be renewed and rule and reign over our soul. As we yield and forsake every self-centered aspect of our soulish life and willingly obey God, our spirit will gain control of our thoughts, emotions and desires. As Ephesians tells us, we are to "be strengthened with might by His Spirit in the inner man" (3:16) and be "strong in the Lord and in the power of His might." (6:10)

This strengthening of our spirit occurs through the Holy Spirit at the Incense Altar of our hearts. "Strengthened" is the word *kratos* in the Greek, meaning *power to rein in, mastery over self, self-control,* or better yet, *spirit-control.* God's Spirit gives our spirit strength to *put off* the habits of our flesh and to *put on* Christ.

Again, remember the saints in the Valley of Baca.[229] Even though they experienced the darkness of the Valley of Weeping, they were able to turn it around and "make a well." They went from "strength to strength." *They were overcomers!* In other words, they knew how to trust the Lord in the midst of the darkness and let the whole experience make them stronger. These pilgrims made this valley, this gorge, this canyon, a valley of praise and a well of water. It says they went from strength (in the Lord) to more strength (in the Lord). Remember also Isaiah 40:31, which says: "those who wait in the LORD [those who see the LORD in the midst of their difficult circumstances] will renew their strength." This is exactly what is happening here.

The Old Testament word for "strength" is *gibbor*, which means *to overcome.* Overcomers are simply those who choose, no matter what is going on in their lives, no matter how they feel and no matter how others are treating them, to "put off" sin and self and "put on" Christ. *An overcomer is simply one who is freed from self to serve God.*

Overcomers are the ones God will choose to assist Him in His coming kingdom. Listen to Revelation 21:7: "He that overcometh shall inherit all things; and I will be his God, and he shall be My son."

Consequently, if our "soulish ways" are not broken and our spirit has not been set free and strengthened, we really have not grown at all. ***Real advancement with God is only measured by the growth of our spirit.***

## God's Comfort

What is another important result of intimacy?

Scripture promises us that "as the sufferings of Christ abound in us, so our consolation also aboundeth by Christ."[230]

What this is saying is that the more we suffer for Christ (the more we "bar ourselves" from following what we think, what we feel and what we desire and chose instead to unconditionally follow Christ), the more He will show us His comfort, His encouragement and His support. The word "comfort" or "consolation" here is the Greek word *paraklesis* (*Strong's* #3874), which means to "call to one's side or to come to our aid." It also means "one who pleads another's case." This is exactly the role of the Holy Spirit, and 1 John 2:1–2

Overcomers are simply those who choose, no matter what is going on in their lives, no matter how they feel and no matter how others are treating them, to "put off" sin and self and "put on" Christ.

tells us that Jesus is our advocate and our defender. ***Comfort combines "encouragement" with "the alleviation of grief."***

"Comfort" simply means knowing that God is with us. Nothing else in the world matters if we know He is holding our hand. That comfort may come in the form of a Bible promise, an encouraging word from a friend or a special event in our life, but the best comfort of all comes from God Himself, who is the "God of all comfort."[231]

In Psalm 145:14, God promises to "uphold all that fall and raise up those that are bowed down." He promises to be close to those that call upon Him in truth. He promises to heal the broken in heart and bind up their wounds. He promises us that if we call upon Him, He will deliver us[232] and remember us in our low estate. He promises to free us, to liberate us, to keep us from evil and not to leave us.

What is God's purpose then for having us endure such difficult trials and suffering? Second Corinthians 1:4 tells us so that we can comfort those who are in any trouble "by the comfort wherewith we ourselves are comforted of God." *The Commentary on the Whole Bible* by Jamison, Fausset and Brown states: "Though the sufferings are many, they are swallowed up in His comfort." And later it says, this ***"comfort is likened to hope (elpis)."*** Wow!

***"Hope" is not only important in believing the Word of God for ourselves, but it's also important in walking the Word of God out for others.*** We mentioned earlier that one of the reasons why the Lord allows the trials in our lives is so that others will be encouraged by seeing how we ourselves endure affliction and suffering.[233] This is what ministers to others. They can now identify with us. We've had troubles too. And telling them how God ministered to us through our trials is what comforts them.

The first night I was in the hospital, I had a Christian nurse, and while she was bathing me, we talked about the Lord. She was having huge trials in her own life and our conversation seemed to really minister to her. Sharing our lives with others and seeing how that helps another person become our purpose as believers and are so encouraging.

### "THE FULLNESS OF JOY"

Another result of intimacy with the Lord at the Incense Altar is that when we hear His voice, we'll be overwhelmed with *joy*. Remember Psalm 16:11, which tells us: "...*in Thy presence* is fulness of joy."

The word "joy" actually means "to brighten up, to rejoice or *to be happy*." But the definition I find absolutely fascinating is that the root of the word "joy" means "to join" or "to bind together." In other words, "joy" is the result of waiting on the Lord, coming into His presence, *catching on fire with His Love and being joined or consumed in it* (which is exactly what happens at the Incense Altar as the fire and smoke envelop each other). *Joy is the result of that union and the continuing communion of our spirits.*[234] Scripture tells us that this joy is our strength (Nehemiah 8:10) and what enables us to overcome and to endure whatever situation we find ourselves in—to go from strength to strength.[235] Proverbs 17:22 validates this by saying that a merry or joyful heart makes us strong, but a broken spirit saps our strength.

If you search the Scriptures, you'll find this principle of "joy" being associated with the Lord's presence validated over and over again. For instance, consider Psalm 51:11–12: "Cast me not away from Thy presence...restore unto me the joy of Thy salvation."[236] In other words, this kind of joy is a gift directly from God and comes only as a result of our being before His presence in worship. Joy comes from being overwhelmed with His Love and His faithfulness and from *knowing that He cares* about what we are experiencing.

James 1:2–4 even tells us "to count it all JOY" when we encounter various trials. Are you kidding? Count it all joy when we get clobbered? Who can do that?

But here's the Scripture that really gets to me. It is 2 Corinthians 7:4, where Paul says, "I am **exceeding joyful** in all [my] tribulation." Now, who can say that? Have you read the "tribulations" that Paul experienced? He went through every trial and difficulty you can imagine. I, personally, have never been able to genuinely express that I was "exceedingly joyful" with all the storms we have experienced. But the deeper I go into the Holy Place of my heart and His presence at the Incense Altar, the more I understand what this Scripture is saying, and at times I can say yes, it brings me "exceeding joy."

# "JOY"
## *is the result of waiting on the Lord,*
## coming into His presence,
### *catching on fire with His Love*
# *and being joined
or consumed in it.*

When trials hit, most of us fall prey to our own emotions that can quickly spiral us *downward.* James, however, goes on by saying, *"the trying of our faith* worketh [or produces, if we allow it to] *patience. But let patience have her perfect work, that ye may be* [for the moment] *perfect and entire, wanting nothing."* In other words, we will be "entire," having learned what God was teaching us.

"Joy" is said to take possession of our whole man, which means that when we are "in the presence of the LORD," this joy gives us the strength *to withstand whatever circumstances the Lord has allowed.*[237] In other words, we will be so full of joy from being in the Lord's presence that it won't matter what our circumstances are.

Can you say this in your situation?

Jesus tells us in John 15:10–11: "If ye keep my commandments, ye shall <u>abide</u> in My Love; even as I have kept my Father's commandments, and abide in His Love. These things have I spoken unto you, that My joy might remain in you, and *that your joy may be full* [or complete]." Jesus had perfect joy because He always did the Father's will and was in constant communion with Him. Consequently, as we do the Father's will (deny ourselves, pick up our cross and follow Him), and as we commune with Him in the Holy Place of worship, our joy also will be complete.

The question is then: Why wouldn't every believer want to experience the presence of the Lord like this, with its accompanying joy and comfort?

The answer is that intimacy not only allows us to experience God's presence, comfort and joy, it's also the vehicle God uses to expose more sin and self in us. Obviously, many Christians *do not* want to see or hear any of this. Most of us know that we have more things to deal with, but we'd rather not see them yet. We'd like to be the ones who choose the time and place they are revealed. Those of us who are willing to risk the exposure of these things and who are willing to deal with them will be allowed to repeatedly enter His presence in the Holy Place. Others of us, who are not willing to follow Christ to that degree, will simply remain in the Outer Court.

Another reason we don't have that daily intimate relationship with the Lord is because of our misplaced priorities. The saying goes, "the urgent preempts the important." And this is often the case with us. Things such as work, parenthood, ministry, busyness, etc., have become more urgent in our lives than sitting at the feet of Jesus. I know; I've been there. But no matter what our reasons are, if we aren't worshiping the Lord as He would have us, we'll not only miss out enjoying His comfort but also His joy.

## HOPE FOR THE FUTURE

Another incredible result of enjoying intimacy with the Lord—that private, close and personal communion with the Lord—is that we'll be able to "see Him in the little things" that will give us "hope" that He still is involved and that He still loves us. Hope is what allows us to take that next step of trust, to pick up our cross and to endure all that the darkness brings. If we lose that connection to the Father, we'll also lose our mooring (our anchor) and our security for the future. Once that is lost, we'll find ourselves adrift and afraid. Hope not only connects us to God Himself in the Holy of Holies, it also is what helps us "see" His Hand in the circumstances of our lives. That's why I sometimes call "hope" *the bridge or the path to the unseen.* It's what enables us to spiritually "see" what we cannot see in the natural.

Psalm 146:3, 5 says: "Put not your trust in princes, nor in the son of man, in whom there is not help. ***Happy is he...whose hope is in the LORD his God.***"

We are not to hope in anything else, but the Lord, His Love and His faithfulness. Remember Habakkuk 2:4, which says: "The just shall live by **His** faithfulness." This is echoed in Romans 1:17, Galatians 3:11 and Hebrews 10:38. *The Complete Commentary on the Whole Bible* translates the latter as, "The just shall live **by the faith of Him**," meaning Christ. In other words, no matter what we see or feel, we have "hope" because of God's faithfulness toward us.

It's <u>God's</u> faithfulness and His Love that <u>our</u> hope must be built upon. Here again, we see faith, hope and Love connected. *<u>Faith</u> is the SUBSTANCE (or the belief); <u>Hope</u> is the VEHICLE (or the bridge), and <u>Love</u> is the RESULT (it's that Tree of Life at the end of the bridge). In other words, "faith" is what produces the work; "hope" is what inspires the endurance, and "Love" is the ultimate "fruit."*[238]

First Thessalonians 1:3 sums it up for us: "Remembering without ceasing your *work of faith*, and *labor of Love*, and *patience of hope*..." I find it fascinating that **our faith and our hope toward God (in this lifetime) depend totally upon <u>His</u> faithfulness and <u>His</u> Love**. But then in the future, the whole scenario is turned around and **our position and our responsibility (in the coming kingdom) will depend totally upon <u>our</u> faithfulness and <u>our</u> love toward God here and now**. This, to me, is so ironic! But it's so like God to do it this way.

**So you could say that our life here and now depends upon <u>His</u> faithfulness toward us, whereas our life in the future coming kingdom depends upon <u>our</u> faithfulness toward Him.** Remember the "good and faithful" servants whom Matthew 25 talks about and also the saints in Revelation 17:14 who were not only "called and chosen" but also "faithful."

"Hope" is not only what keeps us from sinking on the road to salvation, it's also what makes us sure and steadfast. Again, hope is the anchor (the grounding and the mooring) that prevents us from tossing and turning and falling off the bridge. When that anchor has pulled loose in our lives and we are adrift, the only way to secure it again is by choosing to rely upon our intimate knowledge of God's Love and by trusting in His faithfulness.

*Our present relationship with the Lord affects everything we think, say and do. And the impact we have on the world around us totally depends upon the impact Jesus is having in our own lives at that moment. We can't function in the present on something Jesus did for us years ago. Our relationship and our intimacy with Him needs to exist in the now.*

Are we relying upon His faithfulness right now? Are we allowing Him to complete what He started in our lives? Or have we returned to our old self-centered ways of relying upon our-selves? In spite of the anxiety and the fear that we may personally be experiencing because of the difficulties surrounding us, we **must choose** *(by faith) to trust Him. He is in control and He knows what He is doing.*

*We are not to hope in anything else, but the Lord, His Love and His faithfulness.*

Remember Psalm 89:33: "Nevertheless My lovingkindness will I not utterly take from him, nor suffer My faithfulness to fail." No matter where we are and no matter what is going on in our lives at the present moment, we must know "He will never leave us nor forsake us" and "He will [somehow] work it all together for good."

The question is: Do we believe Him and will we trust Him?

## THE FRUIT OF THE SPIRIT IS LOVE

Probably one of the most important results of intimacy with the Lord is genuine "Agape Love." "Love out of a pure heart" is the ultimate fruit that God is looking for in all of our lives. And it only comes from being one with the Lord.

Scripture tells us that the "fruit of Love" is the barometer or the measuring stick that determines whether or not we will receive the prize at the end of the "race." Being conformed to His image of Love is the "mark of the high calling." First Corinthians 3:12–15 validates this: "If any man's work [or fruit] abide which he hath built thereupon, he shall receive a reward. If any man's work shall be burned, he shall suffer loss: but he himself shall be saved; yet so as by fire." The difference here is that one man's work or "fruit" (gold, silver and precious stones) is "produced by the Spirit of God," whereas the other man's work (wood, hay and stubble) is "produced by his flesh."

The "fruit" that God is talking about here is His Love, the ultimate "fruit of the Spirit." *Agape* Love is received and poured into our hearts the moment we invite Christ to take control of our lives. He is that Love. "Everyone that loveth is born of God, and knoweth God. He that loveth not knoweth not God; for *God is Agape*." (1 John 4:7–8) But the whole reason God gives us His Love is so that we can pass that Love on to others.[239]

"Works of the Spirit" might be as simple as reaching out to someone who in the past has ignored us or snubbed us; it might be doing something Godly for someone who has betrayed us, belittled us, or used us, and it might be praying for someone who has told lies about us. Works of the Spirit are things that we allow the Holy Spirit to do through us; things we know we cannot do in the "flesh." In other words, it's *doing what Jesus would do.* It entails smiling at someone on the street who looks sad or telling someone they "look pretty" or commenting on someone's skill. You will be so surprised at how these little things put a smile on that person's face and how good it will make you feel to have shared God's Love. These are the kind of "works" (from the heart) that the Lord will classify as gold, silver, and precious stones.[240]

Our motive in doing these "works" is not trying to *earn* or *work* our way to heaven, but simply allowing God to have His way in us. We have already surrendered our lives to Him, and we have chosen to be cleansed vessels, so He is now free to produce *HIS* fruit through us.

The defining line between "works of the Spirit" and "works of the flesh" is not only *who* accomplishes the work but also *who* gets the glory. The Lord or us?

## Glorifying Him

Speaking of glory, another result of intimacy with God is that we will be able to genuinely glorify (reflect) God.

The word "glorify" is *kabod* in the Hebrew and *doxazo* in the Greek. It means to reflect, show forth, demonstrate and express the image of an object or person. *It means to add something to someone's character that in itself it does not have.* It's the result of being conformed into "Christ's image of Love." In the New Testament, *doxazo* can mean to signify, extol and ascribe honor to.[241] According to the Bible, to glorify God simply means to manifest or reflect Christ's innate image and His character.[242]

God doesn't want us to just have a *revelation of Christ,* He wants us to be *a reproduction of Christ.* He wants to form Christ in us so that inwardly we can continue to commune and fellowship with Him, but outwardly we can reflect Him in all that we do.

The proof of our being "like Christ" is shown by *what we do.* All that we do—whether at home, at the office, shopping, on trips, every place we go and everything we do—should bear "fruit" and show that we belong to God. It's not that our life will be "perfect" and that we will breeze through all our trials and storms, but at least all our actions will prove that we belong to Him and that we also have an intimate Love-relationship with Him. Isaiah 24:15 exhorts us to even glorify Him *"in the fires."*

Paul elaborates in 2 Corinthians 6:4–10: "...approving ourselves as the ministers of God, in much patience, in afflictions, in necessities, in distresses, in stripes, in imprisonments, in tumults, in labors, in watchings, in fastings; by pureness, by knowledge, by long suffering, by kindness, by the Holy Ghost, by love unfeigned, by the word of truth, by the power of God, by the armor of righteousness on the right hand and on the left, by honor and dishonor, by evil report and good report; as deceivers, and yet true; as unknown, and yet well known; as dying, and, behold, we live; as chastened, and not killed; as sorrowful, yet always rejoicing; as poor, yet making many rich; as having nothing, and yet possessing all things."

Glory seems to be the vehicle that conveys and reveals the true presence of God in our lives. In Scripture, *"glory" means to possess the character, beauty and majesty that belong to the Lord. It means an exact representation of His being, His presence, His essence, His soul, His Life and His Name.* To glorify God is to manifest all that He is.

"Ye are the light of the world. A city that is set on an hill cannot be hid. Neither do men light a candle, and put it under a bushel, but on a candlestick; and it giveth light unto all that are in the house. Let your light so shine before men, that they may see your good works, and glorify your Father which is in heaven." (Matthew 5:14–16)

Glorifying God is showing forth *His Self,* not our own. It's *His* glory brought to light in us.

Christ wants us to mirror His image to all we come in contact with—to our spouses, our children, other family members, our friends, our coworkers, and so forth. "But *we all*, with open face beholding as in a glass the glory of the Lord, are changed into the same image from glory to glory, even as by the Spirit of the Lord." (2 Corinthians 3:18)

### A Personal Example

My whole desire this last year with my horrific illness is that somehow God would use it all to glorify Himself. I want Him lifted up and that His ways would be manifested through all that has happened to me. That, in truth, is the motivation for this book.

Thousands of people have been praying for me and anxiously watching what God is going to do.

In the last chapter I shared that I had a relapse in January and the doctors feared that the cancer had come back and had now gone to my brain. They took scans and this is what it seemed to show. However, four weeks later (February 4, 2014), the Lord gave me some incredible Scriptures from Psalm 118:17–18 that said that I would live and not die. These Scriptures so ministered to my heart that I cried all night long, knowing in my heart they were true and directly from the Lord. The next week, the doctors called and confirmed that the cancer they thought (and the scans showed) had gone to my brain was not there anymore. In other words, I was touched by the Lord. I shouted the good news to the world!!!

The enemy, of course, was furious and wanted to destroy any witness, any glory and any victory I wanted to attribute to the Lord. And he knows

Christ wants us to mirror His image to all we come in contact with— to our spouses, our children, other family members, our friends, our coworkers, and so forth.

just how to get to our hearts. Remember Luke 22:31–32: he wants to "sift us like wheat."

The very next day (after the doctors had given us the miraculous news), my heart began to act up. As I mentioned before, I have AFib, which means your heart doesn't pump regularly, but irregularly. I've been on heart medication for years and haven't had any problems at all. Well, evidently, when they thought the cancer had spread to my brain, the doctors automatically put me on "steroids" to reduce the swelling and to control the pain and the vomiting. Those steroids, at the very beginning, were fabulous. But after one month of being on them, they began to mess with my heart and sap all my energy and strength. I began to feel so lightheaded that I could hardly walk across the room; my heart raced, my body sweated and my feet felt like noodles. The more the doctors tried to take me off the steroids, the more my body began to go through horrible withdrawals, messing with my heart.

For the first time this year, I began to really "fear" that I might now have heart failure and would die and the witness that I so longed for God to use would be gone.[243] When He gave me Psalm 118, I thought it meant I would be healed "completely" and thoroughly.

It took me awhile to realize that any kind of "fear" is obviously not of the Lord. What He does in my life and HOW He does it is His business, not mine. Again, His ways are not my ways and are totally passed finding out. That night after I had confessed my sin of fear, He directed me to Matthew 14:31: "O thou of little faith, wherefore didst thou doubt?" I confessed my doubt and unbelief and chose by faith to trust Him. Once I did that, He led me to John 11:4 in my daily reading: "This sickness is not unto death, ***but for the glory of God, that the Son of God might be glorified thereby.***" That settled my mind and gave me back my hope.

He also confirmed the Scriptures He had given me earlier, such as Isaiah 41:10: "Fear thou not; for I am with thee: **be not dismayed**; for I am thy God: **I will strengthen thee**; yea, I will help thee; yea, I will uphold thee with the right hand of my righteousness." He is the One who will restore my strength, but it will be in His timing and in His way.

The question is: Will I trust Him to do so? Yes, a thousand times, yes—I do and I will.

## Live the Truth

God not only wants us to know Him intimately, abide in His presence and glorify Him; He also wants us to "live the truth."[244]

Living the truth simply means being a genuine witness of Him. The definition of "truth" is *where our words and our deeds match and become one.* The Greek word for "truth" is *emunah* (*Strong's #530*), which means firmness, a fixed position, security, fidelity and *faithfulness.* Interestingly enough, the Hebrew word for "**truth**" and the Hebrew word for "*faithfulness*" are the very same word *emunah*, which we studied in Chapter Five.[245] In other words, God not only wants us to know His faithfulness, He also wants us to walk in faithfulness toward Him (with our words and our deeds matching).

It's interesting to note that throughout Scripture, God's truth (His faithfulness) and His Mercy (His Love) are always linked.[246] For example, Hosea 2:19–20: "I will betroth thee unto Me for ever; yea, I will betroth thee unto Me in righteousness, and in judgment, and *in lovingkindness and in mercies.* I will even betroth thee unto Me *in faithfulness*: and thou shalt know the LORD."[247]

*Once you start being aware of these two attributes of God being linked, you will see them everywhere. For example, Psalm 89:14, 24* says: "*Mercy and truth (faithfulness) shall go before Thy face.... My faithfulness and My mercy shall be with him.*"

James 1:22 says it another way: "Be ye *doers of the Word* [live the truth], and *not hearers only*, deceiving your own selves." Being doers of the Word *means not only hearing God's Word but also choosing to do it.* Luke 6:46 tells us: "Why call ye Me, Lord, Lord, and *do* not the things which I say?" And finally, Hebrews 3:14 encourages us to be "partakers of Christ." Being partakers of Christ's Life is not automatic! It's God's will, but only our continual choice will implement it.

If our souls are sanctified and our spirits purified, it will be Christ's Life that will be showing forth.[248] Living the truth is how we prove our faithfulness, our fixed position and our fidelity to the Lord. If, however, we don't choose to be sanctified body, soul and spirit, God's Life will be quenched in our hearts and self-life will be shown forth instead. The result is that we will be "living a lie" and proving ourselves unfaithful. This, unfortunately, is what causes so many Christians to be "hypocritical," *saying* one thing and yet *doing* something totally different. This not only proves us to be poor witnesses to others, but it also affects our future position in the kingdom.

*We are God's "arms and legs" of Love in this world. We are extensions of His Love, if we so choose to be.*

## THE ABILITY TO LOVE OTHERS

One of the most important results of intimacy with the Lord (loving Him) is that we will now be able to love others. "By this shall all men know that ye are My disciples, if ye have Love one to another." (John 13:35)

We are God's "arms and legs" of Love in this world. We are extensions of His Love, if we so choose to be. All He requires from us is a cleansed body and a sanctified life to work through. Just as we received His Love at our new birth, He now wants us to give it out. First Peter 1:22 validates this: "Seeing ye have purified your souls [sanctification] in obeying the truth through the Spirit unto unfeigned Love of the brethren, [now] *see that ye love one another with a pure heart fervently.*" Also remember Matthew 22:37–39, which tells us that we are not only to love the Lord our God with all our heart, soul and mind, but also we are to "love our neighbor as our self."

The verb for "to love" here is *agapao*, which means what we totally give ourselves over to. There's no way, however, that we can love another person with God's *Agape* Love unless we have first loved (totally given ourselves over to) God and have that intimate relationship with Him.

Throughout the New Testament, Jesus commands us to love as He did. In John 13:34, Jesus says, "A new commandment I give unto you, that ye love one another; *as I have loved you,* that ye also love one another." How did Jesus love us? He died for us! He gave up everything for us. He gave up His rights, His will, His desires and His Life—everything. This is God's model for each of us to follow and how the "fruit" of His Love is produced and passed on.[249]

But remember, God's Love has two sides to it: it's a longsuffering Love, but also a tough Love. So we don't become "doormats" when we love with *Agape* Love. God's Love also has *a tough side* to it. God's wisdom will show us how to love "wisely." "Loving others" is the "fruit" that God is looking for in each of our lives. It's the measuring stick upon which He will judge us in the end. First John 4:17 expresses it this way: "Herein is our Love made perfect [complete], that we may have **boldness in the day of judgment**: because as He is, so are we in this world," **and that is Love.**

Therefore, the fruit of Love is the goal not only for us in this lifetime but also the "mark" that determines our role and our responsi-bilities in the kingdom to come.

## How We Live our Lives has Eternal Significance

Therefore, as we have stressed throughout this book, *our life here on earth is simply the training ground, the proving ground, and the testing ground for the life to come!* In other words, how we live our lives here and now—whether we trust God or not; whether we love Him or not; whether we produce "fruit" or not, and whether we glorify Him or not—will all dramatically affect our role, our position, our place, our status and our authority in the coming future Millennial Kingdom and thereafter.

The Millennial Kingdom is *not* heaven; it's that literal, physical kingdom on earth where Jesus Christ will reign *in person* for a thou-sand years. It's a place where we will recognize one another, a time when we will have real intimacy with the King of kings, and a realm in which many will rule and reign alongside of Christ. When we say "rule and reign," I simply mean hold positions of authority or levels of responsibility. It might be authority over a country, over a state, a city, a town, or simply a housing complex. It will all depend upon our faithfulness to Christ in this lifetime.

Most Christians acknowledge the coming Millennial Kingdom to some degree, but many have absolutely *no* idea as to *what criteria is required* (if any) to enjoy a significant role there. Many of us have not been taught the spiritual requirements for this future kingdom. We haven't understood that not only our rewards but also our place of responsibility in that kingdom will either be won or lost according to our trustworthiness and our faithfulness in this lifetime. Consequent-ly, there is an urgent need in the Christian body for a renewed recog-nition of our own personal accountability. It's imperative that we see our lives here and now in the context of eternity. We must understand that once we are saved, we are still responsible for what we do with the rest of our lives. It isn't "cheap grace"! *Saving faith is more than just belief*; it's more than just knowing the Scriptures, and it's more than just going to church on Sundays. **Saving faith is trusting the Lord every minute of every day**. It's called **hoping against hope**.[250] Romans 8:24–25 even tells us: "**We are saved by hope**: but hope that is seen is not hope: for what a man seeth, why doth he yet hope for? But if we hope for that we see not, then do we with patience wait for it."

Being *born again* at our new birth is **not** enough (yes, we're saved and going to heaven, but this is not all that God has planned). God wants us to learn how to reflect His image and produce the "fruit" of

# IT'S IMPERATIVE
*that we see our lives*

*here and now*
in the context of eternity.

His Love. We need to put our actions alongside of what we already possess in our heart. He wants us changed from the "inside out." He wants us to reflect His likeness and His image in all we do.[251] We are to love with *His* Love, share from *His* wisdom and walk in *His* power. We were created and called for this purpose. Our personal fulfillment and our meaning will only come when we align ourselves with His design and His intentions.

Second Corinthians 3:18 describes God's purpose for us: "We all... are [being] changed into the same image from glory to glory, even as by the Spirit of the Lord." And 1 Peter 4:11 summarizes it by saying, "If any man speak, let him speak as the oracles of God; if anyone minister, let him do it as of the ability which God giveth." Why? So *"that God in all things may be glorified"* and our future assured.[252]

## THE IMPORTANCE OF BEING "READY"

Jesus is returning soon, and it's critical for us to be ready and "prepared" for what He has planned. "Preparation" simply means being sanctified both internally and externally. *Internally* means continually washing ourselves, putting off our sin and self, and putting on Christ. *Externally* means putting on the Armor of God, praising and thanking God and making known the mysteries of the Gospel.

"Making ourselves ready" means making ourselves worthy, qualified and fit to inherit the blessings He has in store for us. We must be so ready that when Christ taps us on the shoulders and says, "Let's go!" we won't be surprised, unprepared or caught off guard.

Jesus' exhortation in Matthew 24:44 is crucial for us to understand: *"Be ye ready; for in such an hour as ye think not the Son of man will come."* This is also the readiness that Revelation 19:7 refers to: "Let us be glad and rejoice and give honor to Him: for the marriage of the Lamb is come, ***and His wife hath made herself ready.***"

*Constancy* and *perseverance* are key words in this process. Luke 21:36 warns us to: "Watch ye therefore, and pray always, that ye ***may be accounted worthy*** [in the Greek this means to be "entirely deserving"] to escape all these things that shall come to pass, and to stand before the Son of man." Second Thessalonians 1:5 states: "...that ye ***may be counted worthy*** of the kingdom of God, for which ye also suffer." And finally, 2 Thessalonians 1:11 tells us: "Wherefore also we pray always for you, that our God would ***count you worthy*** of this calling, and fulfill all the good pleasure of His goodness, and the work of faith with power."

(Again, we are not talking about "justification" here—the Blood of Christ cleanses us from all from past, present and future sins. We are talking about "sanctification," where we obtain the "gold, silver and precious stones" spoken about in 1 Corinthians 3:12–15.)

## THE TREE OF LIFE

We began this book with Proverbs 13:12, which says, "Hope deferred maketh the heart sick; but when the desire cometh, it is ***a tree of life.***" This simply says that when our hope is finally realized, grasped and obtained, it will be *"a tree of Life."* In other words, rather than a heart that is sick, we will have a heart that is overflowing with Life.[253] Christ, who is the real Tree of Life, will be able to flow freely through us.

It's fascinating, because if you ask Christians, Bible commentators or teachers what the "tree of Life" is, you will get a hundred different answers. After doing much research in this area, I've come to the conclusion that reference to the "tree of life" *can* mean several different things, but they are all connected. What's fascinating to me is that they are all connected to "hope." Job said it perfectly: "...mine hope that he removed like a tree." (Job 19:10)

First of all, the divine Tree of Life is Jesus Christ. He is the One at the end of the bridge of hope in the Holy of Holies. He is the One who gives Life without death to those who choose to believe in Him and to those who eat of His fruit.[254] He is also the One who fulfills His promises by equipping us with wisdom and understanding as to the future kingdom. All of creation hangs on the life that Christ gives. All of us receive our vitality and our nourishment from His Life. It's His wisdom, His understanding, His knowledge and His Love that the world is built upon.

"Blessed are they that do His commandments, that they may have right to the Tree of Life, and may enter in through the gates into the city." (Revelation 22:14)

Second, "life" itself is often depicted in the Bible as the "fruit of a tree." In other words, a man's life is evidenced by his fruit.[255] Just as the vitality and quality of a tree is evidenced by the growth of its leaves, so our lives will be known and recognized by the "fruit" we produce.[256] If our roots are based in the divine Tree of Life, we will bear much fruit. If they are not, just as John 15 tells us, we will wither up and die.

Proverbs 11:30 tells us: "The fruit of the righteous is a tree of life." And Psalm 1:1–6, one of my favorite Scriptures, says: "Blessed is the man…[whose] delight is in the law of the LORD; and in His law doth he meditate day and night. And he shall be *like a tree planted by the rivers of water, that bringeth forth his fruit in his season*; his leaf also shall not wither; and whatsoever he doeth shall prosper.... For the LORD knoweth the way of the righteous." Also, Psalm 92:12–14 states: "The righteous shall flourish like the palm tree: he shall grow like a cedar in Lebanon. *Those that be planted in the house of the LORD shall flourish in the courts of our God.* They shall still bring forth fruit in old age; they shall be fat and flourishing."

Consequently, our lives are not our own. They belong to Christ. We gave them to Him when we first became born again and we can't take them back.[257] *He is the Source of our Life; we are simply the branches that produce His fruit. As we stay clean and open for His use, we, too, will continue to produce the "fruit of His life."*[258]

There's an interesting Scripture in Job 14:7–9 that applies here: "For there is hope of a tree, if it be cut down, that it will sprout again, and that the tender branch thereof will not cease. Though the root thereof wax old in the earth, and the stock thereof die in the ground; yet through the scent of water it will bud, and bring forth boughs like a plant."

Why is producing "fruit" so important? Again, it all goes back to our being prepared and equipped for levels of responsibility in the coming Millennial and Eternal Kingdoms.[259] The fruit we produce here and now will determine our future responsibilities there.[260] ***This validates that a man's relationship to God now and the "fruit" that he produces here will determine the destiny God has for him in the future.***

Third, the "tree of life" might simply be referred to as Godly "wisdom," i.e., knowledge of God's plan for our lives. Jesus wants to equip us with this divine wisdom. Proverbs 3:18 states: "She [speaking of wisdom] is a *tree of life* to them that lay hold upon her: and happy is every one that retaineth her." In other words, when we apprehend and understand the real reason *why we have been called*—i.e., the hope of our calling—and *where we are going*, it will put everything together for us and the whole Bible will come alive.[261] This knowledge will be a "tree of Life" to those who understand it. Proverbs tells us that those who embrace this wisdom will be blessed.[262] ***Divine wisdom is what guides us along God's path to Life—from faith to hope and then on to Love.***[263]

How ironic to think that it was the "tree of Life" that Adam and Eve ate of in the Garden of Eden and that took away mankind's privilege to have life without death (immortal life); and yet through Christ—

who is our divine Tree of Life—we have the privilege of receiving that eternal life once again and becoming an eternal "tree of Life." Revelation 2:7 validates that the tree of Life that was lost by the Fall can only be restored by Christ.

His Life flows *to us* as "justified" believers; His Life flows *though us* as "sanctified" believers, and His Life will *consume us* as "glorified" believers. If ***"faith" is the belief and "hope" the bridge, you could say that Love is the "tree of Life" at the other end.*** "Hope" is the key to producing the kind of Love that will determine our destiny in the future. Hope is what allows us to be "fruit bearing" trees in spite of our trials.

In his book *Secrets of the Temple*, Moshe Chaim Luzzatto (an eighteenth-century rabbi who wrote exclusively about the first Jewish temple) ties the "Tree of Life" to the foundation stone in the Holy of Holies of Solomon's Temple. He tells us that this foundation stone— the tree of life—is where all the branches extend outward. This, of course, is <u>not</u> from the Bible, so I don't know if there is any validity to it, but I thought it interesting that there is a connection between the temple, bearing "fruit" and the "Tree of Life."

The Bible says "no other foundation can a man lay than that of Jesus Christ." (1 Corinthians 3:11)

## THE SUM OF IT ALL (JOB 42:5)
So what is the sum of all of this?

God wants our fellowship. As hard as that is for us to comprehend, that's His plan—to prepare us to have an intimate relationship with Him, not only here and now but also in the future.

In order to do this, however, He must conform us into His Image so that we might not only be witnesses of Him here and now, but also that we might be prepared to rule and reign with Him in the coming kingdom. Consequently, not only must our soul be sanctified in order to do this, but also our spirit must be purified. And this is where God often allows "dark nights" into our lives in order to accomplish this. *The key to making it through these dark times is "hope"—trusting God no matter what we see, feel or desire. It's being able to "see Him who is invisible" in the midst of our darkest and deepest trials that will give us the strength to overcome.*

God is the "Tree of Life," and only *He* holds the entire understanding of His plan of redemption. We are not to lean to our own understanding, but in ALL OUR WAYS we are to acknowledge (depend upon, let our security come from) Him. Then He can direct our paths—from being born again by His Spirit in the Outer Court, through the sanctification of our soul in the Inner Court and the purification of our spirit in the Holy Place to the reward of inheritance in the Holy of Holies. This is what the Christian life is all about.

When we don't understand God's purpose or His plan, however, we will easily misunderstand what He is doing (especially in the dark times), doubt His Love for us and lose our trust. This not only crushes our hearts, it also leaves us despondent, discouraged and despairing. This, in my opinion, is why the enemy is making such huge inroads in the Body of Christ right now. *If we don't understand God's plan and His purpose for our lives, then when the trials and battles come, we'll get confused, paralyzed and unable to move forward.*

Again, consider Proverbs 13:12: "Hope deferred maketh the heart sick..."

*"Hope" can only be realized when we understand what our future inheritance in Christ is all about.* (See Romans 8:24.) That's what Ephesians means when it talks about "the hope of our calling" and "the riches of our inheritance."[264] This hope is the anchor of our soul and the mooring by which we must live.[265]

Now, of course, this future hope does *not* replace our temporal hopes (our hopes for marriage, careers, family, ministry, etc.), but simply enhances and magnifies them. In other words, when our temporal hopes fade (and they will because they are temporal), our eternal hope will always be there to carry us through. Our *temporal hopes are fleeting* (brief, they pass away quickly), *but, the "hope of our inheritance in Christ" is eternal.* (Romans 15:13) It's just like God's *Agape* Love—when the human loves fade away and die, which they often do because they are human, God's Love (*Agape*) will always be there to carry us through. It's the same thing with the "hope of our salvation"—when the temporary expectations fade, our hope of inheritance in the coming kingdom will always be there to carry us though.

We must continually remember Psalm 89:33 that says God "will not take [His] lovingkindness from [us], nor let [His] faithfulness fail." His "faithfulness and mercy (Love) shall always be with us." (v. 24)

"Nay, in all these things we are *more than conquerors* through Him that loved us. For I am persuaded, that neither death, nor life, nor angels, nor principalities, nor powers, nor things present, nor things to come, nor height, nor depth, nor any other creature, shall be able to separate us from the Love of God, which is in Christ Jesus our Lord." (Romans 8:37–39)

"Hope" can only be realized when we understand what our future inheritance in Christ is all about.

In response to this, the Lord wants us to "make known His faithfulness to all generations."[266]

*One of the purposes of this book is to do exactly that: to make known God's faithfulness (His Truth) in the congregation of His saints.* My intention is to shed more light on God's specific plan of redemption, to give encouragement for the future and to reinforce the criticalness of God's Love and His faithfulness in times of despair and hopelessness. God has arranged circumstances in my own life right now so I can share from personal experience. *I pray I can help to unveil the real meaning of "hope" and show how essential it is in all of our lives in order to endure the dark and difficult days leading up to the fulfillment of God's plan.*[267] If I didn't have "hope" right now, I might as well give up and die.

Truly, I've finally learned how to HOPE AGAINST HOPE!

As an older Christian, who has blown it many times, I have learned through the grace of God not only how to recognize my sin and self, but also how to identify my times of hopelessness and lack of faith. I've learned how to choose by faith to give it all to God (the four sanctification steps in Chapter Eight).[268] And as a result, God has allowed me to experience incredible intimacy with Him, revelation from Him, the ability to see Him in all the little things and to be able to hope for the future.

Like Job, I can truly say "I had heard of You [Lord] by the hearing of my ear, *but now mine eye sees You!*" (Job 42:5) And, "according to all that You have promised, there has not failed one word of all Your good promise..." (1 Kings 8:56)

My prayer for you is that "the God of hope fill you with all joy and peace in believing, ***that ye may abound in hope,*** through the power of the Holy Ghost." (Romans 15:13)

# CHAPTER TEN—THE SUM OF IT ALL

1. How does Scripture say Moses was able to endure all that God had allowed in his life? (Hebrews 11:27)

2. What is the "dark night of the spirit" all about? Explain in your own words. How is it different from the dark night of the soul?

3. God's plan is to conform us into His image, not only so we can fellowship here and now but also so we can be prepared to rule and reign with Him in the future. What does this mean to you?

4. What's the difference between the two kinds of "knowing" expressed in Matthew 25:11–12?

5. When we talk about abiding in God's presence, in light of all of the above, what exactly does this now mean to you?

6. What is it that connects us to God's presence "behind the veil"? What keeps us there?

7. What is one of the main and most important results of intimacy with the Lord at the Incense Altar?

8. What exactly is a renewed spirit? What happens to the functions of our spirit when it is renewed?

9. What are some other results of intimacy with God and being in His presence?

10. Explain how the way we live our lives today has eternal consequences. How do all these things affect our future role with Him in the coming kingdom? Why is it so important to be ready and to be equipped?

11. Are you a "tree of Life" to others or are you a "tree of defeat"? (Proverbs 11:30) Is your heart sad so you can't really glorify God or are you "a tree planted by the water bringing forth much fruit"? (Psalm 1:4–6)

12. What is the sum of all of this?

# KNOWING GOD LOVES ME

The following Scriptures are paraphrased with emphasis added.

- *Herein is Love, not that we loved God, but that* **He loved us** *and sent His Son to be the propitiation [substitute offering] for our sins.* (1 John 4:10)

- *He bowed the heavens also, and came down.* (Psalm 18:9)

- *He sent from above, He took me, He drew me out of many waters.* (Psalm 18:16)

- *The Lord appeared unto me saying, "Yea, I have loved thee with an everlasting Love."* (Jeremiah 31:3)

- *I have engraved thee upon the palms of my hand.* (Isaiah 49:16)

- *I will never leave thee, nor forsake thee.* (Hebrews 13:5)

- *For the mountains shall depart, and the hills be removed; but my Lovingkindness [chesed] shall not depart from thee, neither shall my covenant of peace [rest] be removed, saith the Lord that hath mercy on thee.* (Isaiah 54:10)

- *As the heaven is high above the earth, so great is His Mercy [loving-kindness] toward them that fear Him.* (Psalm 103:11)

- *Many are the afflictions of the righteous: but the Lord delivers him out of them all. He keepeth all his bones; not a one of them is broken.* (Psalm 34:19–20)

- *When you pass through the waters [trouble], I will be with you; and through the rivers, they won't overflow you; when you walk through the fire, you won't be burned; neither shall the flame kindle upon thee. For I am the Lord...You are precious in My sight and* **I love you**. (Isaiah 43:2–4)

- *God commendeth His Love toward us in that, while we were yet sinners, Christ died for us.* (Romans 5:8)

- *For God so loved the world, that He gave His only begotten Son.* (John 3:16)

- *Greater Love hath no man than this, that a man lay down his life for his friends.* (John 15:13)

- *Behold, what manner of Love the Father hath bestowed upon us, that we should be called the sons of God.* (1 John 3:1)

- *...having loved His own which were in the world, He loved them unto the end.* (John 13:1)

- *What shall separate us from the Love of Christ? Shall tribulation, or distress, or persecution, or famine, or nakedness, or peril, or sword?...I am persuaded that neither death, nor life, nor angels, nor principalities, nor powers, nor things present, nor things to come, nor height, nor depth, nor any other creature shall be able to separate us from the Love of God which is in Christ Jesus, our Lord.* (Romans 8:35, 38–39)

STUDY QUESTIONS
*and*
ANSWERS

# Chapter One—Valley of Baca

1. Memorize 2 Corinthians 4:8–10.

2. Why does hopelessness occur in our lives?

   **ANSWER**: It occurs when we pray and pray and pray and yet everything continues to turn out against us. When we expect miracles, yet everything just gets worse. Our confused and doubtful attitude then prevents us from "seeing God's Hand in all the little things," which causes us to give up and the enemy wins.

3. What is the connection between having faith to believe, confessing our own sin and seeing God's Hand in our trials?

   **ANSWER**: We can't see God's Handprint of Love and faithfulness or receive strength to endure if we haven't first confessed our sin and chosen by faith to trust God regardless of what is going on.

4. In Psalm 84, what does the "Valley of Baca" stand for?

   **ANSWER**: It was an arid desert that the believers had to pass through in order to worship the Lord at Solomon's Temple in Jerusalem. It was known for its difficult terrain.

5. Psalm 84:5–7 tells us that even though believers experience much darkness in this "valley," they were able to turn it around and "*make it a well*" **of blessing.** How did they do that? What does going from "strength to strength" mean?

   **ANSWER**: They knew how to trust the Lord in the midst of darkness and how to let the experience make them stronger. They went from strength in the Lord to more strength in the Lord. (Isaiah 40:31) They were overcomers.

6. Second Corinthians 12:9 gives us the answer as to how our strength is renewed. Write this Scripture out and explain it as best you can.

   **ANSWER:** The only way our strength can be renewed is by first being emptied of self and then filled with Him.

7.  In order to go from "strength to strength" in Psalm 84, what did these believers have to do? In other words, before we can go on to having more strength, what must we do first?

    **ANSWER:** We must first "put off" our old clothes (our old man) and then we must "put on" our new ones (the new man).

8.  The place where God answers our prayers and turns them into "a well of blessing" is our own Valley of Baca experience. (Psalm 84) Are you in a similar place right now? Has God encircled you with darkness, confusion and trials? Explain.

9.  Psalm 81 tells us that sometimes when we call upon the Lord and are in trouble, He will answer us at the "waters of Meribah." What does this mean?

    **ANSWER:** It means that this is the place He tests our faith. In essence, He answers us by testing us.

10. How many times does David refer to the temple of God in Psalm 84:1–10? Why is this important?

    **ANSWER:** Three times. These verses refer to weeping, darkness and black shadows on the way to worshiping God in His temple. This is important because we will encounter the same things in our approach to worshiping God in the Holy Place.

11. Why does God continually "test" us?

    **ANSWER:** To see if we really trust Him. Will we still hope in Him when the unthinkable happens? He is preparing us and equipping us for a future reign with Him.

12. How does Hebrews 4:12 fit into this testing place?

    **ANSWER:** It's the Word of God that tests us. It's like a sword that pierces and divides our soul and our spirit, our joints and our marrow. It is also the Word of God that is a discerner of the thoughts and intentions of our heart.

13. Why the darkness and the loss of light? (Isaiah 50:10)

    **ANSWER**: God tests and refines us like gold. He puts each of us through the fire. It's His way of "cornering" us. (Matthew 9:49) Job equates darkness with "loss of hope." (Job 19:8–10)

14. The Bible says that God's presence is often obscured in darkness. What are some of the Scriptures that validate this?

    **ANSWER**: Exodus 19:9; 20:21; 2 Chronicles 6:1; Psalm 97:2; Hebrews 12:18.

15. What is one of the most important and helpful Scriptures as to how we can SEE God in the midst of our trials?

    **ANSWER**: "Trust in the LORD with all thine heart; and lean not unto thine own understanding. In all thy ways *acknowledge Him*, and He shall direct your paths." (Proverbs 3:5–6)

16. What happens if we don't do this? Explain.

# CHAPTER TWO—WHAT IS HOPE?

1. Memorize Hebrews 6:18–19.

2. What exactly is "hope?"

   **ANSWER:** Hope is the Greek word *elpis*, which means expectation, trust and to have confidence in. Hope is confidence in God's Word and His promises no matter what we see going on around us. (Romans 8:24–25) Hope is knowing that God will be faithful to accomplish these promises in His timing and in His way. (2 Corinthians 1:10; 1 Timothy 4:10) Hope is what allows us to see Him who is invisible in the middle of our trials and thus endure and overcome. Hope is "never doubting" God's Hand.

3. What are the two types of hope, and how do they differ?

   **ANSWER:** "Eternal hope," which is our hope in God's promises for His future return and our salvation. "Temporal hope," which is our day-to-day personal promises from God.

4.  Why is it that when our hope is "deferred," our hearts become sad and we wither and die? Have you ever been here?

    **ANSWER:** Without seeing His Handprint of Love during our trials (becoming encouraged and able to endure), we'll become empty, dry and lifeless. We will have cut His Life off.

5.  Hebrews 6:18–19 tells us that "hope is the anchor of our soul." What exactly is an anchor, and why is hope associated with it?

    **ANSWER:** An anchor is made up of two parts: The anchor itself and the chain that connects it to the object holding it in place. Hebrews is telling us that hope is not only the mooring holding us still; it's the chain that connects us to God's presence.

6.  Hebrews 6 tells us that "hope" is like the chain that keeps us tied to the Lord "behind the veil" (in the Holy of Holies). Explain exactly what this means. Can you give a personal example? (Hebrews 11:27)

    **ANSWER:** Hope is the lifeline that allows us to penetrate behind the veil and lay hold of God in the midst of our trials.

7.  Scripture tells us that hope is not only like an "anchor" holding us in place, it's also like a chain, bridge, link or a cord between what two things? (2 Corinthians 1:10; 1 Timothy 4:10) Explain that.

    **ANSWER:** Hope is like a bridge or a link between God's promises and their fulfillment in our lives. It's the connection between our faith in Him and His Love toward us.

8.  Romans 5:5 tells us that "hope never disappoints." Can you explain what this means?

    **ANSWER:** Hope makes it possible to be satisfied with the here and now, even though we don't know what's going to happen or how it will turn out in the future.

9.  How are the words "hope" and "trust" related? Define each of them.

    **ANSWER:** The words hope and trust come from the same Greek root word. "Hope" means unconditional confidence in God, acknowledging Him and seeing Him even though He is invisible. Hope assures us that what we have believed is true and will come to pass. "Trust" means not only depending upon God's Word for the future, but also relying upon His Spirit to get us through our difficulties today.

10. Why is trusting God in the darkness so very difficult? Give a personal example.

    ANSWER: Because we often "feel" one way and yet, by faith, we must choose to act in another. It's easier to trust God if we can see Him at work.

11. Why is this type of unconditional hope and trust so very important?

    ANSWER: It's important because trust and hope are not only what hold us in place during the trials (like an anchor), they also are our connection to God in the Holy Place during our trials. (Hebrews 6:19) Hope is the connection to intimacy with the Lord. And hope is what helps us to see God's Hand during the hard times, which then helps us to withstand and endure the fire.

# CHAPTER THREE—HOW DOES HOPE DIFFER FROM FAITH?

1.  Memorize Hebrews 11:1

2.  As simply as you can, define what *faith* is, what *hope* is and what *Love* is.

    ANSWER: Faith is believing in God's Word. Hope is trusting God to perform His Word. Love is the fulfillment of God's Word. Faith is a promised believed; Hope is a promise walked out, and Love is the promise fulfilled. (1 Corinthians 13:13; Colossians 1:4–5; 1 Thessalonians 1:3–5, 8)

3.  Define faith according to Hebrews 11:1. What does the word "substance" mean? And what does the word "evidence" mean? Now, define "faith" in your own words.

**ANSWER:** Faith is the substance of things hoped for and the evidence of things not yet seen... "Substance" means support, whereas "evidence" means proof of something.

4. What then is "hope"? Have you ever struggled in this area of hope?

   **ANSWER:** Hope is trusting God's Spirit to bring His Word to pass in His timing and in His way. It's the confidence to endure the struggle between receiving the promise and its fulfillment in our lives. Hope is seeing God's Handprint of Love in the darkness.

5. What's the difference between faith and hope? Have you ever gotten these two confused?

   **ANSWER:** Faith is believing in God's Word, whereas hope is relying upon His Spirit to bring His Word to pass in His timing and way.

6. What is the secret to holding fast to God's promises? Give an example in your own life where you held on to His promises "against all odds" because you knew He would be faithful and He would come through.

   **ANSWER:** Knowing God is faithful and continually acknowledging Him will give us the endurance we need to see Him in the deepest trial.

7. Why do we lose our hope? Have you ever lost yours? (Job 49:14) Explain.

   **ANSWER:** Many of us don't know what to do when we lose hope and our emotions begin to take over. If we don't know how to renew our minds (go through the sanctification process), we will end up in the pits. We don't understand that God is testing us to see if we really trust Him, and He is using our present situations in order to do that. (Romans 3:3–5)

8. "Night Seasons"—what are they, and why does God allow them? Have you ever experienced a night season in your life?

   **ANSWER:** Night seasons are periods of time when God deprives us of the natural light that we have always relied upon in order to teach us to trust Him in the dark. (Isaiah 50:10) Night seasons are God's way of exposing our hidden secret motives or natural habits and our self-centered ways.

9. What is God trying to accomplish in us by allowing night seasons? (James 1:3)

   ANSWER: He is trying to conform us into His image. He is forcing us to trust Him unconditionally, strengthen our endurance and equipping us for a future reign with Him.

10. The three pillars of the Christian walk are faith, hope and Love. 1 Corinthians 13 tells us the greatest of these pillars is Love. Can you define Love?

   ANSWER: 1 Corinthians 13:4–8 defines it perfectly. (Jeremiah 31:3)

11. What are some of the characteristics of this kind of Love?

   ANSWER: God's Love is an unconditional, one-sided, freeing and other-centered Love. It's totally opposite from human love, which is a conditional, two-sided, bondage and self-centered love.

12. Why must God's Love be the basis of our hope? Do you know God's personal Love?

   ANSWER: We can't trust the Lord or lay our lives down to Him if we don't personally know His Love. (Psalm 136:1–9)

# Chapter Four—Two Kinds of Hope

1. Memorize Romans 4:18.

2. There are two kinds of hope. What are they and, in your own words, explain their differences. Can a non-believer enjoy these two kinds of hope?

   ANSWER: *Eternal hope* is the belief that life here on earth is not all there is, but that Christ will soon return to earth and bring with Him an incredible future and eternal kingdom that we will be a part of. (1 Corinthians 15:51–53, 58) *Temporal hope* is believing in the personal promises we have received from the Lord that affect our everyday life. Non-believers cannot have eternal hope because they don't belong to the

Lord. Neither can they depend upon the temporal hope that the Word of God brings them, because God is not involved in their lives.

3. "Hope against hope" then really means what? (Romans 4:18) Can you give a personal example?

   **ANSWER:** Hope against hope means that in the midst of our trials, when our temporal hopes fade, we must stand on God's eternal hope. In spite of what we see and feel with our natural eye, we must have hope in God's faithfulness to work our circumstance together for good in His timing and in His way. (Romans 11:30, 33) When our temporal hopes become "deferred" and our hearts sad, that's when our eternal hope helps us wait for God's direction.

4. Why is the Word of God so important while we are waiting for our temporal hopes to materialize? (Hebrews 4:12)

   **ANSWER:** The Word of God is what divides our soul from our spirit, and it's what combats the enemy and his lies. It's critical we understand the Word and how we can speak it forth (Psalm 1:1–3). Hope is the connection by which the Word of God is implemented in our lives.

5. The Bible talks about the authority believers have in Christ. What is this authority, and how does it work?

   **ANSWER:** Through the Holy Spirit, God not only gives us the authority to choose His will by faith, He also gives us the supernatural strength to actually do His will. The Word of God is what gives us the authority and the Spirit of God is what gives us the strength to accomplish it.

6. Matthew 16:19 speaks about the "Keys to the Kingdom." What is this referring to, and how does it work?

   **ANSWER:** The "Keys to the Kingdom" refer to the *authority* that God has given to every believer "to bind" the enemy and "to loose" his strongholds. (Matthew 18:18) Binding and loosing are Hebrew idioms for experiencing the Lord's authority and His power. They are definitely the "Keys" to the coming kingdom.

7. In your own walk with the Lord, have you ever had an opportunity to "bind the enemy"? Can you give an example? How about loosing strongholds in your life?

8. Ephesians 6:11–19 talks about putting on the whole armor of God. What does this mean, and how do we actually put the armor on? Explain each step.

    **ANSWER:** Read Ephesians 6:11–19

9. What are some of God's promises from this chapter that really ministered to you. List them here.

# CHAPTER FIVE—CAN WE TAKE GOD'S PROMISES LITERALLY?

1. Memorize Galatians 2:20.

2. Can we take God's promises in the Word personally and literally? Give some examples in your own life.

    **ANSWER:** Yes, absolutely. We can trust and believe and hope in God's promises in all the details of our lives, even though we might not understand how they apply to our situations or how or when God will fulfill them. (Psalm 38:8–15, 23; 66:9)

3. Define "faithfulness" as it relates to the Lord. Why is this so important to understand?

    **ANSWER:** Faithfulness is God's trustworthiness, His security, His truthfulness, and His honesty toward us. His faithfulness means He is staying in a fixed position and not moving an inch. (Exodus 17:12) *His faithfulness is the basis of our hope, the anchor of our soul and the only thing that allows us to keep on walking toward Him in the difficult times.* (Hebrews 11:11)

4. So it's our faith in His faithfulness that is going to give us "hope" for the future. Is this what Habakkuk 2:4 is really saying? What do you think?

**ANSWER:** Possibly. It could mean both things. The truth is we live by our faith in Him. But I also believe we live by seeing God's faithfulness toward us, which then gives us the hope we need to endure and to overcome.

5.  Seeing God's Hand (His faithfulness) in the midst of our trials is what will help us persevere to the end. Can you give a personal example of this in your life.

6.  There are a couple of conditions to claiming God's promises personally and literally. What are they? (Acts 2:38)

    **ANSWER:** We must be "born again." We must have asked Christ into our lives to become our Savior and have received the gift of the Holy Spirit. (Acts 2:38) This must be done before we can claim God's promises. Then we will have the authority and the power to walk His Word out.

7.  Speaking of receiving God's Spirit, what exactly is our spirit? What are the functions of our spirit? And why is it so important we let God sanctify our spirit?

    **ANSWER:** Our spirit is like the power source or the energy source of our lives. It's the place that God unites with our human spirit. In order to have light, our spirit needs to be "turned on," i.e., controlled by the Spirit of God. The functions of our spirit are our conscience, our intuition and our personal communion and fellowship with the Lord. Our conscience is where God reprimands us or approves us. It's like our teacher and mentor. Our intuition is like having knowledge directly from God. It's His discernment. And, finally, fellowship with God is like having an intimate relationship with someone, a friendship. It's seeing Him who is invisible. However, if our spirit is not sanctified, none of these functions will work.

8.  What does it mean that we "become a dual man" when we are born again?

    **ANSWER:** It means we not only have a human spirit, but we now have God's Spirit united with our own spirit.

9.  Why does our spirit need to be purified? (2 Corinthians 7:1)

    **ANSWER:** Our spirit needs to be free of all soulish influence so God's Spirit can be free to direct our lives.

10. What then is our soul? "Hope" is what holds our soul in place. What does this mean?

    **ANSWER:** Our soul is like a neutral area that either will show forth *God's Life* (His Love, Wisdom and Power) if our spirit is purified, or it will show forth *self-life* (our own thoughts, emotions and desires) if God's Spirit has been quenched.

11. Why is it so important that our soul be divided from our spirit?

    **ANSWER:** Only God's Word can enable us to see what is of the spirit and what is of the soul, what is carnal and what is spiritual, what is natural and what is of God. Only God's Word can reveal exactly what we are and enable us to see ourselves in the true light. We cannot do this for ourselves. The more of our soul we allow to be stripped away from our spirit, the clearer we will be able to walk in the Spirit.

12. Finally, what exactly is our heart?

    **ANSWER:** Our heart is where God's Life (His Spirit) dwells—His Wisdom, Love and Power. Ezekiel 36:26–27 tells us that at our new birth we "get a new heart." This is the time God takes away the "old stony divided heart" and gives us a new pure one. So our heart is the place God's Life resides, whereas our soul is like a neutral area that either God's Life can be shown forth or self-life shown forth. An analogy might be: Our heart is like the roots of a plant, where our soul is like the flowers or the weeds that have grown on top.

13. What does "sanctification" mean?

    **ANSWER:** It's the process of becoming holy. It's the removal of anything in our lives that is sinful or unholy. It's simply the dividing of the soul and spirit. (Hebrews 4:12)

# CHAPTER SIX—WHAT IS GOD'S PLAN?

1.  Memorize Philippians 3:13–14.

2.  Is our goal as Christians simply to get saved? Is that all there is to life here on earth? Share from your heart what you think God's overall plan is.

    **ANSWER:** God loves us so much He wants us to have intimate fellowship with Him. In order to be in His presence, however, we must be holy and conformed to His image. The reason He wants us holy is not only fellowship and intimacy with Him here and now, but also to train us for ruling in His future kingdom. The prize of the high calling of God that Philippians talks about is that we will one day be able to rule alongside of Him in His coming kingdom. (Hebrews 2:7–10; Romans 8:29; Philippians 3:14; James 2:5)

3.  Why does Hebrews 12:1 tell us the Christian life is like "a race"?

    **ANSWER:** In a race, there's always a "prize" at the end. In a race, we are moving toward something or running toward someone, and also in a race, other people are competing alongside of us. The Christian life is very much like that.

4.  How does God accomplish "conforming us into His image" so that we might be able to rule and reign with Him in the coming kingdom?

    **ANSWER:** He daily wants us to sanctify our souls (our own thoughts, emotions and desires) and purify our spirits. He does so by exposing our sin and self. Sanctification deals with our sin, whereas purification deals with our self.

5.  In Mark 9:49, it says: Everyone will be "salted with fire." This simply means we will all be tested by fire just like when gold is refined. What are the three steps in the process of gold refinement? In your own words, how does this relate to what God is doing in our own lives?

    **ANSWER:** God wants to separate the impurities in our lives (our flesh), just like they separate the dross from the gold in the gold process. First, they melt the gold, then they bind it and finally, they melt it into pure bars.

6. Just like the gold process, God wants to separate the dross (impurities) in our lives (in our souls) and from His Spirit (in our hearts). How does He do this with us? What is the "self" that He wants to expose?

   **ANSWER:** He allows difficult times into our lives that expose not only our sin but also our tainted spirit—our self-centeredness, our own plans, our own desires, etc.

7. What are some of the "root systems" in our human nature that He wants to expose?

   **ANSWER:** Our presumptions, our expectations, our disappointments, our dreams and goals. These are values and beliefs that we are sometimes not even aware of. (Psalm 139:23–24) These are not necessarily sin, but they will quench the Spirit if left alone. (2 Timothy 3:2)

8. Does God cause our "Night Seasons"? Explain.

   **ANSWER:** Obviously, God does *not* cause them, but He does allow them and uses them in our lives to help conform us more into His image in preparation for His coming kingdom.

9. Philippians 3:10 tells us that God wants us to know "the fellowship of His suffering." What exactly is the "fellowship of His suffering"? What does this mean? Have you ever experienced it? (Philippians 1:29; Romans 8:13; Hebrews 2:10)

   **ANSWER:** The fellowship of suffering means the place we "die to self"— it's our own Calvary. Jesus is our example and He showed us how to do this. (Philippians 2:5–8) It means dying to self and then letting God's Spirit lead and guide us. This is how we go from "strength to strength."

10. Through the fellowship of suffering, the dark times and the trials, what is God teaching us?

    **ANSWER:** God is teaching us to unconditionally trust Him without seeing any evidence. That's the bottom line. He wants nothing in our lives before Him. (1 Peter 1:13)

11. What is it that defeats the enemy more than anything else? (Psalm 23:4–5)

    **ANSWER:** Being a "living example" of Christ: unconditionally trusting in Him, seeing Him in the little things, hoping for the impossible and enduring everything.

12. What more can we do to help further God's plan?

    **ANSWER:** Learn to love God. Loving God means "totally giving yourself over to Him" in everything. It means obeying His Word, trusting His Spirit to perform His Word in our lives and worshiping and serving Him only. (Matthew 4:1–10)

# Chapter Seven—What Is the Enemy's Plan?

1. Memorize John 10:10.

2. In your own words, what is the enemy's game plan, and how does he use our loss of "hope" to accomplish it?

    **ANSWER:** The enemy's plan is to steal our hope, kill our vision and destroy our faith. He wants to devastate us through our circumstances, so that he can steal our hope and ruin our faith. He wants us to lose our anchor and drift away from faith. Hope is the "key" to seeing God's Hand in the middle of our trials and to ultimately making it through. That is why if the enemy can steal our hope, he's got us. (Proverbs 13:12)

3. Why is hope so important in the scheme of things?

    **ANSWER:** Hope is the only thing that allows us to see the Lord in the midst of our trials and gives us the endurance to overcome. *Without hope, we would lose our way, our faith and our ability to overcome.*

4. The spirit of Jezebel is mentioned quite often throughout the Bible. (1 Kings 18—19:21; Revelation 2) What does she represent, and why is it important for us to understand?

**ANSWER:** She represents the enemy's "spirit of control"—Satan's whole objective.

5. What are some of the things the enemy uses to steal our hope? Share from your heart.

   **ANSWER:** Relationships, finances, arguments, illnesses, circumstances, negative emotions, etc.

6. Which do you see yourself in, either in the Cycle of Trust or the Cycle of Defeat? Share from your heart.

   **ANSWER:** The Cycle of Trust—is knowing that God loves you and has a plan for your life, which gives you the confidence to make "faith choices" to do His will, which allows you to lay your will and your life down to Him and frees Him to show you His Hand in your circumstances, giving you enough hope to endure the trial.

   However, if you are in the Cycle of Defeat, you aren't sure that God loves you and has a plan for your life, thus you won't have the confidence to make "faith choices" to do His will, which will force you to hold on to your life but prevent the Lord from showing you His Hand in your circumstances, which will collapse your hope and your endurance to make it through the trial.

7. What exactly is the "spirit of control"? Why is the enemy so intent upon having control?

   **ANSWER:** The enemy wants to direct our lives. He gains control when we yield to the "flesh." (Galatians 5:19–21)

8. Again, Satan wants to destroy our "hope"—Why? (Proverbs 13:12)

   **ANSWER:** So he can get full control of our lives. Once he has control, he wins. Hope again is the KEY! And it seems so easy for him to destroy it in our lives.

9. How do we know if we are controlled by the "flesh" or by the "spirit?"

   **ANSWER:** Either the "fruit of the Spirit" will be apparent in our lives or the "fruit of the flesh" will reveal itself.

10. What does Scripture say is our defense against the enemy?

    **ANSWER:** Christ has given us the authority "to bind" the enemy (break his control) and "to loose" whatever it is that is keeping us captive. In other words, binding and loosing free us from being his captives. In Jesus' Name, we are to renounce him, stand firm against him and tell him to leave. (James 4:7; 1 Peter 5:9) Then we are to put on the "armor of God." (Ephesians 6:11–19)

11. Second Corinthians 4:8 tells us that we can be troubled, perplexed, persecuted and cast down, but not distressed, not in despair, not forsaken nor destroyed. How is this possible? Have you ever been here?

    **ANSWER:** We are, in fact, supposed to be "joyful in all our tribulations." (2 Corinthians 7:4)

# Chapter Eight—What Is the Answer to Restoring Our Hope?

1. Can you quote Proverbs 3:5–6? This is one of the most important Scriptures of all to memorize.

2. When our circumstances, other people in our lives, pain, or the flesh triggers discouragement, despair, or depression, what must we choose "by faith" to depend upon? Why is this so important?

    **ANSWER:** We must always depend upon the faithfulness of the Lord no matter what. Then He is free to answer our prayers and show us His Hand. We must confess and repent of any lack of faith on our part so that He is in control of our soul. Then He can freely work.

3. What must "we" do in order for God to direct our paths? (Proverbs 3:5–6)

    **ANSWER:** We must **acknowledge Him** (make faith choices to depend upon Him). **Our** "seeing Him" in the middle of our situation allows **Him** to direct our paths.

4. Once we are in the enemy's grip, how do we get out of it?

**ANSWER:** Lack of hope is what gives us over to the enemy. It gives him "a hole." By confessing and repenting of it and giving it to the Lord, we can once again put our lives back into God's control. (Job 13:15)

5.  There are three essential steps to restoring our hope. What are they?

    **ANSWER:** Knowing He loves us, learning to make faith choices, and being sanctified.

6.  Sanctification is critical. What exactly is it, and why is it so important in restoring our hope?

    **ANSWER:** Sanctification is simply the process of becoming holy and set apart. God not only wants our body to be sanctified, He also wants our soul to be sanctified and our spirit to be purified. (1 Thessalonians 5:23) There are four sanctification steps—we must confess, repent, give to God and read the Word. These are important to do because this allows God to work in your life in a much deeper way.

7.  What are some of the other things we can do to restore our hope?

    **ANSWER:** Be faithful to Him, have perseverance, see Him in the small things, praise His name, do warfare and worship Him.

8.  What does worshiping the Lord really mean to you?

    **ANSWER:** Worshiping the Lord means being in His presence, fellow-shipping with Him and adoring Him. It means bringing the Love He originally put in our hearts full circle back to Him. It means becoming one with Him—the fire and the cloud.

9.  The definition of worship that I really like is to "catch fire" with the Love of God. Has this happened to you? Explain. (Psalm 16:11)

# Chapter Nine—God's Pattern for Our Lives

1.  Quote 1 Corinthians 3:16–18. What does it mean that our "body" is a temple?

**ANSWER:** This is one of the most important Scriptures that connects the temple of God not only with our bodies but also with our walk with the Lord as we advance from the Inner Court (after being cleansed) to the Holy Place and toward the light of God's presence at the Incense Altar, giving us the hope and the endurance to overcome.

2.  First Corinthians 10:11 tells us that all that is written in the Bible is for our learning. "Now all these things happened unto them for examples and they are written for our admonition, upon which the ends of the world are come." Are you beginning to see the connection between the temple of God, our bodies and our walk with the Lord?

3.  What does Hebrews 6:19 tell us is the only thing in our lives that will penetrate "behind the veil"? In other words, see God's Handprint in our lives during the difficult times.

    **ANSWER:** It tells us that there is a connection between *hope* and *God Himself, behind the veil of the temple.* Hope is the "bridge to the unseen."

4.  As simply as you can, explain the ritual the priests went through, first in the Inner Court to cleanse sin and then the purifying ceremony at the Incense Altar in the Holy Place for a deeper cleansing. What's the difference between these two places?

    **ANSWER:** The Inner Court ritual is where the priests stood in place of the people to cleanse their sin; in the Holy Place ritual the priests carried the "hot coals of fire" to the Incense Altar symbolizing a deeper cleansing and God hearing the people's prayers.

5.  What then does the Outer Court represent in our own walk with the Lord? How about the Inner Court, what does it represent? And the Holy Place?

    **ANSWER:** The Outer Court represents our own natural and worldly lives, the place we first come to know Christ and choose to follow Him. The Inner Court represents our souls (our own thoughts, emotions and desires) that must be continually be sanctified. This is where we must lay our own wills down to the Lord continually. And the Holy Place represents our new hearts (filled with God's Spirit—His Love, His wisdom and power) (Ezekiel 36:36), which will pour forth *if* our spirits are purified; but if His Spirit is quenched by our self-life, it will be blocked.

6. Explain as best you can what the priests did in the Inner Court. What pieces of furniture did they encounter? How does that apply to what we must do in our own sanctification process?

    **ANSWER:** In the Inner Court there were ten Lavers of Bronze—where the priests confessed and repented for the people's sin; the Brazen Altar—where they gave their sacrifices, and the Molten Sea—where they bodily bathed in order to be totally cleansed.

7. The Holy Place to me is the most exciting and most intriguing place in all the temple. What did the priests do here, and how does that correlate with what we must do in order to see God's Handprint in our lives?

    **ANSWER:** The priests changed their clothes, carried the hot coals of fire and found their way through the dark cloud of His presence to the Incense Altar where they said their prayers and put the ashes on the fire. This is the same thing we must do in order to see God's Handprint in our lives—put off the old man, put on the new, make our way through the confusion and see God's Hand at the Incense Altar.

8. What is the significance of the "hot coals of fire" in the Holy Place, and what is meant by the priests having to "change clothes"? (2 Samuel 22:13; Psalm 18:12)

    **ANSWER:** The hot coals of fire represent a deeper cleansing and a purging of self. They represent the difficult situations in our lives that test our spirit. *This is where, in spite of our temporal hopes being smashed, we must have that eternal hope drawing us on. This is where we hope against hope*.

9. The Incense Altar is one of the major themes of this book. Tell what you now know about this interesting altar. What is its significance? Where did it sit?

**ANSWER:** In the Bible, the Incense Altar is usually spoken of as sitting in the Holy of Holies, but actually it sat in the Holy Place just in front of the veil. (Exodus 30:6; Revelation 8:3; Hebrews 9:3–4) The Incense Altar represents our "dual man," the place our spirit is united with God's Spirit. It represents the place we experientially fellowship with the Lord (become one with Him) and the place He hears our prayers. (Numbers 16:9)

10. As briefly as you can, give a little history about this fascinating altar. (Exodus 30:1–10; 1 Kings 6:22; 1 Chronicles 28:18)

    **ANSWER:** We must always keep in mind we are talking about the Incense Altar in Solomon's Temple, not the one in the tabernacle. (1 Kings 7:48) This will clear up a lot of confusion. The spiritual significance of this Incense Altar is that it was not pure gold like the other pieces of furniture in the Holy Place. Again, it is symbolic of our "dual man"—the place where God's Spirit (gold) unites with our spirit (wood).

11. What is this telling us we must do when we face the confusion of our own storms and valleys? Explain.

    **ANSWER:** We must keep on walking toward God's presence, acknowledging our own self-life, but letting that "chain of hope" show us the way. If we can see His Handprint of Love, we'll be able to endure to the end.

12. Why has God's presence always been portrayed in a cloud of darkness? What is the significance here? Is this true in the Holy Place also?

    **ANSWER:** All throughout Biblical history, God's presence is shrouded in darkness. (Exodus 19:19; 20:21; Genesis 15:12; Hebrews 12:18; 2 Chronicles 6:1; Psalm 97:2) Thus, it stands to reason that the Holy Place experience with the Lord would be no different.

13. Give an example in your own life of where you had to walk in the darkness and confusion, but knew that God's Hand was there guiding you.

14. Explain how "hope against hope" comes into play in the Holy Place.

**ANSWER:** The only way we can traverse and walk through the cloud of God's Presence in the Holy Place is by hanging on to our ***eternal hope***, but at the same time "by faith" choosing to believe in God's faithfulness and Love to answer our ***temporal hopes*** in His timing and way. Only our faith choices will allow us to do that.

15. The Incense Altar represents "what" special place in our own walk with the Lord?

    **ANSWER:** It represents the place where God meets with us, the place we see His Hand, His presence, His Love and His friendship in our lives (Malachi 1:11; Hebrews 10:20–24)

16. Some prayers are answered right away, others we have to "wait" for. "To wait for" has an unusual meaning, what is it? What does this mean to you personally?

    **ANSWER:** To wait for means "to bind together by twisting" or to become one. (Psalm 40:11)

17. Becoming one with God's Spirit is the ultimate goal. Only Jesus really has done this perfectly, because He is God and He is perfect. Have you ever experienced special moments such as this—where you really felt God's presence? Share from your heart.

    **ANSWER:** John 17:17 is all about becoming one with the Lord. "That they may become one as Thou, Father, art in Me and I in Thee, that they also may be one in us..." This oneness is what marriage is supposed to be a model of and what we have to look forward to in the future.

# CHAPTER TEN—THE SUM OF IT ALL

1. How does Scripture (Hebrews 11:27) say Moses was able to endure all that God had allowed in his life?

   **ANSWER:** It says Moses was able to endure by "seeing Him who is invisible." This is the "key" to having hope and to being able to overcome.

2.  What is the "dark night of the spirit" all about? Explain in your own words. How is it different from the dark night of the soul?

    **ANSWER:** The dark night of the spirit is a time of purifying of ourselves—our self-centered thoughts, motives, desires, etc. The dark night of the soul focuses on eradicating sin in our lives.

3.  God's plan is to conform us into His image, not only so we can fellowship here and now but also so we can be prepared to rule and reign with Him in the future. What does this mean to you?

    **ANSWER:** This is the climax of our Christian walk. (Acts 2:25)

4.  What's the difference between the two kinds of "knowing" expressed in Matthew 25:11–12?

    **ANSWER:** In Matthew 25, He talks about two kinds of knowledge—beginning knowledge and intimate knowledge. Beginning knowledge is knowing by name only. The Lord validates this in Matthew 25:12 when He says to the second five virgins: "I know you not." In other words, He didn't have an intimate relationship with them. The second type of knowing is being intimately acquainted with someone. (John 10:4–5) It's being able to see them and to perceive them. The first five virgins had this type of intimacy with the Lord.

5.  When we talk about abiding in God's presence, in light of all of the above, what exactly does this now mean to you?

    **ANSWER:** Being able to stay in His presence, continually confessing and repenting and staying sanctified and purified. It's choosing by faith to follow Him no matter what is going on in our lives.

6.  What is it that connects us to God's presence "behind the veil"? What keeps us there?

    **ANSWER:** Hope is what connects us to the Lord—acknowledging Him, seeing Him in all the small things. And His Love and faithfulness are what keep us there.

7.  What is one of the main and most important results of intimacy with the Lord at the Incense Altar?

    **ANSWER:** A renewed spirit.

8.  What exactly is a renewed spirit? What happens to the functions of our spirit when it is renewed?

    **ANSWER:** When our spirit is renewed, we receive a clear conscience, a supernatural intuition and a restored communication and fellowship with the Lord. We go from "strength to strength" just as they did in the Valley of Baca. We now have the strength to overcome.

9.  What are some other results of intimacy with God and being in His presence?

    **ANSWER:** God's comfort. Comfort not just for ourselves, but comfort for others who are watching. Also, God's joy. The trials can, if we allow them to, bring such light to the Scriptures and to seeing God's Hand-print in the little things that it results in unexpected joy. Some other results from intimacy are the fruit of the spirit that is the barometer as to where we really are with the Lord, hope for the future, glorifying Him (reflecting His nature) in all things, living the truth where our words and our deeds match, and the ability to love others.

10. Explain how the way we live our lives today has eternal consequences. How do all these things affect our future role with Him in the coming kingdom? Why is it so important to be ready and to be equipped?

    **ANSWER:** We are being conformed to His image now and learning to have abiding intimacy. This is the testing ground and the training ground. These are the things that will determine what our role with Him will be in the future.

11. The question is: Are you a "tree of Life" to others (Proverbs 11:30) or are you a "tree of defeat"? Is your heart sad so you can't really glorify God, or are you "a tree planted by the water bringing forth much fruit"? (Psalm 1:4–6)

**ANSWER:** Christ is the Source of our life. We are simply the branches that pass His Life on to others. In order to do this, however, we must first be cleansed, sanctified and purified. Being a tree of Life means having wisdom from above…about faith, about hope and about Love.

12. What then is the sum of all of this?

**ANSWER:** Simply, to know God has a plan. And we must continually choose by faith to believe and trust and hope in Him, no matter what is happening in our lives. Then He can show us His faithfulness even in the little things, which will give us the strength we need to endure and to overcome the trial. If we don't understand God's plan, then when the battles come, we'll get confused in the darkness, paralyzed and unable to move. When our hope gets "deferred," Satan wins! We must know that God's overall plan is to conform us into His image so we can enter the Holy Place and continually abide in His presence. Thereby, we are qualified to be able to rule and reign with Him in the coming kingdom.

# ENDNOTES

1. Psalm 84:5–7
2. 2 Corinthians 4:8–9
3. Romans 8:28; 1 Peter 1:21; Titus 2:13–14
4. Romans 8:24–25
5. 1 Thessalonians 1:3
6. 1 Peter 1:3
7. Luke 22:42; Mark 14:33–36
8. 2 Corinthians 12:9
9. James 4:3
10. Hebrews 11:27
11. Psalm 78:15–16; 105:41; 114:8
12. Numbers 21:22–25
13. Job 3:9; 10:21
14. Psalm 84:7
15. 2 Corinthians 12:9
16. Isaiah 52:1
17. Genesis 35:2; Judges 14:12
18. Psalm 2:9; 45:6; Exodus 21:20; 2 Samuel 7:14
19. Exodus 21:19; Judges 6:21; Zechariah 8:4
20. Romans 11:33
21. Numbers 20:1–5
22. Matthew 9:49; Revelation 3:18
23. Luke 9:34
24. Hebrews 12:18
25. 1 Kings 8:10–11
26. Hebrews 11:27
27. Jeremiah 2:11–13
28. 2 Corinthians 1:10; 1 Timothy 4:10
29. 1 Timothy 1:1; Romans 15:13
30. Job 19:10
31. Philippians 4:4
32. Isaiah 40:31
33. Romans 15:13
34. Ephesians 1:18
35. Acts 27:29–30
36. 2 Corinthians 1:10; 1 Timothy 4:10
37. Philippians 3:14
38. Titus 1:2; 1 Peter 1:21
39. Romans 5:3–8
40. 1 Thessalonians 1:10; Hebrews 6:18–20
41. 1 Peter 1:13
42. Isaiah 42:4; 51:5; Habakkuk 2:3; Psalm 62:5; Jeremiah 29:11
43. 2 Corinthians 1:10; Matthew 12:21; Romans 15:13; 1 Timothy 6:17
44. Romans 8:28
45. Matthew 5:8
46. Job 13:15
47. 1 Thessalonians 1:3
48. Jeremiah 17:7, 17; Joel 3:16
49. Romans 8:24–25; 1 Thessalonians 1:3
50. Hebrews 6:18–19
51. Romans 4:18; 5:2–5; 15:13; 1 Thessalonians 5:8; Galatians 5:5; Colossians 1:4–5; Hebrews 6:13–15; 10:22–24; 1 Peter 1:3–8, 21–22
52. Philippians 2:7–8
53. Habakkuk 2:4
54. Hebrews 11:27
55. Hebrews 11:33–37
56. Ephesians 2:8–10
57. Hebrews 11:6
58. Job 10:15
59. Philippians 3:14
60. James 1:2—2:26
61. Job 14:13; 16:9
62. Hebrews 12:6
63. 1 Peter 4:12–13; Philippians 1:29; 2 Corinthians 1:4–5
64. Matthew 16:24
65. Psalm 119:92
66. Psalm 16:8

67  Romans 8:38–39; Proverbs 3:5–6
68  Romans 8:29
69  Ephesians 2:8
70  Luke 22:29
71  1 Corinthians 13:13
72  Galatians 6:9; 2 Timothy 4:2;
    Ecclesiastes 3:1, 11
73  Philippians 3:13–14
74  Romans 4:18
75  1 John 5:4; Revelation 2—3;
    Romans 12:21
76  1 Corinthians 13:13
77  Psalm 111:28; Ephesians 1:18;
    1 John 3:2–3
78  Romans 8:24–25
79  Hebrews 3:14
80  Job 1:12
81  Job 13:15
82  Romans 11:33
83  Luke 2:25, 26, 34
84  1 Samuel 13:14; 2 Samuel 5:3
85  Genesis 37:5–10, 20–24
86  Genesis 30:22–25
87  John 11:17–25
88  Haggai 2:5–23
89  1 Kings 18:21
90  Hebrews 6:18–19
91  Proverbs 13:12
92  1 Peter 1:3
93  Hebrews 10:23
94  1 Peter 3:15
95  Romans 4:18
96  John 14:6
97  Psalm 43:5
98  Psalm 146:3–5
99  Psalm 34:22; 1 Peter 1:3; Colossians
    1:27; Romans 15:13; 1 Timothy 4:10;
    Titus 1:1
100 Romans 5:2, 4–5; 1 Thessalonians
    1:13; Hebrews 6:11

101 James 1:6
102 2 Corinthians 1:10; Philippians 1:20;
    Hebrews 3:6; 1 Peter 1:21
103 Hebrews 4:12
104 Matthew 18:18
105 1 Peter 2:24
106 Acts 14:9
107 Psalm 103:3
108 Psalm 138:7
109 Psalm 56:9
110 Psalm 66:9
111 Deuteronomy 28:7; 1 Chronicles
    17:10
112 Psalm 112:1–2; 115:14–15; 128:3–4
113 Psalm 141:8
114 Psalm 112:1–2; 115:14–15; 128:3–4
115 Jeremiah 17:7–9
116 Exodus 17:12
117 Psalm 89
118 Acts 2:25; Hebrews 10:36; Job 42:5
119 Ephesians 3:19
120 Acts 2:38
121 Romans 3:10
122 Acts 23:1
123 Psalm 51:10
124 2 Corinthians 7:1
125 Romans 7:18–23
126 Hebrews 4:13
127 Job 30:17
128 Lamentations 3:4
129 Psalm 51:10; 2 Corinthians 1:22
130 Colossians 1:27; Deuteronomy 5:29;
    Psalm 57:7; Jeremiah 24:7; Exodus
    11:19; Luke 8:15; 2 Corinthians 5:17;
    Galatians 6:15; Ephesians 2:15; 4:24
131 Isaiah 30:15; Romans 5:2–5;
    1 Thessalonians 1:3; Hebrews 6:11
132 James 1:6
133 2 Corinthians 1:10; Philippians 1:20;
    Hebrews 3:6; 1 Peter 1:21

134 Romans 4:18

135 Hebrews 2:7–8, 10; James 2:5

136 Romans 8:29

137 Isaiah 40:31; 2 Corinthians 5:8;
2 Thessalonians 2:16; 1 Thessalonians
4:18; 2 Thessalonians 1:3; Hebrews
6:18–19; 1 John 3:3

138 1 Peter 1:7; 4:12

139 Psalm 12:6; 66:10

140 1 Thessalonians 5:23

141 Job 33:13

142 Philippians 1:29; Romans 8:13

143 James 2:21

144 Matthew 26:30–41

145 Job 7:11, 20; 9:17; 17:15;
Luke 21:16–19

146 Psalm 107:6; 145;14; Joshua 1:9

147 Hebrews 2:10

148 2 Corinthians 1:5

149 Proverbs 13:12

150 Hebrews 10:23

151 1 Peter 3:15

152 Acts 20:24

153 Isaiah 41:20

154 Matthew 22:37–39; Romans 13:10

155 1 Kings 21:13–14

156 1 Kings 21:23

157 Matthew 4

158 1 Kings 18:4, 13; 2 Kings 9:7

159 2 Kings 9:22

160 2 Kings 9:36–37

161 Revelation 2:20

162 Matthew 18:18

163 Ephesians 6:11–19

164 1 Corinthians 10:10; Philippians
2:14; Jude 16; Exodus 15:23–34;
Numbers 11; 14:27

165 2 Corinthians 11:25

166 Psalm 119:92; Ephesians 4:22–24;
Colossians 3:10

167 Isaiah 40:31

168 Philippians 1:12–13, 20–21

169 Hebrews 12:14

170 1 John 4:1–6; Mark 6:7

171 Ephesians 5:26; Hebrews 10:22

172 Psalm 43:15

173 Hebrews 11:27

174 Romans 8:28

175 Psalm 150:6–8

176 Psalm 116:17; 107:22

177 Philippians 4:7; 1 Thessalonians 5:16

178 2 Chronicles 7:3; Luke 7:45–46

179 Revelation 4:10–11; 5:8, 14; 7:11–12;
11:16; 19:4, 10; 22:8; 1 Corinthians
14:25

180 Revelation 5:8; 1 Peter 2:5, 9;
Hebrews 10:19–24

181 Psalm 16:8

182 Psalm 2:6; 3:4; 20:2; 146:10;
Ezekiel 40—48

183 1 Chronicles 28:11–19

184 1 Kings 8:22–29

185 1 Kings 5

186 Ezekiel 40—48

187 Isaiah 56:7

188 Hebrews 8:5

189 1 Corinthians 3:16; 6:19; 2 Corinthians
6:16; Ephesians 2:20–21; Hebrews 3:6;
1 Peter 2:5; 4:17

190 Exodus 25:8–9

191 1 Kings 7:48–50

192 Leviticus 16:12–13; Exodus 30:6, 36

193 1 Kings 8:10–11; 2 Chronicles 5:13;
Nehemiah 9:19

194 Psalm 93:5

195 Hebrews 11:27

196 Psalm 33:18–22; 147:11;
Proverbs 23:17–18

197 Romans 12:1

198 Psalm 24:3–5

199 Hebrews 4:12
200 1 Kings 7:48–49
201 2 Corinthians 4:8–10
202 2 Samuel 22:13; Psalm 18:12
203 Mark 15:38; Hebrews 6:20
204 Exodus 30:10
205 Leviticus 4:7, 18; 16:18
206 Leviticus 16:12
207 Exodus 30:34–37; 25:22
208 Exodus 30:1–10; 1 Kings 6:22; 7:48; 1 Chronicles 28:18; Ezekiel 41:1–4
209 1 Kings 5:5; 8:22–29
210 1 Kings 6:22
211 Revelation 5:8; 8:3–4
212 Hebrews 10:22; 1 Peter 3:15–16
213 Psalm 119:105
214 Malachi 1:11; Hebrews 10:20–24
215 Philippians 4:6
216 1 John 5:14–15
217 Psalm 145:15
218 Psalm 25:5; 37:34; 62:5; 123:2; Proverbs 20:22; Isaiah 8:17; 40:31; Hebrews 12:6
219 1 Chronicles 16:29
220 1 Thessalonians 3:13
221 Numbers 6:24–26
222 Psalm 135—136
223 Psalm 146—150
224 Psalm 92:3
225 Psalm 84:7
226 Romans 1:9
227 Zechariah 4:6
228 Psalm 24:3–4
229 Psalm 84
230 2 Corinthians 1:5
231 2 Corinthians 1:3–4; Ephesians 6:22
232 Psalm 81:7
233 2 Corinthians 1:4–7
234 Acts 2:25–28; 1 John 1:4
235 Psalm 84
236 Psalm 43:4; Matthew 25:21; John 15:11; Acts 2:28
237 Nehemiah 8:10
238 1 Corinthians 13:13; Colossians 1:4–5; 1 Peter 1:21–22
239 Ephesians 3:16–19
240 1 Corinthians 3:12
241 Matthew 5:16
242 John 17:1
243 Job 3:25
244 3 John 4
245 Psalm 98:3
246 Psalm 61:7
247 Psalm 115:1
248 Matthew 7:16
249 John 12:24–25
250 Romans 4:18
251 Galatians 4:19; Romans 8:29
252 Psalm 115:1; 1 Corinthians 6:20; Romans 15:6
253 Proverbs 11:30
254 Genesis 2:9; 3:22; Revelation 2:7; 22:2
255 Psalm 1:3
256 Matthew 7:16–20; 12:33; Luke 6:44
257 Galatians 2:20
258 John 15:16
259 Proverbs 11:30; Jeremiah 17:7–8
260 Matthew 16:27
261 Ephesians 1:18
262 Proverbs 3:13–18
263 Proverbs 4:5–9
264 Ephesians 1:18
265 Hebrews 6:19; 1 John 3:3
266 Psalm 89:1
267 Hebrews 10:24
268 1 John 1:9